Frank and Me

A Priceless bond with an Amazing Dog and Soul Mate

By Malc Collier.

Frank and Me

Malcolm Collier

Paperback Edition First Published in the United Kingdom in 2016 aSys Publishing

eBook Edition First Published in the United Kingdom in 2016 aSys Publishing

Copyright © Malcolm Collier

Malcolm Collier has asserted his rights under 'the Copyright Designs and Patents Act 1988' to be identified as the author of this work.

All rights reserved.

No part of this book may be reproduced or transmitted in any form or by any means, electronic, mechanical, photocopying, recording, or otherwise, without prior written permission of the Author.

ISBN: 978-1-910757-55-0

aSys Publishing
http://www.asys-publishing.co.uk

*I would like to thank each and every person and animal(!) who has become a part of my story here. My journey would not have been possible without any of them, the good and equally bad events all contributing towards Life's lessons. I acknowledge fully that the memories of those events described in this book are **<u>completely my own.</u>** In my opinion, they are the honest and truthful account of everything that occurred. The book is not in any way intended to hurt my family and friends. I would sincerely regret any unintentional harm resulting from the publishing and marketing of **"Frank and Me."** It is my intention to HELP people, NOT HURT.*

To all you guys out there that are going through or have suffered the turmoil of losing a Business and / or Marriage . . . IT DOES GET BETTER! More importantly, it helps to talk about it as I have done here with my book! (See Pages 224, 225 and 226).

Malc.

Foreword

I just wanted to begin by explaining this didn't really start out as a book about my Dog, Frank! Well, to be precise, it was originally about the 5 / 6 year period following the break downs of both my business and then my marriage. In essence, it was a diary, **warts n' all**, cataloguing my journey in life at that time. There was a lot of content in that first draft I managed to keep intensely private until I got it down on paper . . . and then allowed a select few to read it at raw manuscript stage. It was therapy, a cathartic exercise for me, a reminder to myself that we are all on a journey that has its trials and tribulations but, with perseverance and lessons learnt along the way, can lead to a better place. Revisiting all the things I had been through in that time of my life allowed me to properly destroy my demons by exposing them, then eradicate them forever.

Writing intensely about my past allowed me to bury it and not live in it as I think I had been doing for far too long. I found peace in my mind, heart and soul and, in achieving that, knew that everything else would eventually fall into place. There were times in those years that I didn't think I had a future. I read something somewhere where a guy said that "when he got all his problems sorted, he would find peace in his life." WELL, frankly I learnt that if you find Peace in yourself, you can then sort out all your problems or, at least, your problems don't seem half as bad! I learnt to LIKE myself, respect myself and how I have lived my life. I don't like or condone some of the things I have done in my life, but I have learnt from them and the effect they have had on other people. I have done some bad things but I am NOT a BAD person. It took me a long time to realise that. I am a Good person who cares for and loves those that are special to me and always tries to do the best for them. The secret to life is learning and continuing to learn by our mistakes, misdemeanours, misjudgements and bad decisions. I have learnt to live with my failings and understand why they occurred and know I would not let them happen again.

But, then what I also realised in setting that draft down on paper was that throughout that part of my journey . . . **and thereafter,** I had one common denominator, a focus, a reason for being and a very special connection and relationship that endured. Something that brought me through the hard times and made me appreciate the simple things in life, the straightforward, inexpensive pleasures you can embrace to fulfil your life . . . the outdoors, nature, the coast and moorland, but, most importantly, spending quality TIME with someone you care for and enjoying every moment we are on this planet. Of course, I AM talking about Frank . . . that wonderful dog . . . Christ, I am talking about **a Dog!** But not just any old dog, a quite unique, special, mad, scintillating, effervescent, energetic, carefree, devoted, loyal, loving . . . DOG! Fate is a strange thing and there was a reason for getting that dog in the first place and another reason why I ended up his only master . . . No, I am going to retract that statement, well the Master bit. I never thought of myself as his Master, nor he mine. Frank was so, so much more than that. Let's clarify this here . . . I never was, never will be your "normal stereotypical dog owner", never got into the dog walking fraternity . . . "Oh, you have a lovely dog, what's he called, how old is he, what's his name?" . . . all that malarkey, nah not for me. I acquired the dog, soon accepted he'd be my responsibility, aware Wife and kids would lose interest after Christmas and so just took on the mantle and got on with the task in hand. He then became my soul mate, my Best friend, my purpose and we just developed this unexplainable bond that was just a given. **Me and Frank against the world!**

Where it all Began

We both sat there in bewilderment at the top of the hill in the field. It was a warm, sunny, Spring day. All around us were a sea of bluebells and wild garlic which seemed endless, a small scattering of sporadic yellow buttercups gate-crashing the dominance of blue and white. Beyond that the trees, bushes and wild plants and, yes, more bluebells and garlic, only broken up by the maze of naturally created paths and walkways through the woods that we'd explored, discovered and walked many, many times over the years. Our view in front of us was an expansive one. In the foreground was the estate of houses, two of which we had previously lived in! From our chosen sitting point on the hill, we could pick out those 2 houses and, already, the memories were starting to flood back. From this Special vantage point, we could see pretty much the whole of the little town in which we had once lived. Admittedly, there were lots of houses, the odd industrial unit and a hospital in the distance . . . but, there were plenty of lovely green belts to savour too and, in the far distance but very visible from **Our Place**, was the appreciation of the wonderful moorland, again a place we had lived in, briefly, on our journey. Stunning and tranquil, the inviting hills and wild moorland that we could see as we sat there on this beautiful Spring

Day, again stirred many memories... thoughts of times when we bonded strongly after probably thousands of hours spent amidst that landscape.

We sat there, side by side for what seemed an eternity, just staring in awe at this scene. So much of our lives had taken its course in the place we were sat, behind and in front of us. So many twists and turns, good and bad, so much to recount. It had been a Journey for me and this Special, wonderful relationship had been its guiding light. It had been the one thing that had remained constant, solid, simple and uncomplicated throughout. The one and only thing I could ALWAYS depend on... I had been through some tough times over the years but this relationship had endured all that and come through it. Indeed, there were times that if I hadn't had this special, unique connection, I wouldn't have got through.

I turned to him, my beautiful black Labrador; of course, he was greying at the sides by now and looking a tad worn and tired. Still a wonderful looking dog though and those deep, brown, radiant eyes were oozing still with a desire for life... those eyes told me he still wanted to bound through those bluebells, sprint into the woods, disappear into the wildly growing bushes and reappear hundreds of yards away... but still back on the path we'd been walking, as he'd always done! Clever and mischievous all rolled into one. This dog was Special, remarkable and our bond was undeniable. He had never asked anymore of me than my time and affection; okay, I had to feed him too! But this dog had been there for me, unconditionally and gave me his loyalty, company and devotion in endless amounts.

"What a Journey FRANK; It All started Just down there" ...

Chapter One

12 years ago
Frank is the Chosen One!

"No, Tom, for the millionth time, You ARE NOT having a dog!" ... I screamed out in utter determination and steadfastness, with the firmest of tones I could muster. "But please Dad, all my mates have a dog and my Teachers and you had one when you were a kid", Tom came back at me. You could write the script; it was the same old record I had heard from my Son for, what, 4/5 years now? Tom was nearly 12, a Real lad, typically boisterous, football loving and full of energy. Despite these tough, rough qualities, he could still turn himself into this sweet, "butter wouldn't melt" little boy, looking up at me with his big blue eyes and spiked up brown hair, in his begging mode! Very hard to stay firm and refuse his constant pleas.

Once again, as I had done on many occasions when this subject arose, I reminded Tom that he had never even looked after little Molly, the rabbit, which, I also reminded him, he had craved and begged us to buy with his whims when he was a 5-year-old little boy! After the initial cute stage, it was me who cleaned, fed and cuddled that rabbit till it eventually died as they do naturally. With me sorting her out, she'd had a great life. I remember the day my little white rabbit died ... she'd been poorly for a couple of weeks and I had given her even more TLC than normal to bolster her, but that inevitable day came when I found her rock hard in her house . . . I had gone to clean out the hutch as normal and picked her up, lifeless. I started crying my eyes out . . . Me, just me! Remember going into the house to tell the Wife and kids, blubbering . . . "It's Molly, she's dead, Molly is dead." I was distraught, loved that rabbit I did! . . . They were sad but not as sad as me . . . I am a wet-wipe aren't I? So, after the Rabbit experience I went for years turning down Tom's requests for a dog.

But, yes, it had been a bad year in our house. My Business had gone bust thanks to the good old recession. I was now trying to rebuild my life, all of our lives; I had tried to get a job after the Bankruptcy but there just wasn't much around for an old Dinosaur like me. I had also been Self-employed for several years and so potential employers weren't too keen on that adaptation. My business was print and advertising related and (in the way I had done it) this was a diminishing trade thanks to the good old Internet and the advances in Digital technology. The demise of my business had by now had a crippling effect on our Marriage, the financial stresses and pressures of my reluctant wind down of what had been my dream (to run my own business) had taken its toll on us all. I had not handled this period in my life with ease . . . to see a Business that I had worked so hard for and actually do very well for a few years, just slip away despite my constant efforts and tenacity right to the end, was a bitter pill to swallow. We had once made great money out of it which allowed us a good, not wealthy, but comfortable life style. On the back of it, the kids had been afforded a pretty exciting childhood full of foreign holidays, caravan beach weekends, nice presents, eating out regularly, trips away (many visits to our beloved Stamford Bridge to watch Chelsea play and countless Theme Park excursions). We did it all . . . and the Wife and I had fantastic **benefits** too. As well as the sheer pleasure of seeing smiles on our boys faces, we also got away a lot together, just us two . . . Paris for her 40th, Oxford for a 5-star long weekend, Cardiff (many times), the Headland Hotel at Fistral Beach, Cornwall (our favourite, where I proposed to her and we revisited many times) . . . the list goes on; not forgetting nice cars and a lovely house . . .

The Business went down in the July of that year. I had to make redundant 3 staff and pay off a Business Partner. I had tried for the last 6 months or so to run it alone and keep it going but to no avail. It had been like clutching onto the side of a mountain and finally my grip had given way and I had to freefall down into the abyss of reality. As I said, despite my efforts, I could not get work immediately. Did a bit of low paid commission work for a while and scratched around but nothing permanent. Times were tough and, despite writing off all our debt with the Bankruptcy, we had still managed to keep the house (for now) so there was still the mortgage to be paid, bills and food to be put on the table for 2 growing boys. Daniel, my other Son, was nearly 18, still in full time education so both boys needed to be fed, watered and clothed!

At that juncture, I decided all I could do was try to resurrect my business, or at the least try and do something with what I knew with all my experience gained over the years in the print industry. At my company's peak, we had handled the design and production of half a dozen monthly community, advertising magazines so this was an area in which I had great knowledge. With this in mind, I researched then launched our own local monthly magazine for our little town. At that time, no one else had done it successfully there so I thought Why Not? The initial thought process was to get it off the ground, then when established, put my efforts into something more permanent . . . and lucrative. However, this pretty much became our only source of income. LOTS of hours and hard work for very little return.

So all in all, it was a torrid time; as I said, a Bad, bad year in that house. The collapse and fall of a Business, money worries, insecurity about the way ahead and lots more problems fuelled by the sheer stress of it all . . . For now, though, we ALL needed a lift as that year was coming to an end . . . something, just something to put a big smile on our faces . . . enter Frank into our lives!

Yes, I did it, I finally caved into Tom's pleas . . . he could sense I was down, my resolve weakening, my body language was showing a sign of vulnerability. . . . he Had me and those big Blue eyes came out incessantly to wear me down! We sought out all the ads. in the local 'paper for breeders selling Black Labs; in our hypothetical discussions over the years about this dog request thing, we had at the least decided that IF we ever did get one, it would have to be a "Real" dog, not one of those token gesture hand-bag accessories that seemed to be the in thing these days! Don't really see the point in those little things you see people with! No ... time to hold back Malc; don't want to upset loads of dog lovers here! It was just that if I was going to be talked into this, we agreed on a Black Lab, hardy and strong, ready for the challenge of a predominantly male dominated house-hold. A dog that would be up for a playful scrap in the garden, chase around whilst we all play footy, be lively and fun, take to the beach and throw in the waves! ... but also have its mellow and soft moments so it could be a warm, loving, family dog. We'd done a little bit of research and decided on a Black Labrador Retriever as opposed to any of the other flavours available, hearing that the black ones are meant to be the most intelligent of the breed? They are strong dogs, used for a variety of trained jobs, such as hunting and aiding the blind or deaf. We liked the advantage of having a short haired dog. We both had dogs in our childhood and I also had a couple of Border Collies during my brief first marriage, but between us we were by no means dog experts so this was still a massive step. We found a suitable breeder in the 'paper, a lady who lived out in the sticks on a farm with her husband. They had an import furniture business too but this was a side-line for them, the breeding of pedigree black labs, which they'd done for many years apparently. So we all drove out to the farm on that day towards the end of November. It was a mild day for that time of the year, no rain, just a little breeze in the air. We were all very excited I have to say, especially little Tom. This was the culmination of years of moaning at his old Dad and he was finally getting his dog! We found the place after navigating a few dodgy country lanes. We were welcomed by Mrs. Pawley, a tallish, middle-aged, quite posh lady who ushered us straight away into the large, stone floored kitchen, steeped in character. A typical Country residence with a few outbuildings where they ran their main business from but also a couple of old barns where they kept horses...and other farmyard animals, chickens, geese and...dogs! As soon as we entered the kitchen we were greeted by the proud Mum of the litter, don't remember her name but she was a tired looking, bedraggled old Lady...Well, after what she'd gone through, giving birth to 6 pups, this was quite understandable. And there they were!...6 gorgeous little, adorable, sweet, cute black Labrador puppies! Until we came, they had just been curled up with Mum in a big, comfy looking dog bed underneath the large, oak kitchen table. But, on hearing and seeing us, Mum first, then the puppies made a bee line towards these visitors to their abode, curious to find out more. Not ALL of the puppies ventured towards us; a couple just stayed quiet, perhaps pretending to be asleep, shy and, maybe, a bit intimidated by us...or humans in general? Those two were definitely, immediately off our "pick list"...sorry guys but there's a lot of noise and madness going down in our household and you aint gonna survive all that tucked up in your cosy bed! The other 4, at varying speeds, made their way towards us. All...but ONE of them, seemed to be checking with Mum first that this was ok before plodding their way awkwardly over the slippery kitchen floor. They were only around 6 weeks old, had just had their first vaccinations, so were naturally a bit cumbersome and understandably fragile...Apart from This One! He was slightly bigger than the others (still a little bundle of cute black fur) and he was just different from the rest! Though he was the chunkiest of the 6, he was also, by sheer determination, the fastest and liveliest and this made him the most awkward! He just wanted to get to us First and, in this spirited endeavour, he was comically falling about all over the place! But he had something about him, a big personality oozing out, a will to play and "get out there" and explore! They were All bloody cute in their own way but this one, he had something different that stood out. I asked if I could pick him up and Mrs. Pawley said that was fine. So I scooped him up as soon as he was at my feet, held him into my arms...then (I had to do it), did the Lion King type gesture of holding him up with one hand neatly tucked around his four legs, the other hand supporting his back. I lofted him high above my head and just looked at him in the eye ... I thought to myself "You'll do for Me little guy, we're gonna have some fun!" Of course we looked at the other pups and played with them, even picked up a couple but, me, I had silently made my mind up on this one. But I said nothing until they all made their decision and, thankfully, brilliantly they had decided on him too! Great stuff. He just seemed to take to us all and from that moment wanted to come and join our family. We asked Mrs Pawley if he was the runt of the litter as he seemed a bit "different" but she ran through the order of birth and he'd been second to the runt I think. It didn't matter anyway, he was the one that stood out for us ... the chunkiest, most boisterous, with the biggest personality out of the half a dozen we could've chosen. Fell in love with him straightaway.

Of course we couldn't take him there and then. Mrs Pawley said to come back in a week or so just to make sure he'd suffered no after effects from the vaccines. We paid her the agreed £450 (don't know how we'd mustered that up amidst our skintness!), got a receipt and paperwork proof of his Pedigree etc. and left. Before we went, we all had one last look at him, just to take in the moment and a parting cuddle! We noticed that on his chest, just below his neck was a distinguishing, small, white in colour, parting mark in his otherwise black shiny fur. Like a birth mark. He was the Only one of the 6 that had this so this was great as when we came to pick him up, we could make sure we had the Right one, no mistake! Don't think we'd have made an error there ... He was Different, NO MISTAKE!

Now to have a family conference ... to pick a Name! ...

Chapter Two

Frank comes home . . .

We'd already had several discussions about possible names for our new addition to the family. It had been a humorous debate for some weeks, since I conceded that we would be having a dog! Indeed, though, the conversation had sporadically popped up in its hypothetical sense many times in the preceding years. Most names had gone along the football theme, me being a lifelong Chelsea supporter, none of this band wagon stuff . . . I was the Real thing, a truly dedicated, through thick and thin, supporter. And the boys had followed my lead . . . both very much into their footy, playing and watching. As a result, they had become Chels fans too and we were fortunate (during the good times when the money was rolling in) to have got up from Plymouth to London to see the boys in Blue play at the home of football, Stamford Bridge! Happy Days and great memories . . . as a Dad, there is nothing better than seeing the sheer pleasure and excitement written all over the face of your Sons. Football and more to the point, Chelsea does that for us . . . I have literally seen my boys tremble with the thrill of being at the Bridge on match day. Priceless!

Sorry to non-football addicts if these words are meaningless, but some of the names that were thrown around were **Drog** or **Didier** (after Didier Drogba, superstar and legendary goal-scorer), **Ossie** (my own childhood hero, Peter Osgood, now sadly deceased), **Zola** (the little Italian once voted the most favourite all time Blue), **JT** (after John Terry, perhaps our collective favourite player and Captain) and **Jose'** (obviously, of course, after the Messiah that is the man himself, Jose' Mourinho, Manager and God!). Forgive my digression into football mode but these great names just drool from my mouth at the thought of my passion that is CHELSEA! I have often said that they were my First love and will be my Last... no other Love comes close! Of course I mean this in jest and play but have to say it still remains the longest relationship I have had in my life, though I guess very one sided!

Of course we threw around the obvious candidates for a big, sturdy canine... Rover, Butch, Buddy, Buster, Duke but none of the alternatives seemed to make the mark. There were none to match or beat or even come anywhere close to our out and out favourite... **FRANK!**... Frank, as in Frank Lampard, again an all-time legend at the Chels, a player that we all loved and admired for his long time consistency, loyalty and ability on the footy field... a true Blue and good bloke to boot. **Lamps** was a follow up option to this but, somehow, **FRANK** seemed to still come out in front and we began shouting it out in mock commands: "Frank, Frank, Sit"... "Frank, Stay Boy"... "Come on Frank, Come here"... That's it, we had Our name, all agreed, all Happy.

The day to pick up Frank couldn't come around quick enough... and the kids were excited too! I gave myself the day off and again we made our way out into the sticks to visit the farm. This time, we would return with a dog, Our dog! We had a little blanket ready to wrap him in and a dog cage we'd bought in preparation... brand new, of course... nothing but the best for Frank! We had some spare towels and newspaper... Just in case any accidents on his first car ride. Mrs. Pawley was waiting for us and she'd already prepared for our visit by keeping Frank's Mum away from the house so we had a hassle free exchange. As the first time, Frank bounded over to us in his awkward but cute fashion. It had been nearly 2 weeks since that first visit and, by God, had he grown already! Mrs. Pawley said he had put on a couple of pounds in that time and certainly more than the others who were lagging behind him! Labs are good at eating we'd been told but we hoped we hadn't got an over greedy little beggar here!

Including Frank there were 4 of the 6 left from the litter. The first two had been picked up earlier that day by their new owners. As before, we just knew Frank was our choice, even though the remaining 3 were still bloody cute and we were sorely tempted to add at least another one to our "shopping basket!" God, what had happened to me? Where was that resolute bloke who'd said No all those years to even having a dog? ... here I was, my legs like jelly, my heart pounding, encompassed in this pathetic state of gushyness! I elected Myself to carry Frank out safely to the car, obviously in the interests of health and safety! Nothing to do with the fact I'd fallen in love with the little chap there and then! "No, I'll carry him Tom, just in case, you never know." Then I whispered in Tom's ear ... "and you don't want him weeing on You if he gets scared in the car" ... further justification to my cause! Clever I thought. As cute as Frank was and as misty eyed as we All were, kids don't like the thought of dog urine all over them! So the wife drove and I cuddled the little chap in his blanket all the way home; he wriggled a little at first but soon settled in the safety of my lap, contentedly resting his chunky head on my arm. Dog basket? What dog basket?

So here we were, a couple of weeks away from Christmas. Our family had a new member and boy did he change the whole dynamic of our life! He was bought that year to give us, as a family, a massive lift to what had been a terrible year with the business going down and everything. Yes, he was a Christmas dog for Tom predominantly but I knew, in my decision to buy him, that it would be ME looking after him properly; after the puppy phase, Christmas a distant memory, the reality was all the shitty stuff had to be done and I knew that would fall to me! The toilet training, the discipline, the cleaning up, the walks ... all eventually would end up with me. They would sort of pitch in at first in the cuddly bit but we all know **that** fizzles out. But for now, I was determined to focus on all of us as a family enjoying this new acquisition, embracing it for the purpose it had been brought into our lives ... to make us forget, albeit temporarily, the terrible time we'd had of late. Frank gave us an escape, a different purpose, something else to think about rather than our troubles.

I took a lot of time off that Christmas, probably more than I'd done in all my years of working. I was still self- employed, of course, but in previous years THAT had meant me working right up to the last minute and taking sporadic time off for the festivities. This year I was in a nonchalant mood, almost couldn't care less attitude ... totally Not like me and very alien to my normal, hard- working ethic I had all my life. I just wanted to spend quality time with my Family and enjoy this Christmas as best we could after the horrendous year and, of course, bond with Frank. In those couple of weeks, I honed in on some basic training with him and mastering the toilet habits! I spent many hours alone with that dog that Christmas (a sign of things to come in the far off future I wasn't even aware of at that time). The kids did all the nice stuff of cuddling him, playing with him and rolling around on the carpet whilst I got the mundane chores of cleaning up his odd accident in the kitchen, making sure he was settled at night, popping down in the early hours to deal with his yelping and ... the training, constant, endless training!

But it was All worth it ... we had a lovely, in fact very well-mannered doggy who just seemed thankful to have been chosen by US! Despite the hard work of it all, this dog was Special from Day One and every moment I spent with him was a pleasure not a pressure. I just seemed to strike up a bond with him instantly. There was a Circus going on around us with our family life, next door's two even younger boys, kids the other side too contributing to the mayhem ... but me and Frank already had developed our own, unique "balloon" to live in! ... I would spend hours in the garden with him just doing simple things, spending quality time in his company. It was all important to use those two intensive weeks over the Christmas to install the ground rules, get him to understand the basics of being a domesticated dog. Any dog owner will confirm that if you can get the dog into good habits from the start, then these will stick and make life far easier all round for the rest of his time with you. I feel I achieved that with Frank. Though, yes, I felt like cuddling and playing with him all the time, there was a need to be firm too.

I got him sitting and staying to attention in the garden... then advanced onto walking away from him, whilst he sat patiently waiting for me to turn around and then, when I was ready, gave him the command to "come, come on Frank." He then happily bundled his way over to me, still falling about all over the place, his little but cute and chunky legs getting used to proper exercise. He was still a baby, I had to keep reminding myself! Some things he didn't take to like "DROP!"... Once he had hold off a toy, ball or plastic bone between his teeth, he just wasn't letting go. Every other command he seemed to embrace but not this one!... It almost seemed that when he was refusing to loosen his grip on whatever item he'd claimed, this gave him a chance, just one little opportunity to rebel... like he was saying, "look you got me to do every other bloody thing, sit, stay, come, fetch, roll over, even wee and poo in all the right places; and I aint given you any hassle really, but this, this one thing I am gonna do this my way!"... it also gave him the opportunity to snarl a little and gnaw his teeth as he would "fight" with my grip on the item in hand. His little head was going ten to the dozen, backwards, forwards, side to side, his snappers encrusted around his catch and he wasn't letting go! A statement to Me that he was still a dog that liked to play a bit rough now and then. But... if those sharp, little teeth (getting bigger by the week) even hinted at doing any damage, made any uncomfortable contact with me or my skin, I immediately stopped the "fight" and chastised him for going too far. He very soon knew the line between playing and biting. He knew, he just knew... they are just so intelligent those dogs but you still have to teach them the ground rules. This lesson was up there on the priority list, even more important than toilet training as we had lots of friends, as well as the neighbours, with kids. Kids, including my own boys, would just pull him around all over the place and kids are oblivious to any danger or natural reaction to anger from a dog. I didn't want to turn my dog into a big softie, but just an all- round dog that could adapt to the requirements of any situation or behaviours of those weird human things he would encounter!

So, Christmas that year was a good one. We'd achieved our "escape" as planned. Frank had been a saviour. But the stark reality of January beckoned and this meant me knuckling down and getting my head around a proper future for us all. We were now a family of 5 and money had to be earnt and plans had to be made. I could no longer scratch around, the odd job here and there. I had to get something more stable than that and make sure we could pay our way. I had, before Christmas, done a little bit of mutual business with my Nephew, Andy. He had invested an amount of money into helping me get back on the self- employed ladder but, frankly, we didn't achieve the volume of sales needed to keep 1 of us in bread and water, let alone the 2 of us! The only concrete income stream I had was the little, monthly, community magazine I ran in our small town. I worked hard at this to evolve it as best I could but these kinds of mags are limited in what they can bring you in, money wise. But I knew nothing but Working Hard is what you have to do. I had done it All my life, been brought up with that ethic... Council House, working class upbringing. Reap what you Sow, all that malarkey! I could do No More... get up early, put the hours in and hope a few doors would open on the back of this too.

At 10 weeks, Frank had his second lot of vaccines and was now ready to be taken out into the big, bad world! We could start taking him for proper walks and teach him more good habits. Again, he was brilliant and so receptive to my commands and training. It didn't take long to get him disciplined on a lead and then to appreciate the freedom of being off it too. We kept him on the lead until we could let him off in the woods where he would do his stuff in private then always come back to us for commendation and attention. He was just such a great dog... still had all that energy, character, mischievousness and personality we had seen in those first two visits to Mrs. Pawley's farm house, but he coupled that with a respect for us, a need to please and generally very good behaviour. He would run and run, whether we were throwing a ball or not and he just seemed to have a zest for life, making the most of every minute he was out! We can learn so much from dogs can't we?

I can't really remember the boys taking Frank for a walk much in those early months... I think Tom joined me on a few occasions to see how it was done but, in the main, It was me that this pleasurable chore fell to. I was already beginning to forge a relationship with this canine companion that was strong and, for me, it was just an escape from my daily pressures. I must admit, although I am a morning person, in the puppy stage, his first "outing" of the day invariably involved just letting him out the back door to pay a brief visit to our big garden. There he would relieve himself and leave his deposits for me to pick up at a later time! At least he was trained to go outside. I always have prided myself on my work ethic of getting started as soon as possible in the morning. Indeed, as soon as I awake I am thinking work, work, work, pressures, problems... call me a Stresshead! But just have a need, an in built desire to get on with the day and get things done. I had not organised a proper dog walk into this strategy yet... but that would come!

In fact, as the next few months went on, I seemed to be spending much, much more time with Frank, mostly alone and our walks were getting longer and longer. I had found an escape! By now, Christmas and its emotion and excitement seemed a million years ago and we had ourselves a vibrant, boisterous dog that was growing daily into a big, strong beast... and he devoured exercise, he needed it. I began to explore and found some lovely dog walking places that I never knew had existed before!... we are very fortunate in Devon to have a great mixture of moors and coast, all on our doorstep and, now, me and Frank were embracing this. I began to talk to Frank along these walks about my problems. Yes, he became my confidante! It does sound mad even just admitting this but our dog walks became therapy for me, a chance to think away from the circus of my life. I savoured every moment, the peace and tranquillity of being out in the open in whatever the weather, finding many spots where me and Frank could just be predominantly alone and exploit each other's company. In return for me getting him out there to exercise and have fun, Frank would listen to all my woes and put up with me waffling on, probably repeating myself over and over about my situation and unhappiness. My life was in a quandary. I began to realise in those reflective moments that added up to probably 100's of hours(!) just how much the Bankruptcy and losing my business the year before had affected me. It had been my life's dream to start, build and run my own business. I had achieved it, I had done it and I was good at it but then, last year, it had all crumbled. On those tumultuous walks, I realised the extent of my anger, disdain, bewilderment and the sheer reality of my life now. Our marriage had been hit for six by it all and we were not happy together, if the truth be known. But we had plodded on, despite everything. You do, don't you . . . sometimes you just bury your problems away and just get on with things. All marriages hit bad times don't they? And we had 2 kids that needed us.

But this business breaking down had probably had more of an effect on our relationship than I had ever imagined. That was until I got out into the wide open with Frank and came "up for air" myself to actually analyse it all. If I am honest, I think I realised that the pressure of it all had actually forced me into a bit of a meltdown . . . that last year in the business, desperately trying to cling onto the "mountain" to keep things going had taken its toll. I remembered the countless late nights of working in the office, just tearing my hair out, looking around for inspiration, something that could eradicate the mess. Perhaps if I tender for that, quote on that job, knock on their door tomorrow, make THAT call . . . it was all pointless in the end. The debts were too high and not enough coming in. BUT I TRIED . . . Boy, did I try, right to the end. A good Captain goes down with his ship right at the end when there is nowhere to go, when he's done his best to keep it afloat . . . that was Me. In that last office (before I returned to work from home), I remember the Security Guard knocking on my door a few times because I was working late, just checking I was ok because I was pretty much the only one still in the building at 9, 10 o'clock at night ... he even showed me the exclusive trip switch for the lights as they were on a timer. Some nights I just sat there in utter disbelief of my plight and just cried, head in my hands wondering where it had all gone. I would think back to the good old days when there were ½ dozen people buzzing around the office, all busy, vibrant, energetic people, all generating profits! ... those days seemed ages ago now but, frankly, they were not that far behind me. That bloody Recession just seemed to have attacked us like a Shark ... one minute we were all swimming in the beautiful, clear waters, the sun was shining and the weather was sweet as Bob Marley said but then this bloody venomous recession swept us off our dancing feet in a whisper.

"So thanks Frank, thanks for getting me out here to think again about all that ... realise just how bloody unhappy I am, bloody dog, it's all your blimmin' fault!" Of course I meant this in jest but those walks did bring it all clearer in my mind, put things into perspective. I was extremely down, my marriage was hanging by a thread and I was scratching around for a living. "Frank, what the hell shall I do mate?" ... "Give me some inspiration here boy; don't worry, If I have to leave I'll make sure you are ok, you'll be fine mate, I won't leave you!" He just looked at me in a state of nonchalance ... all he cared about was that these walks, his fun and his little life would not change. If he could speak, he'd have probably just have said to me "I don't give a damn what you do with YOUR life ... I just need to be fed, watered and taken out to these nice places!"

... **Why can't our thought processes and needs be as simple as a dog?**

Chapter Three

I leave home

Brave, stupid or whatever opinion you might have, I chose to get out of it and "try my luck" at another Life at 46 Years Old! I finally plucked up the courage to leave the family home, split up the relationship, caused heart-break, devastation and hurt all round. I left an *avalanche* of problems in my path behind ... and, though I didn't know it then, caused many more to follow! Of course, purchase that big bottle of HINDSIGHT of the top shelf and, maybe, I would not have left ... If only I knew what lay ahead! My thought processes were just All over the place and, as I had said to Frank, I just knew I had to get away, perhaps just to clear my mind of everything.

What was I doing? My life wasn't that bad was it? Lovely Wife, 2 brilliant Sons, a great Dog, smashing house, car, not huge amounts of money but we had always found a way to do stuff and "others were a lot worse off" weren't they? But I was just so unhappy and had been for such a long time. My walks with Frank had really got me thinking about my lot and the time I spent with that dog, alone, just thinking became crucial in my decision making process. I'd made no plans, had no real thoughts on the way ahead, just knew I had to leave.

I Remember that pivotal day I left the home. I walked out that day, after yet another argument. That was it, I had reached the end of my tether. Enough was enough. I drove to a local beauty spot by a lovely river where I'd been to many times with Frank, with a carrier bag of basic belongings. Sat there by the Bridge at 6 in the morning, crying my eyes out trying to contemplate what I'd done, recalling the image of little Tom's face, my 12-year-old Son, begging me to stay and, for the First (And I don't think since!) time, telling me he Loved Me! . . . Stayed an hour, brushed myself down then got over to my mate Dan's house, turning up for a Shower, Man Hug and . . . 8 months later, I was still there! Dan is a Teacher, young man, then 26, living on his own in "batchelor land", fully enjoying life as a 26-year-old! He had a lovely 3 bed house and had JUST, literally a couple of days before, got rid of Rich, another mate who had lodged with him for over 2 years! Then I turn up on his door step! "Dan, you know we discussed Many times that **IF** It ever got too bad, you would put me up for a little while until I got sorted? Well, here I am mate . . . need your help, a shower and a room for a couple of weeks max? That ok?" . . . What could he say? He is a great mate and saw the state I was in, blubbering mess, full of confusion, all over the show. At my lowest . . . or So I and He thought . . . little did I know this was NOT my lowest moment; this act of leaving was purely the start; the beginning of a series of downs, problems, a bloody 3 Ton tin of worms being opened! Let the "Games" begin . . . bit like a play on that film "The Hunger Games" where you never quite know what's gonna come next to deal with! What I have learnt from this Chapter of my life is that, when you make that massive, massive decision to go, break the norm, rip up the marriage certificate, go down the unconventional route, it just starts an avalanche of hurt, despair, issues, problems, encounters, challenges, few good but mostly bad to contend with. Little did I know! And THIS IS WHY people Stay in loveless marriages, unhappy relationships, boring jobs, mundane life styles because THEY KNOW, they bloody know . . . or they will in abundance AFTER they've read my waffles here, what the Alternative is!

So, I end up at Dan's! . . . 46 years old, shacking up with my 26-year-old mate! We always used to say, still do, that our friendship works as "we meet in the middle" . . . I was 46 going on 36, he was 26 going on . . . 36! I have pretty much watched Dan grow up . . . knew him from about 9, played footy with his Dad, John. Dan used to come along, at first to watch the footy then later, when he was around 15 ish, actually join in with us old fuddies! We used to say that it was our YTS scheme, bleeding in the youth, giving them the benefit of our wisdom! Dan started to join in, learn from the Masters. This evolved into playing regularly or, even if he didn't play, certainly at 17 / 18 onwards falling into the Bar afterwards. That's around when he became one of my Best mates . . . confiding in me, asking for my advice, talking to me about the World, his life, his plans, his ambitions. I have a lot of time for Dan as right from that early age he always had his 5-year plan and goals and pretty much stuck to it. Indeed, he set himself to be a teacher by the age of 21 . . . and fulfilled That ambition. Top Man.

He said I could stay as long as I needed . . . a statement not made lightly but as a Genuine friend. But I think he'd be the first to admit, he said it thinking that me and the Wife would probably sort things out, I'd lay low at his for a few days, week or 2 even and then go home. Didn't expect to have me there for Christmas and beyond (this was late June!). Only a few days before, he'd got rid of his last lodger! . . . I knew Rich from footy circles, like Dan had seen him grow up. He had been renting Dan's spare room for a couple of years, on /off with the girlfriend . . . now he'd gone back to her. This time, with me in situ he couldn't come back to Dan's! So from my 3 bed, comfortable, nice house and my family to Dan's spare room in his Batchelor House. It wasn't the cleanest of abodes . . . typical Single Man's paradise . . . Dan would come home from work, grab something to eat, slob out or go to bed leaving a trail of dishes, clothes, towels, whatever. He would perhaps, have a "clean up" of the house at the weekend? And the bin, the refuse bin in the kitchen, not to mention those outside . . . well I had to put on me "anal hat" asap and get that one cleaned out! Indeed, I spent that first weekend just scrubbing, cleaning and hoovering the house . . . If I WAS going to live here, at least I was going to do my bit and get it looking half liveable! Call it my feminine side kicking in . . . this set a bit of a precedent as I ended up being the house skivvy and did the majority of the cleaning. Wasn't a problem to me really. 1. I like to clean and 2. It took my mind off all the emotional stuff going on around me.

Dan had this really dodgy shower that took a lifetime to get hot water out of and when it did eventually come out it scolded you to make you screech in agony. The flush was dodgy as well, taking a few attempts to get yer deposits down t' system! And he was so bloody tight he hardly ever put the heating on ... was like living in the North Pole! Little did I know this was good practice for some of the dodgy places I'd find myself living in on my journey to come! But, despite everything going on in my life with the family, the subsequent depression in this period, there were times when me and Dan had a ball in those months, living together under the same roof, adapting our friendship to co-habiting.

I certainly got an insight, starting from Day One into Dan's life! As I said, up to now, he'd been a great mate but we had only seen each other once a week at footy for years. Occasionally, he'd have come down to visit us if we'd gone away to a Caravan for a weekend or whatever. But in the recent years, the weekly footy social thing hadn't happened as our normal venue had been knocked down ... we weren't That bad at footy were we? And Dan's teaching career had taken off so I hadn't seen a lot of him really ... we used to get together for an odd "treat" day, drinking all day or swimming or something where we'd catch up but here we were ... Living, eating, breathing, NO NOT SLEEPING together! Though there were a few nights we had Quilt nights on the sofas and just watched rubbish TV all night and got pleasantly drunk together.

Dan's "switch off" from his very demanding Teaching role was TELEVISION ... it just gave him an escape from everything and it's fair to say was a huge part of his life. Probably only a few days in, he called me into the front room and said: "Relax Malc, sit down and watch this programme with me" and there I was being initiated into the world of Dan and his TV escapes ... 'Enders (well it's Real isn't it?), endless footy, Extras, The Office, Waterloo Road of course, the list goes on! But nothing could prepare me for Mr Trawlerman... "Watch this mate and then tell me what you see!" I watched this programme, snuggled under me duvet, glass of Red in tow, watched it whilst trying to keep awake. For me, it was so damn boring!... "Well", I responded to my Teacher mate's request or was it an order being a teacher... "these bunch of fishermen jump aboard their big Trawler boat, go out to sea as far as they can, catch as many fish as they can, as big as they can, then they sail back into shore, offload their catch, sell it, then they all fall in t' pub, get bladdered, then go to sleep, get up the next day and go out and do it All over again! Day after day after day after... same bloody thing mate! Why the hell do you watch this pile of crap?"... "Well mate", he quipped, "because it's such a simple, hard but simple life with JUST ONE GOAL, to catch fucking fish"... For Dan, it was so far removed from his complicated, very stressful and sometimes demoralising job as a Teacher, he just loved to be confronted with the diversity... as I said, his Escape!

I found out so much about him in those months, what makes him tick, his likes, dislikes, his ups, his downs, habits and ways, moods good and bad, it was like being bloody Married without the sex. Don't ever believe that Teaching is an easy job... far from it. Yes they get their long holidays and it aint as dirty as working down a pit but boy did I find out how hard it is and how intensive an effect it has on their lives at home. Though he found those moments to switch off, Danny would have to force himself to switch off the mobile and / or laptop to get away from the constant need to be "on call." There was always a problem to sort out, a colleague to speak to or a parent, a report to write, a lesson, assembly or presentation to prepare or books / papers to mark. It was endless, not to mention the day to day stuff they have to contend with and "bring home." During my 7/8-month tenure there, Dan had a pupil "die" in the swimming pool on his shift (they brought him round thank God), had to find a kid that had bolted out of the School and gone missing after being taunted by other kids about his Dad who'd gone down for 9 years for sexual abuse and dealt with an internal complaint from another Teacher who said that one of his colleagues had caressed her boobs! That one dragged on for months! Aside from this were unruly kids, drugs, under age sex and pregnancies etc. etc . . . God, I wondered how they found time to actually teach! But I lived through this shit with him, advised him where I could as a Parent and a Friend but, most importantly, shared these life experiences. Even more than the house-work, it gave me a deflection from my troubles at that time.

We had many light moments too! . . . He re-taught me how to cook . . . of a fashion! In my marriage, I pretty much had everything done for me for 16 odd years. I was institutionalised and came to his without the knowledge of how to even switch the cooker on! He showed me how to make Pasta, Lasagne, Spag. Bowl . . . oh all pretty much the same! Cottage Pie, Shepherd's Pie and Roast . . . basic stuff. Many a night in those early days would we shut out the world, that 'orrible bloody jungle out there, stick on the music LOUD in the kitchen and sing & dance our way through the making of the latest gourmet . . . To be fair, Dan was a pretty good cook and I his pupil . . . again he took on Teacher mode!

There was this one memorable night when Dan had gone to bed early, shattered from his long day and Mr. Trawlerman had "finished him off!" Sent himself to bed to wind down to snooze time by watching More TV on his ever so slightly smaller screen in the bedroom! I was downstairs in the kitchen in my "makeshift" office from home i.e. Laptop on the kitchen table, doing some work stuff. About 10 ish though, I heard Dan come hurtling down the stairs, shouting out loud "Malc, Malc, have you heard the News, have you seen the telly?" . . . Of course I hadn't had the telly on, too busy with my work & personal stuff but . . . earlier that day I had heard that Farrah Fawcett Majors, the most famous (and gorgeous) of the Original Charlie's Angels, the Boys' pin up of the 70's, beautiful body and long, flowing blonde hair, had died in her 50's of Cancer. Sad, very sad, one of my earliest crushes gone. So this was my retort, "Dan, yeh, so sad, lost one of the Angels, sign of getting older I know, poor old Farrah" . . . "What the fuck you on about, get the telly on, see the news!" He replied ... Of course it was Michael, Michael Jackson who had died and it was all over the news! He'd been one of Danny's childhood heroes and of course he loved his music. For me, the greatness he achieved in his pop career had become somewhat tainted by the more recent events and rumours circling his personal life and, though I empathised with Dan and tapped into his emotions that night, I think it's fair to say I wasn't As devastated as Dan! But we watched all the footage into the early hours, cracked open a few beers and put significance on "where we were and who we were with" the day Jacko ... and Farrah died!

Of course, despite all the shit going on in my life, on occasion it was like the 2 guys in Men Behaving Badly except because I was in such a bad place emotionally all the time, we could not evolve this properly. I never had any money to do the "join in with the footy lads" and go out with Dan and them on a Saturday night after the game that day. Indeed, I never had any money per say! So even when we had the chance to go out for a few beers together or get some tinnies / wine in, I was always lagging in that department. What little I was scraping from my little business, I was still paying the mortgage and bills at home, getting to Tom's footy, training and matches, dropping Dan a few bob when I could, and just about eating! Managed a couple only nights out with Dan and the boys and "paid my way." I had left with nothing, left behind anything I owned and now the reality was I was shacking up in my mate's spare bedroom with nothing but the clothes I stood up in! She sent me over a couple of bags of my clothes to keep me going ... To be fair to her, being the "Shopper", she bought all the family's clothes, hers, mine and the kids and she had great, though expensive, taste. So the clothes she bought have lasted as they are quality! One day they will undoubtedly come back into fashion!

So the money thing became an issue early doors at Dan's. As a proud Man I was paying him what I could when I could, keeping things going at home and trying, really trying to keep my head above water. It was tough, really tough. As much as Dan tried to empathise, because of his age, yes sometimes immaturity but, above all, his lack of true life experience and hardship, it was a situation he was never going to understand. How could he at 26? He had never seen such emotional and financial hardship at such close quarters. His Mum and Dad were still together after 300 years and, though his Dad had lost his job in recent times, had been clever enough as an Accountant to steer that one correctly when he saw it coming. Respect to John, he made sure he and his family did not suffer too much through that redundancy and bounced back soon after to another job. So Dan had only seen this and his own strategic planning of his own life which, at 26, was looking pretty stable and on the right path. Here he had a guy in his mid-40's, went bankrupt only a year before, just left his Wife, family and house, no money, earning very little from a small business . . . destitute or what? . . . STAYING in his house! Dan dealt with it in his words with "tough love" . . . not really what I wanted or needed but just his way of handling things. He would constantly remind me how this was "character building", "the only way is up", karma, all the old clichés! THOUGH I did not want pity, never wanted that, I did need now and again a man hug and some compassion and understanding. This happened on occasion but in the main it was the tough love thing.

He got it totally wrong one day when he took me out to this POINT TO POINT races day, at Ashburton, in Devon I think it was. He'd just met Jen who went onto become his Wife and he had asked me to come to this day out as it was to be the first time he'd met up with her family who all lived around that way. Being honest, they were a little posh and perhaps a bit "different" to Dan let's say . . . spoke with a plum in their throat and probably owned half of Devon! Certainly "horsey" peops. from the sticks, very far removed from Dan's normal circles! But he'd fallen for this lady and wanted to meet them all, with me as moral back up i.e. warn him to mind his p's and q's! Me . . . why me? Mr. "say it as it is" merchant! Though, yes, I can have my more sensible, diplomatic moments and I AM older (and wiser?) than him? So along we went, actually had a good day really, "spiffing" some might say old chap! Under our breath we both spent the day taking the piss out of the Plummies but we joined in with the Day's Events as best we could and wandered around like Del Boy and Rodney! I even scraped up enough to put on a few bets on the gee-gees for the fun of it. But I am no gambler and won nothing! Got through the day and then headed home late afternoon; Jen driving, me in the passenger seat, Dan in the back, spreading out! And here's where He spoiled the day, showed off his immaturity, reminded me he WAS ONLY 26 . . . just like when he'd pulled that chair out from under me a couple of years back and watching as my pint of beer swirled all over my nice clothes! Young little bastard! Was this to be another lesson in tough love or just that immaturity, naivety perhaps if I were to give him the benefit of the doubt? He sat in the back of the car, on his 'phone . . . was Always on his 'phone! Talking to his mate Lee who had just moved to Canada with work and Dan was organising a trip out to see him. "Yes mate, me and Jen are coming, you sort it all out, book it, we'll be there, couple of grand?, No problem" . . . something on those lines was how the conversation went but the gist was I had just scraped up £20 or so to jump in a car with them and force myself to have a day out which in the end I had enjoyed and here was Dan rubbing my nose in my situation by spending thousands in front of me (can't get away when you're in a car!). But he wasn't finished there . . . on the way back, he'd said to Jen to pull into Tesco's to get some food in . . . thought we were just going to do a bit of mundane, every day essentials stuff but, instead, he jogged off upstairs to the household section and proceeded to spend a couple hundred quid on bits n' bobs "they needed" . . . pressure cooker I think, etc. etc., whatever; he then said to me, "maybe one day Malc you'll be able to do this again!" . . . i.e. spend stupid money on unnecessary items purely because he could! His "final kick in the teeth" was to say "pop down to the pasta aisle and get yerself some pasta Malc." Another slur as it was, I didn't need much more of an invite to get away from him at that point and despatched myself downstairs to . . . get some pasta! Eventually we met up and went back to the car; this time complete silence for the rest of the 10 odd miles before getting back to his house. I was fuming. As soon as we pulled up at his house, I bombed it upstairs to my room, closing the door behind me and just sat there on my bed crying my eyes out. Here I was, 46, living with my 26-year-old friend, with nothing and Totally beholden to him. I could see no way out at that point, no way back to the previous "glory days." But I still had my PRIDE & DIGNITY. About an hour later, Dan came up to see me, knocked on the door then came in. "You ok mate?" . . .

"Ok, OK? . . . You're having a fucking laugh aren't you?" . . . I ripped into him. "Dan, you will NEVER, NEVER, EVER do that to me again . . . you put me down, you made me feel like shit; you have a short memory mate; it wasn't that long ago I was the Man buying you meals, inviting you to the caravan holidays we used to go on, drinks etc. etc. and I COULD pay my way. YOU KNOW where I am in life now mate and no matter what you think of my reasons, decisions and the way I conduct myself, I will not take that shit you just gave me back there in Tesco's . . . not taking it, don't fucking deserve it; I WILL claw myself out of this mess and I will get out of your house as soon as I can. I thank you for your kindness in taking me in but you don't get off on treating me like a homeless dog." Dan did apologise as he saw how emotive I was BUT his explanation was that it was this "tough love" . . . the only way, in his naïve, inexperienced mind, he knew of "dealing with me." I was not looking for Sympathy, just a little respect towards someone who was in the worst place of his life at that point . . . though, little did I know, it could get WORSE! – That's the next chapter!

Two or three occasions we cooked up a nice stew or hotpot the night before. Then we got up early and went out for an All Day walk with the dog (Dan let him stay over on those times). These were great days as it gave me a chance to see Frank, catch up with him and apologise for leaving him behind. When I had walked out that day, I must admit I had not really considered the implications of what would happen to Frank. Looking back, I just knew on that day I had to go, hadn't planned it to be **THAT** day and naively thought I was JUST leaving and that everything else, my routine and relationships with the kids and the dog would just stay the SAME! So Dad was leaving home but not leaving his life behind! Yes, so naïve and blinkered but, in my defence, you don't leave home every day do you?

Being a teacher, Dan knew all the walks the kids do for Ten Tors on the Moors. I let Dan lead the way and plan our walks out in true Teacher fashion. And I had never been in the Scouts so didn't have a bloody clue! He borrowed waterproof maps, compasses, ruck-sacks etc. etc. from School and away we went. Loved those few excursions with Dan and Frank, quality time away from it all, challenging ourselves to climb tors, beat the elements, push our fitness levels in all weathers. We did over ten miles generally, through bogs, up steep inclines, walking through streams, getting utterly lost in the fog, wind and rain! Brilliant Boys Own stuff! I can remember the first time we went out. At the start of the walk, Dan said he was going to call / text a few people, family and friends. As the weather was looking pretty bad and we were venturing into unknown territory on the moor that day, he thought he should let his close ones know just in case we went missing! I remember thinking, actually saying out loud, there was no one really for me to call as "I was alone in the world and no one would give a stuff about me or even know I'd gone missing!" ... SOUNDS needy I know but just an indication of how I was starting to feel at that time and the start of huge depression ... By this time things were terrible between me and the Wife, the kids weren't speaking to me properly and I had shut my family out, Mum and Sisters etc. as I wanted to just get through it all alone. What friends I had left at this time had pretty much had enough of me, were tired of hearing the same old record. If I'd not been living with Dan, think he would've tired of me too ... well towards the end of my stay he did actually!

But I still had Frank. By taking him out on these days, it kept my connection with him intact. I would also pop back to the house and take him out for the odd walk here and there, when I was allowed. Again, we would spend quality time together. In fact, if I hadn't of made the effort to do this, I realised that he actually would not have had a decent walk. Whilst she and the boys loved him, he was by now spending a lot more time doing his stuff in THAT garden than on proper dog walks. I could gauge this by the amount of poos I offered to scoop up on my odd visit back to my old house, mainly at the weekends when I was free from work and had time to take Frank for good, long walks.

So back at Dan's, it was nearing Christmas. Bloody Christmas and I had now been in situ for 6 months . . . Sorry Mate! Didn't expect to be spending my first Christmas away from the family at Dan's house! Indeed, I did actually stay over at my old house on Christmas Eve; slept downstairs on the sofa so I could wake up and see the boys open their pressies . . . that was nice but very emotional and I thought I had cried enough that year! I left around 10 ish as they had to spend the rest of the Christmas with her family. So I was on my own at Dan's for the festivities . . . Dan was around his family home. BUT, he did allow me to have FRANK with me . . . me n' Frank cooked a tasty roast for us which I'd prepared and I spent the whole of Christmas / Boxing Day with Frank at Dan's . . . getting pissed on red wine (me not Frank!), crying over emotional Xmas telly crap and, generally, feeling a little needy and sorry for myself! BUT, get through it I did, another challenge overcome. Part of my "Course-Work" in my Degree Course in LIFE! I had a rule of never letting Frank in the bedroom . . . I'd brought out his bed to put downstairs in the kitchen but, drunk and emotional, I said "sod it, come on Frank, come up and keep me company" . . . as I lead him to my bedroom at the end of Christmas Day. I regretted that decision the next morning . . . never go to bed with a big black Lab; the hairs are a nightmare to get off the duvet the next day!

Hey, then New Year's Eve . . . that first year. Again, what do you do? When you're single, alone and "not in a good place" in that bloody head department. Still down, depressed, skint and trying to deal with all the shit being thrown at me! Wherever I went, there were inevitably going to be people who didn't want me there, friends of the scorned Ex, "friends" who had already made their mind up about me and thrown me out of their lives. You know those ones . . . those shallow people that live in glass houses and throw stones! Quick to judge but not as quick to look at their own shitty lives and behaviour! I could go on and write another Sermon but they aint worth the energy or my creative writing time! Needless to say, they will know who they are and if they wanted to abandon me from their lives so quickly after being a part of it for so long, purely based on their warped judgements of events that had occurred in the split up, their shout! Their call, their loss! I am sure they are all much better people than me and oh so Perfect!... NOT! Well, anyway, here's what 'appened... Dan was throwing a party at his house for the footy team, all his teacher friends and anyone whom he knew! Plenty of booze, open 'ouse! By this time (couple of months back), he had met Jen and she too was a teacher. So the whole dynamic had changed anyway at "home" and there were "3 people in this relationship" now! So Dan asked me to be at the party... obviously because I was living there! And the Wife, on the other hand, had invited me round to the house to see New Year in with her and the lads. But... emotionally I could not do either! Just wasn't up to partying and actually pretending to enjoy meself... and could not face the emotional barrage either way. So I went into work that day, went on Tinternet and found a last minute cheap night at the Future Inn in the City! -Told Dan I was going round to the house and told her I was going to the party so neither would be worried or bothered about me or wondering where I was that night! Sneaked a few bits in a bag, booked meself in around 2ish in the afternoon... had bought myself a couple of 'papers and mags, some Wine gums and just laid on me bed watching telly and trying to forget the outside world and all that was going on in "normal" land! I did actually venture out for a walk by the sea, had a quick meal and beer in the local Weatherspoons but, not in the mood to party, wandered back to the sanctity of me hotel room alone... no partying, no getting drunk, no call girls or funny business! Just a sad old git on his own reading the local 'paper, drinking Red wine, watching the crap on New Year's Eve telly! Did call me MUM and texted a few people but still didn't give the game away!... More Character Building!

Around the Christmas period, I had a big Man to Man talk with Dan. As I said, Jen was on the scene now and things had changed. Even despite this, it was clear "my time was up" and, to save our friendship and our Sanity, it was important that I must think seriously in the New Year of moving on. It was obvious by now that I was not getting back together with the Wife and I needed to sort myself out... in All ways! I promised Dan in that chat I'd be out by Easter one way or another!... We shook hands, had a hug and agreed on this. It WAS time to start the Next Chapter!...

I actually sorted something out and turned the next page by mid Feb...

Chapter Four

BedSHITland!

So, done the "living with me mate bit" . . . now it was the stark reality of living ALONE! . . . It was obvious I had to move out of Dan's at some point. No chance of me crawling back to the family home, kissing and making up and pretending nothing had happened, All live Happily Ever After! Nah, none of that was going to happen. I now had to face the prospect of finding somewhere to live that was cheap and near to my little business. To be honest, it didn't take long; looked at a couple of places and came across a former Old People's Home that a property developer had snapped up on the cheap and was in the interim stage of getting Planning permission to do up. Meanwhile, he was renting out all the rooms to get some dosh in whilst all the legal stuff was going through. Something like that anyway! I didn't really care about his business. The house was literally a couple hundred yards away from the office (above a shop) that I had been renting for a few months anyway to keep my little magazine business going. So I could get up in the morning and just walk to the office! Save a bit of petrol I thought. If I could've worked from "home" I would've done but the noise in that bedsit, no internet connection and landlords rules wouldn't allow for that. Anyway, as it turned out, the office became a necessary ESCAPE from "that room" and its demons! To be fair, it was an airy room, one bedroom / lounge, little (minute to be honest) kitchen bit and me own toilet! Though I had to walk down the corridor to the shower room . . . it wasn't a shared one but I had to keep it locked to keep all and sundry out of it! Being an ex-Care home, the whole house had its own distinct smell of disinfectant, cleaning chemicals and ... probably urine and Death!

But I overlooked any negative thoughts and just saw it as a means to an end at this juncture. If anything, the biggest thing I let upset me about this move was the fact that the landlord's rules were "no pets" allowed. This of course meant that Frank would have to continue to stay back at the house with the family. I had a word with him on one of our weekend "catch ups" and explained I was sorry but had to do this but I would get around to see him and take him out as much as possible ... which, in fact, because the bedsit was just around the road from them, I anticipated a lot more contact with him and, you'd expect, my Sons as well! I also told him (Frank, that is!) that I would sneak him in to the room when I could!

Up till now, I had been paying the mortgage and bills "at home" and trying to make sure the family had not been affected financially from the split up. It had been a struggle for me as the business was not making much but obviously it had helped living at Dan's where I had only been paying him a token gesture rent as well as feeding myself. But now, there was the reality check of just physically not being able to afford renting an office, renting a flat and all that goes with that AS WELL as paying that mortgage, bills etc. on top. As it was clear we weren't getting back with each other, we agreed we would sell the house (the sensible thing) and make a little bit of profit (at that time) and properly go our separate ways. So I put it on the market and we for once were in complete agreement on something. But then, only a couple of weeks later, she decided she wanted to stay in the house and fight to keep it. She said, "it's the kids' house" and she didn't want to lose it for their sakes. I sort of saw where she was coming from and tapped into this line of thought and emotion. But, in reality, this basically meant she would stay in the house not being able to afford the mortgage herself, somehow Still expect me to wave a magic wand and find another grand a month on top of all my new responsibilities to survive and all would be good! So, on top of emotions, anxieties, a complete change of life for me, so began also an ongoing battle with her to see my point of view. I implored her that if she was going to choose to stay in that house, she would somehow have to find a way to pay for it. I earnestly, humbly tried to reason with her... "I would if I could, believe me, but I just can't pay for all this, please let's sell it!" I DID try, I really did, to pay for it all but I simply couldn't so this meant the mortgage started to fall into arrears... more of all that later, I know I am boring you now!

So, here I was in Bedsit land. Well I did have my own Bed! And yes a new one at that! I had done a deal with one of my clients who had... a Bed Shop as it happened! And he gave me a nice new bed, complete with a lovely memory foam mattress! That's where my luxuries ended. All of my nice stuff we had collected over the years was back at the house. So I had to beg, steal or borrow basic goods like a telly, fridge etc. Got given someone's ancient box of a telly which worked with one of those internal aerials which for this telly was actually the size of something you'd see at an Airport! Had an old fridge from work and bought one of those canvas stand alone "wardrobes" that, within days, went all out of shape after hanging a few clothes in it! The landlord had supplied all the rooms with a Mini –Oven / grill thing... like you'd take camping! How I Cooked on that pathetic little thing for the next 7/8 months I will never know... but I did! And that was it, pretty much the extent of my possessions at 47 years old! Oh I did get my old bike back and some more of my clothes and I think she gave me some old bedding... great!

It would be a case of get up early (have always had an early morning ethic), bomb down the corridor to the shower before any of the neighbours got up, shower then creep back to my room in my towel to finish off pruning in the flat. Then I would get out of that building as early as possible to the sanctuary of my office down the road. Work stupid hours, then get back to the flat, normally after dark to get in, lock that door behind me and shut out the world. There were 3 other rooms in and around that corridor in very close proximity of mine so it was difficult not to hear what was going on in those rooms as, let's say, noises and voices travel quite easily. Immediately next door was a young Polish couple . . . never spoke a word of English, well maybe "hallo!" They constantly had loud Polish music on, they shouted at each other quite a bit and She would be "out all hours" at "work" . . . you can only guess! He didn't seem to have a job but spent the majority of his time doing up an old motorbike in the communal car park with a "For Sale" sign on it! I would pass them on the stairs or in the car park and would just nod my head out of courtesy but if I ever saw them down the local shopping main street, I have to admit I avoided them . . . just didn't want the familiarity, the invasion of my privacy and, I guess, the snob in me didn't want to publicly admit I lived in the same house as these weird people! Anyway, a few months down the line, I found out through the lady who worked in the Landlord's office where I had to go and pay my rent monthly, that they had done a moonlight flit, owing several month's rent!

Across the corridor, there was another young couple who just used to either argue all the time or Shag! I suppose it was "make up sex" but boy, I THINK their relationship was the definition of **volatile**.I had to turn the telly up to blot out the sound of their bloody shouting at each other, not just the noise of it but the sheer ferocity of their language. I can swear but this was swearing with bells on it, Olympic Gold Medal swearing! And, yes, I think there was a bit of violence thrown in on occasion from what I could gather. But the telly didn't go up when the make up sex was going on . . . that was a sound I could put up with! Well, despite everything, I am still a Man at the end of the day. BUT, it just made me jealous more than anything!

In the next room was a youngish girl on her own though her boyfriend visited frequently. And, they too would have Sex . . . grrrrrrrrrrrrr! All this sex going on around me but not in My Bloody room! But to cap it all, in one of the flats downstairs was a Scotch guy who lived alone . . . Oh, Just like me! This guy would get really drunk on many occasions and sometimes would lock himself out of the flat and then bang on his own door to accuse himself of locking **him** out!

I swear I thought I had died and gone to Hell living in that place. It was certainly an eye-opener and the scariest place I had ever lived in. Most of the time I just tried to get through that big Front door, run up the stairs to my flat and get in and shut tight my own door and just wallow in my own company. More Character building? Christ, give me a break! But, yes, this was going to prove a massive challenge adapting to living in this hell hole. So what do you do? There's only one thing to settle this? ... DRINK! ...

I have always liked a drink but in the main have drunk to be sociable, NOT to get drunk! But this was a different situation I found myself in. I guess I was entering a huge depression fuelled by the stark Reality of what my life had come to. And to "shut it all out", one glass of Red each night turned into a bottle, sometimes two plus. Have to say that I ventured into shorts or alternative drinks **only occasionally.** The Wine seemed to do the trick thanks very much! I could drink a bottle or 2 most nights and STILL rely on my body clock ... and still to this day nothing has changed ... to wake me up early to get to work. Whether I fell asleep at 3 in the morning in a drunken stupor or I had an early night i.e. just hid myself under the duvet at 8 to "escape", no matter how many hours sleep I mustered, always got up early to get on with my routine! But, in the main, it was getting drunk, then dozing off, but the nights were, as they had been for a while now, either sleepless or lots of intermittent sleep. I had started to sink into a black depression and the early hours of the morning were the worst times as that's when I had time to THINK! And then the Demons started creeping into my bloody head. So much guilt, so much remorse, regrets and so the painful process of "beating myself up" began.

On many an occasion, I sat on my bed, watching my loud telly, drinking wine, only RED of course out of my massive goblet that could hold a whole bottle ... just saved me getting up and refilling all the bloody time! And, of course, red wine has to breathe doesn't it? But on more than one occasion, I fell asleep or dozed off holding said goblet and ended up coming to, having poured red wine all over me and the bed! Initial reaction was that I'd cut myself and was dying! Then more anger that it had all come to this . . . as well as having to clean up – and not a bottle of white in sight!

After over 15 years of living in a family environment, here I was . . . Alone in a shitty Bedsit, alone, drinking, depressed, skint and lonely. But NOT NEEDY . . . Never Needy . . . there is a fine line distinction between loneliness and neediness and I have never been needy. But All I wanted to do was shut the world out, that horrible world that existed in those rooms adjacent to mine AND that bloody world "out there" in "normal people's land" . . . I started to feel (and this feeling lasted for a long long time) that somehow I was no longer part of the Real world, not required anymore, surplus to requirements, useless. Of course, I know now (after years of working through it all and lots of bloody counselling!) that this was just a self - induced mechanism fuelled by depression and anxiety. But I was telling myself it's Karma . . . life's way of paying me back for what I'd done, my punishment for leaving my Wife and kids, the mistakes I had made in life. It was like I had been thrown into Prison to "serve my time."

I started to shut people out including my family, partly my pride kicking in as I didn't want people to see me like this; I can cope alone, I can get through this I said, It's only a phase . . . Tough love, character building, what goes around comes around, it will all be ok in time . . . you hear it all, you say it all to yourself but somehow, at the time, going through it, none of that shit helps you through what you have to endure at THAT TIME! And anyway, by now, most of my friends who'd been around for me at the early stages of the split up, had now become exhausted of the emotional crap. Being entirely honest, with the exception of maybe a few, the majority of my "friends" had jumped onto the Ex's bandwagon and stayed on the side of the only "victim" in all this . . . Another saying: "True friends don't judge" as "there are ALWAYS 2 sides to a story." But I had to pummel myself for a few years first before this sunk in. For now, in the bedsit, I lived everyday thinking, convinced IT WAS ALL MY FAULT and I HAD TO PAY FOR MY DECISIONS THAT CAUSED ALL THIS HURT.

It was a weird, very mixed up time for me. I had for the most of my life been in control of things, a strong, positive, confident man. Intelligent and articulate, always with a plan B in case things went off course. But, here I was, in the worst place I had ever lived, at my lowest ebb, down and desolate with no control or way out. Of course, I still had the little business to get me out of bed in the morning. I was still a proud man that got up, showered and shaved (not as much) and got in there and did my best to scratch a living. Without this, I probably would've cracked up properly. By now, don't forget we were 7 or 8 months down the line. Everyone, even my kids seemed to have "moved on!" It was just me that had his feet in quick sand! I had all these Demons in my head... It was ALL in my head... Demons, demons, they just kept coming at me and my brain was like a bag of nails waiting to explode. And this is mainly why I couldn't make a good go of it with anyone else I met, because I had to rid myself of these demons first... get rid of the emotional cancer that was eating away at my brain.

About 4 months in to my tenure in the bedsit, I did something really stupid, so out of character and, to this day, still unexplainable to me... All I can say perhaps in my defence is that this was the point I was near to my lowest ebb in all this journey of singledom! Danny had thought my lowest point was that day after the races; this was to prove to be worse than that! I had reached a place in my head that was Not a good place to be. A very dark, depressing, scary place. ONE that I was not happy to be in and, quite frankly, didn't know what to do about. On this particular occasion, I had been asked by a client to attend, as his guest (all paid for and on the top table), an "evening with Geoff Hurst", the famous old footballer who had scored the hat-trick in the 1966 World Cup winning England team. It was one of those very boozy, all Male nights, the room full of testosterone, egos and nostalgia. Must admit, the way I was feeling at that time, didn't really relish the thought of actually "enjoying myself!" But, I had really liked these kind of nights in the past, love my footy and I was not really in a position to turn down a completely Free evening out! Apart from playing footy on a Friday, couple of beers after, the odd drink with a mate now and again, my "social life" had been reduced to drinking alone in the Bedsit, drowning me sorrows. I did, very occasionally, wander down to the local village street and meet up with a friend and his Wife in one of the local pubs down there which I hated but, sometimes, it was a necessary evil Just to get me out of that Room!

Anyway, I digress. There I was on the top table, mixing with the snobs and knobs at this do! At these things you always get a mix of people but, in the main, it's full of pretentious, up their own arse, businessmen who have "taken over the world" and been the best at what they do! . . . Mostly in their dreams and alcohol filled thoughts! Very rarely do you meet a genuine person at these things, someone like me that just tells it how it is! Admits when he's up and does the same when he's down. So, in the "place" I was at this time, I just chose to go along, sit at that table and pleasantly take in all the crap going on around me and proceed to eat and drink as much as was available, very quickly getting as drunk as a Skunk! Where does that saying come from by the way? When was the last time a Skunk was spotted with a glass of Red in his hand or slobbering his way back to his den after a few beers down t' pub with his smelly mates? The evening was a good one, great entertainment and football themed. It was the year of the World Cup finals, hence the Geoff Hurst booking and the buzz in the room was the normal anticipation that England were gonna win it Again. Yeh Right! . . . Needed to be drunk to embrace that notion!

However, despite my switch off, letting my hair down, I could not "escape" the demons going on in my head. You cannot legislate for the things that jump into your brain to pester you, eat away and terrorise your well-being. With all this noise, banter, drinking, tomfoolery going on around me, the night's over bearing thought in my head was of my Ex sleeping with her new boyfriend. I knew she was out with him that night. . . . And the rest of the demons jumping in and out of my head that night were ones that had already begun to plague me on those endless sleepless nights in the Bedsit... She was having the best Sex she'd ever had and he was much, much better than me in that department. Bloody insecurity and fucking Demons! **All just going on in my head grrrrrr!** Where does all that come from? By the time I had finished me main meal, he'd done everything with her and was going back for another session whilst I was waiting for the dessert to turn up!... And these demons, these thoughts just kept flashing through my head... I was in a plush Hotel function room but, in my mind, I was on the ceiling of that bedroom or wherever they might be, watching them cavort and do things that I could only imagine... grrrrrrrrrrrrrr!

In essence, they could've just been quietly sat watching telly or out for a drink but, no, I had to imagine they were DOING IT!... So the evening went on and I got through it somehow. Perhaps all my years as a professional Salesman had given me the "tools" to deal with this situation. In sales it's like being an actor; sometimes, even if you don't feel like it, you just have to put on your "make up", brush yourself down and "go on stage." Drunk as I was this night, the persona I gave off was one of a businessman out on an enjoyable evening, holding my own in "the ring." Little did anybody know the horrible thoughts in my head... or what this would lead me to do the Next day...

So the night came to an end; I was extremely drunk, not in a stupid way just in my normal jolly way. Wrong word really to sum up my inner feelings! I had driven to the Hotel and my plan was to leave my car in the car park there, then get a taxi home, then ride my bike out the next day to pick up the car. Well, my mate, Steve, who had also attended the event, offered me a lift home so that was good. Got "home" to the bedsit around 2ish I think, fell into bed and got a few hours kip. As usual, the natural "body-clock" awoke me early, around 7ish I think... a lie in for me! Well I got the bike out, still feeling a bit hungover from the night before, but managed somehow to ride it the 2 or 3 miles back to the hotel. If I am honest, I don't really remember much about that bike ride... couldn't have been the most enjoyable one I'd done! Got to the hotel, put the bike in the back of the car and

THEN I should've just driven back to the bedsit and got my head down again. But no . . . and THIS is where I cannot really explain my actions. The next string of events has no rhyme or reason. But plagued by those stupid demons from the night before, I drove to his house . . . the Ex's new, young boyfriend! Still drink inside me from the night before, I parked outside. . . . I scanned the car park and, sure enough, there it was . . . HER CAR, little black Mini I had bought her for her 40th. I just froze, started crying my bloody eyes out and shook, just shook with emotion. It was like my heart had been ripped out. I guess, if there is ANY reason for being there, it was just to be faced with the reality that she WAS actually with him and that he **did** exist, wasn't just someone she had made up to get me back. But there was her car, she must be in there with him. I just stood and stared at her car, wondering What room they were in . . . My mind was gone, I was a blubbering mess, couldn't make any sense of my thoughts at all. And then, I don't know perhaps 20 / 30 minutes later My Wife finally surfaced and I saw her and Him and still really didn't know what I was doing there! I was screwed up, confused and angry. They walked out of the front door to her car, looking very sheepish and sort of glanced over in my direction to see me squirming behind a fence. I think they saw me; I certainly saw them! Now, at this point, I didn't know what to do . . . I should've just got in my car and gone home and just cried myself back to sleep. After all, I had now seen him, he was real, mission accomplished. And, in my defence, I didn't actually see which way she turned out of the road. I could've missed her altogether and That would've been that; but I just got in my car and drove back towards the main road, still crying, barely being able to see the road through my tears. Pathetic! As FATE would have it, sure enough, in my rear mirror, I just could see her behind me in her little car. We were about ¼ of a mile now away from his house. I pulled into a little layby, she pulled in behind me. I got out of the car, still crying, shaking with emotion, just in a shocking state. She wound her window down and just said: "Why Malc, Why are you here? What do you think you are going to achieve with this?" . . . "I don't know, I just Don't know", I spluttered, is all I could summon.

She just continued to rant how I could've got myself into trouble, just straightforward shit like that. I ranted back a few things at her . . . I just wasn't making any sense; I knew I shouldn't of been there. I was full of emotion, bitterness, anger, jealousy, pent up feelings . . . grrrrrrrrrrrrr! She just said "I'm going now, I'm going to work" and proceeded to wind up her window and go to drive off. With this, the red mist took over. I have NEVER EVER been a violent man but I just instinctively banged hard on her passenger window, shouting and screaming for her Not to go. We needed to talk, we needed to argue more! But what I HADN'T anticipated and definitely didn't plan was that my hand would actually smash the window, it never connected with her but yes she was then sat there with glass all over her lap and a couple of minor cuts. In that INSTANT, I just immediately came to terms with what I'd done! I HAD NEVER intended to hurt her or, indeed, to cause any damage. It was just a cry for help, an appeal for her to listen to me, to help me, I don't know, just help me explain some of the demons. And, after all, she was still my Wife wasn't she?

So what now? . . . We both froze for a moment, in sheer shock, looking at each other contemplating what to do. "Shall we call the Police?", I offered, "I am so sorry, so sorry, Are you ok?" I was just in a state of limbo, hadn't a clue why I'd gone there in the first place or how it had all come to this. After a few moments, she brushed herself down and calmly said: "Malc, look, don't worry, just go, just go . . . get home, I will not call the Police, I'll just clean myself up, call work to let them know I will be in later and get myself sorted, just go now."

"ARE YOU SURE, let me stay and help, please", I said . . . She insisted she'd be ok so I reluctantly got back in my car and drove away. I was still shaking and feeling physically sick from what had happened. My mind was just a daze. I got back, parked up and got into my flat. Within literally 2 minutes of closing the door behind me, there was a knock on the door and there stood 4 policemen! They arrested me and put me in handcuffs and escorted me down the stairs to the car. I saw another 2 police cars in the car park full of cops! It was like a scene out of a film . . . the worst film you ever went to see! Certainly my worst nightmare. They took me to the police station in town and the nightmare continued. This is a guy that had never done anything illegal in his life, never hit anyone, never been in a fight. I'm a lover not a fighter! I was subsequently bunged in a cell where I spent the whole day . . . it was mainly to allow me to cool off and calm down, though I had done that as soon as the copper had put those hand cuffs on! I was an easy arrest, full of remorse and guilt as soon as I had done the deed itself and ready to take whatever they threw at me. As it turned out, the several hours I spent in that cell alone with just a cup of tea and a cold pasty gave me the time I needed to think, really think about my actions that day and how low my life had sunk.

It also gave them time to collect in their statements from her, the boyfriend et al . . . found out many months later it was actually Him who had called the Police; She hadn't wanted to but because she had called him as soon as I had left the scene, he came out to her to help her. That is irrelevant now; I deserved to be thrown into a cell and deserved my Caution I got later in the day. Always remember the really nice civilian policeman who interviewed me; before he turned the tape on, he explained how he had been through a divorce many years ago and that there were times he'd felt like killing his Wife! I said I never meant to kill her, I was just angry with her and lashed out . . . "think you ought to leave that out of your statement on tape!" . . . "just keep to the story as it happened and you'll be home in time for your tea!" . . . He was brilliant that guy. He knew I was not your everyday criminal, just a guy that had lost his way, lost the plot and, anyway, he told me she was not pressing charges. After my interview and Caution, the Inspector actually apologised to me for having kept me so long that day and having to treat me like all the "Real" offenders in the other bloody cells! He said he could see I wasn't one of them as soon as I walked in, I had never been in trouble before and was an intelligent, switched on guy. Pity I couldn't have used that intelligence before driving to that stupid house!

Nice civilian police man drove me home in his own car, shook my hand and wished me well. I got into the Bedsit, slammed my door shut tight and just cried and cried and cried, still not believing what I had just gone through or what my life had come to. I did 'phone me old Mum in Surrey (as I always did at weekends) . . . I broke my heart to her on the 'phone. She was devastated for me. I spoke to no one else that day. Just went to bed to try to shut it out.

So this was my lowest moment, or WAS IT? Could I sink any lower than this? I didn't think so but there were lower times to come. The immediate aftermath of this event was the obvious apologies to everyone, the Wife, my kids, her family and my friends. By my actions, I had let them all down and I had shown publicly that I was a "loose cannon", at the end of my tether. But it was weird really looking back . . . because rather than helping me through this low point, with the exception of my dear old Mum (by now in her late 70's), everyone just seemed to hate me, disown me, in fact some, especially my kids, were a little wary of me and all distanced themselves, choosing to show no compassion. Again I was not looking for any sympathy. As with everything, the decision to leave home and so on, I was ready to take the 100% blame for my behaviour. On this occasion, yes, I was wrong to do what I did and had gone too far. I could've really hurt her . . . but, hold on, FRIENDS, FAMILY (not mine as I had consciously kept them out of my problems at this juncture), give me a bit of slack here, help me don't judge me for Christ's sake. Another example of finding out people's true colours and how they REALLY feel about you. Enough said.

So it took time to get over that one and lots of time before I resumed "normal" relations with my Sons most importantly, then my friends. My boys were understandably angry at Dad for hurting Mum. But they came round eventually and time healed. But not before I sunk into an even deeper depression. My day in Jail was the catalyst for me to enter a very dark time. I was living alone, working alone, alone night times with just my thoughts and wine. I drank Even more and just got more and more into myself, shutting out the world. Still trying to cope alone and sort out all my problems single handedly, refusing any help . . . not that there was much on offer as I said . . . the odd people that wanted to help, I shut out as I thought they couldn't and actually didn't understand the extent of my problems. I had already a long time ago "exhausted" other friends, drained them of their emotional ability to help me. Anyway, blokes just get on with it, don't they? That's what we are meant to do! "Be strong, pull yourself together, grow some balls" ... we are conditioned to bloody well cope. No, apart from Mum (but she was too far away in Surrey), I HAD NO ONE. Alone in this world and with no fight left at this time. I was still getting up every day going through the motions of working in that little office above the shop, running that stupid little magazine, earning a pittance. No, it was all pointless, saw no future, nobody cared, my life was worthless I thought. There was only one thing to do ... kill myself. I was just so low, couldn't see any way out of the hole I was in and my thoughts turned to how and when would be the right time to do it. I was still articulate enough to research it on Tinternet! Analysing the best ways, the quickest, easiest ways to do it. Look at me, even in my gloomiest hour, still the strategist, ever the Planner! I decided the best, easiest way to carry this out would be the hose-pipe trick from the exhaust to the car. One particularly gloomy day, after yet another argument with the Ex ... this time it was about me wanting to go back. Yes, in my screwed up state of mind, I was still convinced we loved each other enough, despite everything that had happened, to be able to put the past behind us and make things up. Get back together, for the sake of everyone, put things back on track. At this point in the process, I was prepared to do, say whatever it took to put my family back together ... and stop Him or any other bloke having her! ... That was a big part in my desire to have her back. The old "if I can't have her, no one else is either!" I wanted her back ... but for all the wrong reasons; yes, I still loved her but when you are low and depressed you just forget the reasons you left in the first place and Only remember the happy times.

So, another argument where she adamantly was not having me back. To be fair, I wasn't the most attractive proposition either was I? Skint, looking shit and quite frankly, a bit of a fruit-cake at this time, not just one screw loose but the whole bloody lot! So I slammed the door, ran out of the house, sped down to Sainsbury's Homebase and bought myself a garden hose! Being pretty skint AND, having always been a bit like Frank Spencer in the DIY department, I bought the cheapest hose going, a thin black one, not your proper, heavy duty one for the job! But, no matters, a hose it was and I drove straight out to the Moors, found an isolated place where I had been many times with the dog for walks but this time there was no idyllic stroll over the moor with Frank, taking in the lovely, natural landscape. No, this time, I parked up, looked around to make sure no one was about and proceeded to put the hose up the exhaust of the car and flow it in through the window where I sat, just like I had noted from my Internet research. I calmly switched the engine on and waited for several minutes for IT to happen. Nothing seemed to be coming through, no fumes, no smoke, nothing... to be honest, looking back it probably was the wrong type of hose, far too flimsy for this job. That said, I have no doubt that if I had sat there for longer than I did, eventually it would have happened. Surely, it has to be the most straightforward way to kill yourself? No, after several minutes, what really "kicked in" was not my frustration of it not working but my thoughts of my Boys and my dear old Mum. As I sat there, alone, crying, very determined to leave this shit existence of a life I was enduring, Daniel, Tom and Mum popped into my head... Only THEM, no one else, absolutely no one else. Everybody else in my life could cope with me doing this, would move on from it. All my friends and family, well they already had their own lives and, at this time were not in mine much anyway. Sad as everyone might be at the news, they would All get over it after the funeral. These were my thoughts, sombre as they seem. Funeral, funeral? What bloody funeral... the way I was going, I'd be in a Pauper's grave!

So it was the thought of how my Sons and my Mum would cope after losing me that stopped me carrying out this ghastly deed. And, I will be totally honest, predominant in those thoughts was Tom, now still only 13. Daniel was 19 and his life as a young man was "on its way" if you see what I mean. He was already at that age, whether me and his Mum were together or not, where he was already independent to a degree and "out there." My dear old Special Mum, nearly 80, had had her life as it were, or the best part of it and, though she'd be devastated, I think she could still find a way of coping with the sadness. She is a tough old bird and has been through so much in her life, I thought she'd have something in her "tool box" to deal with this. But Tom, my Boy . . . I had hurt him so much already by leaving, how would he Move on from this? My mind flashed back to that day I left, that pivotal day the previous June. I remembered him begging me to stay . . . "don't go Dad, Don't go", he shouted at me through his tears, "I love you Dad" . . . he tried to pull me back and I nearly, ever so nearly stayed because of him . . . but my determination to rid myself of the overall unhappiness took over and I went. But, I will never forget that little boy's face that day, the desperation to make his Dad stay. These were my thoughts on this horrible day on the Moors. So after what was in total about an hour or so, I shook myself, wiped my tears and came to my senses. Scurried to get the hose in the car, bunged it into the boot and just drove hurriedly to get back to the sanctity of the bedsit. Another horrible day, another bottle of wine to "drown it out" if possible. Another sleepless night with my black thoughts.

So did I really want to kill myself? I still can't honestly answer that question. All I know is that when you are That down, that alone, with just no answers, it becomes a distinct option . . . I was determined enough to think about doing it and for a period of time in the action of it, I was in that frame of mind to carry it out. But, THANKFULLY, that "bigger picture" mentality took over and stopped me.

I will admit that twice more at various down times, once again when living in the bedsit and, later, when I was back at my old family home, did I attempt the "process" of ending it all. I didn't really get any further than that first time for exactly the same emotional reasons as before but on the 2nd attempt (whilst living at the bedsit), I did actually take some wine and pills out to the moors to accompany the hose-pipe. But still I couldn't go through with it.

After the 2nd attempt, I did realise that I needed Help . . . Professional help.

So here I was . . . a year or so in to this Split up malarkey, living in BedSHITland, two half-hearted but disturbing suicide attempts, drinking myself to oblivion, depressed, lonely, my mind all screwed up . . . Yep, think it was time to pop along to the Docs. Remember walking in there that day. First thing I said to her was "Hi, how are you?" We always do that don't we, up or down, we are there to be sorted out and we ask the bloody doctor how she is? Then I went on to ask her if she could look up on her computer the last time I had been there (to the Doc's). It was about 5 years before when I had a vasectomy! And before that hardly ever. I just wanted to make the point to her that I "didn't do" Doctors and was here because I was absolutely desperate for help . . . I had no answers left, couldn't or wouldn't open up to anyone in my circles, didn't know when my next night of full sleep was coming from and of course I told her about the drinking and the frazzled brain! When they smell Depression, they get out this sheet of 20 odd questions that they have to ask you . . . General stuff to begin with like "how many hours sleep are you getting?" . . . "are you eating regularly?" . . . "do you avoid social situations", blah blah blah; then around question 16, you get: "have you had suicidal thoughts?" Well, I had been nothing but up front with her till then but I did hesitate on this question and then decided I must tell her everything. After all, I had come here for her help, I was desperate for some guidance through my problems. I didn't have any solutions. So I answered truthfully and told her about my aborted attempts. She jotted it all down. She offered me anti-depressants but I had always been against taking pills so declined. She just said she'd like to see me again to discuss a possible course of counselling as there was nothing physically wrong with me but she acknowledged I had issues. Well, I thought that was that for the moment; booked another appointment to see her in a couple of weeks and I walked out of there, relieved I'd got it off my chest but still a bit cynical about the NHS and was it a waste of time? What I hadn't banked on was what came next! The next day I got a 'phone call out of the blue. It was a Counsellor's receptionist who cut straight to the chase and TOLD me I had to come in asap, like Tomorrow for an appointment with ... obviously a Counsellor! She said that I'd been referred by my Doctor and that it was "Extremely important in view of my situation", that I attend this certain Mental Health Clinic NOW! ... Hey, hold on a minute, I wasn't going bonkers here, I didn't need no bloody Specialist Nutter Doctor ... or Did I? She was very firm with me and insisted I HAD to attend ... though she didn't say the words, there was an "Or Else" in there, I sensed. So, I managed to put her off till the Friday of that week, giving me a day to get my head around it ... excuse the pun in there somewhere! But, I just spent that next day I had bought worrying and stressing over the impending appointment.

Not sure what I had opened myself up to by going to the Docs. and laying my soul on the line. I had actually been to one counsellor before ... a Homeopathic counsellor, a lady called Anne, recommended by a friend. Obviously they give you complimentary medicines, if only in very small doses, to combat your defined "ailment." This was before my deep depression had set in and was right at the early stages of my marriage breakdown. My friend thought it would help me to see Anne as she was a very good Life coach and, obviously, at that time it was clear that my head was already all over the place with guilt, emotion and confusion. I went along to see Anne with a Very open mind as I had never sought out counselling before, never! Anne, I have to say, was brilliant. She was a hell of a lot more than someone who Just dished out pills ... At that very first meeting, she let me speak for an hour non- stop about where I was with everything. Quite apart from anything, I was paying her £40 a session, so that bought my confidence in her! But, yes, she was brilliant, lovely, intense and a very perceptive Lady, excellent at what she does. I actually walked in fully prepared (that's me, ever the planner and strategist!) with a note book in my hand with a pre-thought out diagram containing all my "boxes" that I needed her to fix for me. Although my emotions and thoughts were all over the show at that time, I was articulate enough to write into separate boxes, titles of all the aspects of my life that were affecting me and I needed her advice to overcome. And THERE WERE MANY BLOODY BOXES!... "Wife and the Kids"... "Dark Demons"... "Money"... "The house"... "Friends"... "Family"... "Work" and so on and so on!... and we only had a bloody hour for Christ's sake; I was asking her to fix World PEACE here!

Although she allowed me to show her this ill-fated attempt at trying to make some sense of it all, she didn't need my script. She got me straight away in that first session. Had a note pad in front of her but didn't scribble anything on hers which I questioned at the end! But she said she didn't have to write anything... it was all processed in her mind. And, sure enough, on my next meeting with her, she had retained IT ALL precisely! And the one word she used to sum up where I was and what I had to face and deal with was not regret, remorse or guilt but ANGER! I was angry that my life had been so turbulent these last few years but my anger went back further than that... it stemmed back to my childhood when my old Dad (rest his soul) had moved us all down from our stable environment where we'd all been brought up (Brother and 2 Sisters) in Surrey to sleepy Devon!... A sub conscious anger that this was why life had turned out such bloody hard work; rather than going at the 100 miles an hour pace I had been brought up with and knew and liked, I had had to adapt to a much slower pace of life and the people in it, not only in my personal life but in business too. She was spot on as I had always had a problem with the severe apathy in this part of the country, the procrastination and sheer indecisiveness that was "not in my blood." Like my Dad, she made me realise that I had Never really settled down here and now, in a way, was tied by my commitments and responsibilities, mainly my boys, to stay here and fight the fight. And, indeed, I was now a Dinosaur, too old to move back as I would now be like a fish out of water up there! So, this was the core of my problem.

She also identified that, as I thought I had to and so many guys do, I had played out my role of Husband, Father, chief bread-winner for years and years without getting back the real happiness I sought. I had become "institutionalised" into a regimented way to behave. Do the right thing, say the right thing, be an upstanding citizen! If your Wife says we need to spend this or that on the kids, go on holiday, eat out, have a nice car, house etc. etc . . . go with that as **it's the right thing to do!** Keep everyone happy. But, Anne highlighted, I knew all along I was unhappy, these things don't make you happy, spending money is irrelevant to fulfilment and real contentment. Being with the right person, sharing natural (spontaneous) things, being content with each other's company, time and thoughts and feelings are what matters. Not materialism. So Anne gave me lots to think about there but, as is the case with these situations, no over-night Fix! She was realistic with me and very honest. I had a couple more sessions with her but she made me realise that my process of working through all my stuff was going to take a whole lot longer than that. I had read that Divorce / separation, especially after a long relationship like ours, is a bit like bereavement and, just on average, takes at least a couple of years to get over. To work through all the Natural elements of it, guilt, regret, remorse, reflection, jealousy of new partners, anger, sadness, more anger(!), not to mention all the practical, financial, kids issues etc. etc . . . grrrrrrrrrr!

So Anne was great and gave me plenty to think about and to work on in my mind. Aside from my 3 or 4 visits to Anne, I did pop back to see her a couple more times, perhaps a year then 2 after, just for a "top up" of great advice and reassurance that I was "on my way!" She used an analogy at the end of that First meeting that was very apt and is something I will Never forget. She said that where I was then was on the side of a cliff, been trying to climb it but had found myself at a very precarious part of my climb, run out of energy and had been forced to take rest and perch myself on a little crevice that was jutting out. I was clutching on the side of the cliff, firstly looking down to confirm: No I didn't want to fall or retreat my climb. But then I looked up and could Just see the top of the summit and I wanted somehow, some way to get up there . . . but, Christ, I didn't have a clue how to! . . . And again, she was spot on. Didn't know then How I was going to move on with my life but knew I wanted to and had to find the way. Top Lady, will always be in my thoughts; I have kept in touch with her, mainly by e-mail and thanked her so many times for her insight and inspiration.

So... There I was, on that horrible Friday! Must have been the 13th, can't remember! ON ME WAY TO THE NUTHOUSE!... **No that is not fair and a very detrimental,** rude comment to make in view of all the people who suffer with severe mental issues. I am sorry for that lewd comment. But, I just hated what I had to go through at that appointment. I got there on time, as always, never late for anything. Shows at least my faculties were all in order and I hadn't lost the plot completely... well, I could Still tell the time! I was asked to wait in reception for a little while. Could feel the tension in that place and coupled with my stress and nerves, it was a very uncomfortable place to be. However, didn't have to wait too long before a large man in a suit came to get me (no not White coat, phew!), middle aged, smart but, yes, large... I likened him to Robbie Coltrane from Cracker or perhaps better known as Hagrid, the half Giant in the Harry Potter films! Scary Guy! This guy didn't have Coltrane's Scottish accent but, as in Cracker, the TV drama focussing on a Police psychiatrist, he had a very blunt, straightforward, almost curt way of saying things. Showed me into a little side room and sat me down on what seemed like an interrogation chair in the middle of a bare room. Nothing on the walls, just bare. Visions of my police cell came flooding back to me! He introduced me to a lady that had joined us to take notes; she was a mature student and he asked if I minded her being there. I said no problem as, quite frankly, I didn't want to be left alone with Him! Scared the fucking life out of me and what he might do to me! He explained immediately why I was there... "You've been recommended to see me today as your Doctor believes you are depressed, anxious and a possible harm to yourself and, maybe, others"... Bitch, she got all that from me answering her stupid questionnaire? And she went and told bloody Hagrid... Bitch!

I didn't know what to say, I was dumfounded. I looked at the little, meek lady scribbling her notes and thought hey missus, what are you writing? I aint said anything yet! And, whatever you're writing, tell ME cos I don't know what to say! Eventually I think I summoned up a meagre: "Umm, yes, I have been pretty down but I don't think I am any harm to anyone?" "Well", he continued, "Today is all about me deciding where you are with all that: your doctor obviously feels that you need specialist help and advice so let me ask you a few more questions and we'll cover everything I need to know." Well, he'd already frightened the hell out of me, just with his presence and just me being there. So, I answered all his interrogative questions truthfully and to the best of my ability. Again, he touched on my childhood, background and the anger stuff, though not in the NICE, explanatory way Anne had done . . . And I LIKE HER! This guy was a tyrant. Every question seemed to have an agenda and, I think, his aim was to get me to say the "wrong" thing to give him a reason to "throw the book at me." He talked about anger, I think he was perhaps angry at Me being there as I was keeping him from a REAL case he could get his teeth into! Maybe a drug addict, murderer, rapist or Real desperate, perhaps homeless case. Anyway, after about half an hour of intense questions about me and my state of mind, he and lady student "adjourned" into the other room for a resume' between themselves. I was left alone in the bare room with just my (dreaded) thoughts! . . . They came back in about 20 minutes later, sat down and, again, Hagrid just went for the jugular. "Well, my colleague and I have discussed your case and I have to say this: You are really down at the moment, can't see a way out of your current depression, living conditions, financial problems, loneliness and, above all, your emotional state in relation to you missing your family life and the confusion of your failed relationship but" . . . And this is when he leant forward to get even closer to me, looked me straight in the eye, menacingly . . . "We have come to the conclusion that you DON'T REALLY want to kill yourself, do you?" . . . "No", I meekly replied, cutting him off in mid-flow. "And, believe me, if you Do kill yourself, I have seen many situations like this in my time where the Suicide victim IS NOT really the victim here, it is those he leaves behind." "Believe me Malcolm (Think this was the first time he called me by my name), your Son Tom would Never get over this. It would leave him angry and probably change his whole personality, and not for the better I can assure you." Enough said, (although he wasn't finished yet) I got his gist! He only homed in on Tom as he knew that's what would touch the nerve I needed touching! I am sure if he felt it necessary, he would have laboured the meeting and included Daniel, My Mum etc. etc. but he had "done his job", achieved his goal. His parting gesture was to wish me luck, assure me Time would cure All my problems but... reminded me that this meeting was the one that could've had me sectioned if he'd deemed it necessary but he was giving me that chance to show I was above that. He did, however, make sure I had the 24-hour helpline number, as well as his own number and clarified that he would "monitor me via my Doctor!" I thanked him and his assistant and sheepishly walked out of there... just like I had done from the Police Station... another chance, FREE again to "have another crack at getting myself bloody well sorted!" This meeting had frightened me even more than the day in the Cell... being out of my comfort zone was the understatement of the year.

This prompted what evolved into about two years of counselling on and off. Of course, I was Now in the System wasn't I? I'd reached the low point of being a "potential risk" and so they had to keep a bit of an eye on me I guess. I'd gone from being a strong, confident, self-assured, very independent individual to now a guy that had to pay regular visits to the Doctors and play the counselling game to keep me on the straight and narrow. To be fair the 4 or 5 counsellors I had over these next couple of years were very good at what they did and I took something from each of them. I had straightforward one to one counselling at first for around 6 months with a great guy called Dave... saw him for an hour or 2 once a week; just covered all the ground really, him just letting me waffle on and get it all out. He chipped in with some words of wisdom when I came up for air but, predominantly, he just listened to me and, in that way, by airing Everything, he cleverly allowed me to work out my way ahead. I remember the last session I had with him, where I SAID TO HIM(!) "Dave, that's it we're done! You've been brilliant; I walked in here 6 months ago a dishevelled man, depressed, at my lowest ebb . . . I still have my demons, I still can't legislate for what jumps into my head sometimes or my subsequent actions but, Dave, I am not suicidal, I am stronger, I now know what I have to do to get off that cliff!" In other words, I had the "rope attached to the top of that bloody cliff and I was determined to climb it and get the hell off that cliff . . . Bloody annoying Sea gulls were doing my head in!"

So I moved on from Dave, a little stronger but Still a long way to go and, lots of shit still to go through I hadn't planned on! By now, it was Quite apparent this leaving the marital home malarkey in your mid-life was a monumental, tough old challenge I'd set meself!

The other counselling was sporadic and one lot was a specific course (6 weeker) on Stress & Anxiety. Christ, that one was an eye opener! By now, I'd been through enough in my journey, had enough counselling AND learnt "my subject", if you like, enough to know pretty much what the 2 tutors on the course were going to say each week! Indeed, I flicked through the 6-week agenda booklet and skipped a couple of sessions (though I told the Doc I had been!) and didn't really miss much. It was all revisited each week anyway. But my abiding memory of that course was one of the tutors, a small guy, pretty normal looking, very intelligent, knew his stuff. But, when he got up to speak the first week, 3 sentences in he had to apologise because he had a, a, a, a stut, stu, stutter! I looked at a few of my fellow fruit cakes in the cuckoo's nest and it was obvious we were all thinking . . . Fuck, 6 weeks of this! We'll still be here in 6 months! We all had to "bite our tongues", which is probably what he'd done to get a stutter! The people with me on that course were a mixed bunch, around 30 odd in total, all crammed into this one, sweaty room. I somehow still managed to keep myself to myself as I like to do in those situations but also because I just didn't want to get over familiar with any of these cranks that I probably would never see again after the course. I was there because I'd been referred, not because I wanted to be. To be fair, that was probably the case for most of them but there were lots there that were just attending to justify their reason to be off work! But, obviously, there was a lot of Stress in that room because that's why we were there! Though I wonder if MR STUTTERER didn't make things worse for us all!

On a serious note, I'd like to point out at this juncture that my references to the counselling and my descriptions of my observations of some of the things / people I have experienced through it are by no means meant to be disrespectful in ANY way to the subject of Mental Health issues. Absolutely NOT, quite the opposite in fact. I have the ultimate respect and admiration for this area and the professionals that work in it. It is just my humour and My way of coping with the fact that I have had to seek professional help, after a lifetime of ignoring the facts, pretending that I could cope without it and playing the role as most men of the strong, dominant character that the world perceives them to be.

I believe that if men felt able to ask for and find help when they need it then hundreds of male suicides could be prevented. There is definitely a cultural barrier preventing men from seeking help as we are expected to be in control **all the time** and failure to be seen as such equates to weakness.

I DID at one point have specific Sex counselling but this was much later on. I think I am going to save that for a future chapter but, yes, boy Did I "do the counselling" circuit! I didn't ever become addicted to it, just took the Doctor's advice at any one time that it was what I needed. There were times when I felt a failure for doing it but, over and above all, I have to say it Did teach me so much, shaped where I am today and, yes it helped. After all, as I have said, I had chosen to keep my family and friends away from my troubles, not wanting them to see me low, not wanting to be a victim. It is ok to be needy with a Counsellor. They get paid to deal with needy souls, they know how to handle them . . . They are human and probably had days where they went home or down the pub after work and said "had that fucking nutter divorcee' bloke in again today; needs to get a bloody grip", but of course they couldn't say that to me cos then they'd' ve had to give me more counselling for yet another acquired insecurity! They were "my shield" from the outside world and my troubles and I thank them all for their support.

Of course, throughout my tenure in the Bedshit, I was Still a Man after all and a man has his carnal needs! Though with my problems, there had been no real desire in that department for months. The drinking and depression just consumed me really and any thoughts of sex or another woman were inconspicuous by their absence! MOST of my thoughts on that subject were just my intense demons. But, yes, at some point I did start to get the urges back again to actually "get out there" and see if things were looking up! I had met a couple of women but just knew I wasn't ready for anything and it wouldn't have been fair to inflict myself on them in my erratic state. So, it was pretty inevitable that the dreaded drink would be the "tool" I needed to help me "notch my first victim's name onto the bedstead." I'd actually gone out for a meal with the family at an attempt to play "happy families" and see if we had reached a point in all this where we could be civil and at least get through an hour of eating together. But, no, I wasn't ready for this either . . . even before we had ordered our meal, we had started a big argument and the whole dynamic was just not going to work. I just got up, chucked £20 down on the table and said, "sorry, I can't do this, that'll cover my meal, have a good night" . . . and I sped out of that pub, angry and sad at the same time. I hot-footed it up to the little pub in the village, knowing full well my mate and his wife would be in there as they went there Every Friday! They and that pub were my sanctuary, my escape from the anger and bitterness. I very quickly got very drunk and, although I didn't stop being angry, the events of a few hours back were being paled into insignificance by the effects of good old alcohol! My friends knew I needed to calm down, escape from my troubles for a while and let my hair down. They, probably, more than most of my friends knew my life at that time . . . purely because I used to socialise with them the most. If you can call falling into that Den of Iniquity on a Friday night socialising! So, by now, I was snuggled up in the corner of the pub, pleasantly inebriated and humming along to the shit band in the pub thrashing out heavy metal or whatever the din was. It didn't matter, I was pissed and I had escaped my demons for a short while. Then, almost by magic, this woman appeared next to me . . . apparently she had been sat by me the whole time! I hadn't seen her but she'd seen me. We got chatting . . . turned out she was pissed too and also had "problems" . . . well the night was coming to an end, Time was about to be called at the bar: I'd only met this woman 10 minutes ago and already we were both talking about our shit lives. She was called Mandy, wasn't bad looking, a little rough around the edges but looked so much better after that final drink of the evening! On the sound of the barmaid's Bell, I said to her: "so, what do you want to do now Mandy?" . . . it probably came out a lot more incoherent than that but that was the gist of it! . . . she replied: "Where do you live? I want to go back to yours and fuck you senseless" . . . I didn't hesitate; in my drunken state, after the night I'd had and, knowing this was going to be the first sex I'd had (and probably needed) in months, I said: "I live a short walk away, up the top of the street, you ready?" . . . **Now** I was grateful I lived in that bedsit so close to the pub! I don't even remember saying good bye to my mate and his Wife; they were drunk too. I just put my arm around this woman and we held onto each other to stagger (literally) up the street, the 400 odd yards to my Passion Palace, yeah right! Fell in the door and, within minutes we were in bed tearing each other's clothes off. To be fair, from what I can remember, she had a fairly nice body; no fat, everything in the right places! It was SEX, no more, no less, not love-making, drunken, quick, though pretty passionate sex. We fell asleep then woke in the early hours, did it again, still drunk (not so much), bit better this time, fell asleep again. Lucky enough for me, she had set her 'phone alarm for early (6 ish if I remember rightly?) as she had work the next day! So that gave me an excuse to get her out of there before the natives got gossiping about me and I didn't have to spend any more time with her than I had to! I did the gentlemanly thing by dropping her home but when she asked for my number I politely declined and was totally up front with her: "Let's be honest, we got drunk last night, we had a good time, we both wanted it but I am not in a good place at the moment and have a minefield of problems to sort in my life. It wouldn't be a good idea to take this any further at this time. Sorry but thank-you for a good night" . . . the fact I HAD forgotten her name at this point was not a great thing but it didn't matter in the context of my little speech! . . . But, IT WAS THE TRUTH! She thanked me too and said it was a shame as she too had issues in her life to sort and we could've helped each other at least with company but I still declined and waved her good bye. I Never saw her again, well briefly, dropping her kids to school about a year later I think but never to talk to. It was your pivotal one night stand, cleared the "cobwebs" and just served to remind me I am a Man underneath it all . . . and at least all me tackle still worked!

Ok, that was a short term measure that fulfilled a need on that particular night, to allay my thoughts of my spat with the Ex and, yes, satisfy my physical, carnal needs. But, a one-night stand, by pure definition, does not fulfil you ongoing and, in reality, it only served to make me more depressed and realise "what my life had sunk to" . . . pulling cheap tarts in a lousy pub and sleeping with them on the first night.

Of course, as far as women were concerned, in my defence I was still very confused. I think my yearning to go back home and have my wife back was fuelled mainly by my missing the "package" i.e. my family, not so much her but the kids and family life. Also, there was this insane jealousy and anger at her being with another man. So my thoughts towards the opposite sex and quite how to handle them at this time were all over the place. Of course, I HAD to see my Ex regularly because of the Tom situation, making arrangements to pick him up, **money etc. etc** . . . I have no doubt at all NOW that if he wasn't so young and therefore I hadn't needed to have the contact I did with her, I could've done my moving on a lot quicker. It seemed like I had daily contact with her because of the kids mainly and it gave us BOTH an excuse to be aware of each other's lives and, because the situation was still raw and lots of emotion flying about, we didn't handle it well. I continued to bombard her with accusation, insinuation, a damned barrage of innuendo and callous comments about her new found freedom and she, in turn, "threw the book at me" and used every opportunity to get her own back. And when I got anywhere near another woman, somehow she seemed to know about it and spoiled it by 'phoning or interfering in some way! And so it went on ... all part of the process I guess.

So around that time, saddled with this baggage, women were, let's say, sporadic. I wasn't really going anywhere to meet anyone nice and had no money to do anything special when I did meet one! Through work, friend of a friend, I did meet Dawn, a lovely lady whom I am still friends with to this day. She was going through a weird time (They all have a Story!) in that she was living in her house with her Husband but they had an estranged relationship, separate rooms etc. In fact, hadn't slept together in a couple of years I think. She was very unhappy leading this life but, as she explained, felt she had to stay in that house mainly for financial reasons until they split officially and it could all be sorted out. I believed her totally as she was a genuine lady with a massive heart. She listened to my story and totally understood my plight and we confided in each other and actually built up a great rapport, closeness, mutual respect and friendship. This inevitably led to going to bed together and, I have to say, this was much better and a lot more real than my one-night stand! Dawn was lovely, caring, kind, passionate and a great listener. She only came to the bedsit twice; she had her house which was a beautiful 4 bed detached in a nice area and she would invite me around whenever her estranged hubby was away on business which, in the beginning was quite often. Sometimes she would cook for me but, always, there was loads of Red wine on tap! She was a lover of the sacred juice too! It was great to relax in her house which, in comparison to my room, was a Palace ... with proper heating and Sky telly! Though we didn't do a lot of watching telly. We would talk and talk and talk, mulling over the problems in both our lives and wondering how they would ever be resolved. And of course we would drink! Until we'd had enough of drinking and chatting... and retire to bed to play. In some ways, at that time, for me, as selfish as it sounds, it was the ideal situation. My mind was still all over the show and I fluctuated from normal, articulate, sensible guy to warped, screwed up, inconsistent Nut job! So, I could not have a Relationship per say and all that went with it and this lady, for other reasons, more so practical reasons, could not and did not really want to get involved with another man until she knew some way to resolve the financial mess with her hubbie. So our secret nights at her house were a Godsend, an escape for both of us. They went from being quite regular through to very sporadic... he'd had his budgets cut at work and the business trips away became few and far between. But we continued this "arrangement" for around 2 years!... We hardly ever went out... Out, out! I couldn't wine and dine her and we didn't really want to go public. Though there was an awkward stage somewhere in this that Dawn developed feelings for me and, though she never said it directly, hinted that she wanted it to go further. There was an offer to go away for the weekend to a friend's cottage in Cornwall and just other chivvies and comments aimed at unearthing any feelings I might reciprocate her way. I was (still am) very fond of Dawn, admired her, respected her and valued what we had, what we gave to each other and I don't just mean the sex. Our relationship was far deeper than that. But I could not Love Dawn, I couldn't feel that spark, that ultimate chemistry to move it on another stage. Eventually, our meetings became less and less and our "thing" died a natural death. We still kept in touch, had the odd dog walk, drink (in a pub) occasionally but the intimacy fizzled out. In time she did Divorce her husband and met someone else and then the contact went altogether. BUT, towards the end of our time together, she was sadly diagnosed with Breast cancer and subsequently went onto have surgery and chemotherapy. I hear she is in remission and I miss her greatly and wish her well and sincerely thank her for helping me through a bad time in my life. I think I helped her too.

I had actually had a look at Internet dating on the recommend of a friend, a guy who was in a similar situation to me. Left his Wife and was "out there" again in the jungle! He was one of the parents I had met through Tom's footy circles and, though we never socialised or went for a beer, we would meet by the side of the training ground or pitch and swap our stories. He pointed me in the direction of this internet dating site I had never even heard of. To be honest, I was very cynical... and very naïve to Internet Dating and had previously bad mouthed it. Not for me I thought. But he gently persuaded me that for a guy like me(!) who couldn't really afford to go out properly, alone and in need of company, whatever that word meant, it was the perfect medium! So I had a looky, did my research, logged on and registered for this Free site! Wow... within minutes, literally, of shoving my picture on there, (the best one I could find... don't really do pictures but found one on the computer from a year before with my Nephew at my Son's 18th Birthday do!) I had about ten messages from ladies! Talk about a kid in a Candy shop... 10 women wanted to talk to me! Why me? They were a real mix, big, fat, small, ugly, some nice looking, most not! On that first occasion of going on there I must admit I replied to some, even engaged in a messaging situation with a few but, at that time (early Bedsit days) I WAS NOT READY for this or actually Dating in any shape or form. So within a week or so I deleted my Account!... and carried on being depressed! Admittedly, it had given me a flash of humour, some well needed flattery and contact with the female species but I just couldn't handle it at that stage. However, a few months later, I logged on one drunken night! Inevitably, as I was back on there, the messages started flooding in and, this time, I thought Sod it, let's go with it... I am Single, alone, lonely and yes in need of Company! And here were plenty of women willing to give me that. This first time I had gone on it properly, I swear I didn't really know what I was looking for or expecting. I think I just ticked the box that said "looking to date but nothing serious" which can be construed as you're just looking for sex but, as much as I wanted that, it wasn't my first priority. The old Romantic in me still thought that perhaps this was the modern way to find Real Love! . . . Little did I know eh? The key to Internet dating (and I AM NO EXPERT though I have now been on / off this site for a few years . . . let me stress much more OFF THAN ON!) is, like in real life, it all depends on YOU, what state of mind you approach it in and what you are seriously looking to get out of it. This will determine what kind of person you meet on it and, if you're lucky, how good a relationship that follows. If you approach something in a positive manner, you are likely to have a positive outcome; if negative, the same applies. As you know, I was just all over the place at this time. ALL I think the Internet dating site achieved to do was give me a deflection from my shit and day to day problems. A quick fix perhaps, certainly a chance to "talk" to ladies . . . women in similar situations who could empathise with me, sympathise to a degree, understand, offer advice or just an ear.

It did sort of break the loneliness too . . . many a night, I would grab a bottle of wine then wander down the road to my office. Switch on the computer and "talk away"(!), escape the demons and bad thoughts for a few hours. Most times I would stick Eva Cassidy on my old radio / CD player, turn it up really loud and just "shut the rest of the world out" . . . poor people walking past that little office, must of wondered what was going on up there! Thanks Eva, great company, got me through many a night!

So, here I was . . . ON TINTERNET, talking to women, getting engrossed in this new way (to me anyway) of meeting, conversing and flirting with many ladies! I kidded myself this was the way to go, this was the modern way of meeting people. Long gone were the days of actually chatting women up in the pub or asking them for a dance at the disco! Come on Malc, drag yourself into the 21st century. There you go, there was my justification to go down this route . . . quite apart from it was the Only route I had at this time! Sure, I met the odd woman through my work but most were already taken, too young or I just didn't appear on their radar! Long gone were my days of turning heads when I walked into a work place . . . long, long gone! And, it has to be said, my demeanour and body language was showing a broken guy, one well down on confidence, bedraggled and beaten to a pulp, not attractive qualities to reign in the ladies. So, at least on Tinternet I could "hide" behind the façade of my profile initially. That confidence with women I used to have, I could have online. Easier to talk to them in messages and get to know them without seeing them. Initially I did just that - talked to them online. I "met" loads of them on there. And, because of my naivety to this medium, I thought you had to message back Everyone that messaged you! Took me a long time to work out that, in the main, people don't take it too personally on there if you don't answer back a message or if you delete them! I started to get addicted to this thing, revelling in my new found hobby. It is, by the rules of human nature, quite exciting when ladies message you with loads of flattering comments, a desire to meet you and explain their intentions for you! In other words, there are a lot of lonely, horny ladies around! And there were 100's of them on that thing! Although I was courteous enough to reply to them all, there were some on there that were quite scary . . . women I would never ordinarily speak to. But it wasn't long before I put my foot right in the water and ventured out on my first Date! I was to have my first Internet dating Experience! In TAUNTON! I had been talking online to this lady for a couple of weeks, liked what she was all about and, yes, I fancied her! So, I planned to meet up with her on a Sunday afternoon. We arranged to meet by the river, near a pub I knew and had been to before in my past. I drove there in a very nervous state of mind, really not knowing what I was letting myself in for. Totally unsure about all this internet dating malarkey and Taunton? . . . Out of all the women I could've picked locally and I choose one in bloody Taunton, around 70 odd miles away; just about afforded the petrol and a little bit for a drink when I got there. I arrived on time . . . never late for anything. Got out of the car and wandered along near the river where we'd agreed to meet. I saw this lady walking towards me BUT . . . she looked nothing like the pictures of the lady I had been speaking to these last few weeks! Nothing at all like her, a lot older and, though she wasn't ugly, let's just say she was no oil painting! Ordinarily, I would've walked past but, finally, after a few minutes, I plucked up the courage to say Hi! I can't remember her name now . . . the date was That memorable! I think it was Tracie or something like that! Let's call her Tracie then . . . "Hi Tracie, it is you isn't it?" I asked her with trepidation. "Yes, it's Malc isn't it?" . . . IT WAS HER . . . NOT WHO I HAD BEEN EXPECTING TO MEET BUT IT WAS MY DATE! Welcome to Internet dating Malc! Anyway, this lady was pleasant enough AND I had bloody well driven to Taunton so I thought I may as well stay, couldn't be rude, and we wandered along the river to a little wine bar. We chatted about our lives, mostly small talk really, pleasant, simple overviews of our relative situations; what we thought of Internet dating, the weather, Exes, Kids, family, stuff like that really. Had a nice drink by the river on a Sunny day then wandered back to the first pub we had met at and decided on another drink, orange juice for me to keep in control . . . and I was driving. All rather nice stuff and the date had gone ok, despite this nagging thought that SHE was not my Internet contact! I was itching to mention it but, ever the gentlemen, thought it would be exceedingly rude and, what did it matter? We'd had a nice afternoon, though no great spark between us, we had got on ok and SHE had already decided she wanted to see me again. Because of my "imposter" doubts, I in turn had already pretty much decided I **didn't** want to see her again but, at this juncture, was probably still keeping an open mind and might give her the benefit of the doubt. However, my niggles and doubts were cemented when, at the end of the afternoon, she asked me back to her house for a cup of tea. All above board, her Son was actually in the other room playing his guitar! It was just a gesture to drop her home, save her the walk of a mile or so to where she lived. Well, as she was making the tea in the kitchen I sauntered around her living room and had a look at her photos on the side, mantelpiece etc. Many family photos, her and her kids, Ex-husband, family and friends, normal stuff . . . BUT, none, not one of the photos, looked like her! Not one . . . But they were pictures of the woman I had been talking to on Tinternet all these weeks! So Who was this woman I had met today, whose house was she in? She had to be using someone else's identity to get dates, reel us in perhaps!... I don't know, all I know is it spooked me and it was all a bit surreal. I drank my tea in next to no time and made my excuses and got the hell out of there! Driving back, I just felt I'd had a lucky escape and had to be a bit more careful on this online dating stuff in future! We text a few times after that but I never saw her again, managed to keep the excuses up until she moved onto her next victim!

Despite the surreality of this first experience, it had given me a taste for dating and this site intrigued me! The messages, the flattery, the intentions of ladies just kept coming at me! Every day I would switch my computer on there would be at least a dozen messages or women had added me as a "favourite" or pressed the "I want to meet you" button! It was mad! It was like all of a sudden I had become a celebrity or rich and all this attention was for ME! Pretty stimulating for an old, fat, grey and skint bloke living in a bedsit. If only they knew! Though I had been pretty honest on my profile about where I was in life, I hadn't put ALL THE DETAILS on there... I mean you can't sell yourself too well by writing that you are a sad old wino, living in poverty, still pining for love he'd lost as well as his family. Mine was a basic profile, one fairly recent picture THAT WAS ME! But it seemed to do the trick and this attention was uplifting... I was like a kid in a Candy Shop, but this shop was full of WOMEN! Lovely.

I was, I guess, in a "FUCK IT" stage of this whole process. What did I have to lose going out on a few dates, meeting the female species, just getting out there again. It did help to ease the depression, the loneliness of it all. The only thing that really curtailed me was money... I had little or none. But with astuteness and by being honest with these ladies, I managed to go on dates that didn't cost anything or minimal money. Dog walks when I could "borrow" Frank... A quiet drink or coffee somewhere, or the odd time back to the bedshit or their house! In the first 7 weeks of being on that thing, I had 7 dates, one a week! Christ, you can have 1 a night if you can fit 'em in if you want to! I had a friend at the time who did just that! He had a different woman Every night of the week from this site; I don't think I would have the energy! I didn't sleep with all 7 by the way . . . only 2 of them! Good boy me . . . in comparison! But, sorry ladies, I was just Not in a good place in my head to be doing the whole dating thing. Yes, I stuck with it for a couple of months, mainly through intrigue and curiosity but it wasn't really my thing. It seemed a common theme on all these dates. I would turn up, spend a bit of time or, sometimes an evening with them but after a short space of time in their company, I was looking for the Exit door! The final straw for me was Sharon from Newquay! . . . Date number 7! Yes, I predominantly stayed local for money reasons but this lady messaged me and we talked online constantly for a week or so. She looked very attractive (in her pics!) and our chats were good and intense and there seemed like there was a spark between us. However, before I plunged in and committed myself to a date with this lady, I had to ask her the pivotal question: "Are those pics on your profile recent and of YOU?" . . . I did explain why I was asking and she took no offence at all; in fact admired my forthrightness and duly pointed me to her Facebook page to "check her out" . . . now there's another phenomenon I find it hard to embrace and don't really do the old Faceache stuff like the rest of the population! In my view it causes more hassle than it's worth and can be a huge invasion of your privacy. But everyone to their own. I did look at her page though and, sure enough, she had 100's, probably around 500, bloody pictures of herself on there! Pictures alone, dressed up for a night out, fancy dress, in her PJ's, with makeup, without, with her kids, with her dogs, with her family, in pubs, restaurants, holiday snaps, you name it, she had them all on there! And I looked through and studied the whole blimmin' lot of them! After a couple of hours of detective work, I came to the ultimate conclusion that this lady was not an imposter! Coupled with what she'd said in her messages, she seemed a Real person and worth me mustering the petrol money to get myself down to Newquay! She had just said get down there and she'd pay for the rest, a night out in Newquay! SO, this Saturday night I put on my glad rags and hot footed it the 55 odd miles in me old BMW down to the depths of Cornwall, thinking every mile of the way, "what the bloody hell am I doing?" ... When all is said and done, this Tinternet dating is a risk (for both men and women) as you are putting yourself out there, into situations you aren't really sure of. As nice as she seemed on the World Wide Web, she could've been a Wacky, Webbed footed Weirdo just plotting to get me into her lair and do evil things to me and steel all my stuff and my car! But I figured that the evil things might be fun and open my eyes and if she wanted to steel a shitty 13-year-old car, the £40 in me wallet and an extinct Nokia that couldn't do anything but call and text, she was welcome! What's the worst that could happen I thought? In for a penny, hey ho, life's too short, all the old cliché's. So I turn up at her house on the outskirts of Newquay. Nice house, 5 bedroom detached over 3 floors! She had financially come out of her split up quite well, kept the kids (all 5 of them!) and the house. She was a beautician but I THINK the good old Social covered the majority! Well she answered the door in the tightest little black skirt I had ever seen! Hair and makeup done immaculately and yes, she looked lovely. A little bit over glamorous for my liking but, hey, she was sexy, had made an effort for me and for Christ sake, get that open mind working I thought. Most importantly, it WAS the Sharon I had been talking to all last week! She ushered me up to the 2nd floor lounge of her house where she poured me a massive glass of wine, Red of course! She knew I preferred red from our week's ramblings! INTERNET DATING has its advantages! At that point, I realised I wouldn't be **driving** home tonight! I raised this point to her and she just said: "Malc, you're my guest, you're here for a good night out in Newquay with me; if we get on, we get on, if we don't, but I think we will(!), we will have had a good night out ... cool with that?" ... "Fine, Sharon, your territory, your rules!" I said, quite a clever answer I thought! Basically, I had resigned myself to enjoying the night, going with the flow, let me hair down for a change and pretend I had no problems in my life ... Escape for a few hours, why not? We had another glass of wine, I met 3 out of her 5 kids(!) and then we caught a taxi into town. Well, what followed that night was like a script from Eastenders! She took me to probably Every hostelry in Newquay which she seemed to know intimately and the regulars, bouncers, pub staff knew Her! Let's just say she was a girl about town . . . forget that Malc, go with the flow, open mind old chap! But what I didn't anticipate was that, as she got a little more drunk as the evening wore on, her whole life story unfolded. We all have a story behind why we find ourselves split up, divorced whatever at our age but this lady had enough stories and baggage for 5 people! . . . It seemed that at each drinking place, after each drink went down our throat, I picked up another episode of her story. Here goes . . . she had 5 kids, from 4 different Dads, only 2 of whom she still had contact with, the other 2 . . . one was in Prison, the other just disappeared. She had an injunction out on the last husband as he had raped, abused and beaten her up. As a child, she had been sexually abused by an Uncle who had also abused and beaten her Brother. Together they fought to get him put away. On top of all that, she had a child with ADHD, another young girl who'd had a teenage pregnancy and a Son who'd just starting doing drugs. Oh, and she'd had a mild form of Skin cancer a year back. Wow, what a Life! . . . She was not a drama queen and, though she had not volunteered this information in her "sell" to me on TInternet, I had no reason to disbelieve her so just found myself listening, sympathising and wondering what was the next instalment coming at me! And, don't forget, I was just getting drunker and drunker as the evening went on so I was pretty oblivious to it all come the end of the night when we finally ended up in a night club and (I had to be pissed) got out on the dance floor to do me "Dad dancing at a Wedding!" I don't think I got much of **my** story in but I had a great night and, frankly, she had enough stories for the both of us! We ended up back at her house about 4 in the morning, drunkenly fell into her bed (on the first glass of wine I was staying in the guest room), had forgettable sex though I do remember being pretty turned on by her body, as I took off her figure hugging little black dress. We really though just went through the motions, almost as if we expected this of each other to do it. One of those situations where you wake up embarrassed in the morning next to this stranger and not one of you wants to admit what happened the night before. To be honest, my first thought on awakening in the morning was to get the hell out of there as I didn't want to stay and get lined up for the Jeremy Kyle Show! I thanked her for a great night but said I ought to get off as I had an hour and a half drive home and I had my Son to pick up. We kissed awkwardly on the cheek and promised to keep in touch. Yeah right... I had enough of me own baggage without taking on half of Newquay! We texted a few times after and she was keen to pay me a return visit to have another night out but I couldn't put myself through that again! I had to let her down gently... by text! Well, that's how it's done these days isn't it?

So that was that. After THAT date, I got my head around the whole Internet dating thing and just analysed it had screwed me up even more than before. **My** perception of it was that it was full of losers, sad people, weirdos, nutters, strange women with lots and lots of hang ups and baggage... Yeah even more than me! So I deleted my account and went back to loneliness. Well, I still had Dawn... We had kept in touch throughout everything. She was going through a very bad period of time with her estranged husband. We talked by text and had the occasional coffee and chat and she shared her problems with me as I did mine with her. I was always honest with her about my dating and seeing other women and, as a very mature lady who had been through so much in her life (3 marriages to date), she was totally understanding and our friendship remained solid. She, in turn, told me that her husband was trying to be nice to her and, not necessarily make up, but being amicable whilst they worked through their problems and lived in the same house, albeit separate bedrooms! But theirs was a volatile relationship and she confided her desire to just "get out" of that marriage. But, I knew she'd never leave her lovely home for him to reap the benefit... unless she became really desperately unhappy. So, our chat, wine & sex nights were back on and continued!

My dating escapades aside, I guess there were, amidst the sea of depression, solitude, stress and anxiety, some other lighter moments in my time in Bedshit land. There were my fortnightly trips to the Launderette for example! I didn't have a washing machine in my room and the house had a communal kitchen with a washing machine but no one ever used it. I didn't want to take my stinky clothes around to friends so I opted for a trip down the High Street to the "Eastenders launderette!" I would let my washing build up for a couple of weeks into a manageable black bag . . . didn't have many clothes really so it was mainly underwear, socks, towels, footy kit etc. Now this is where the snob in me came out! I found it pretty demoralising that my life had sunk to going to this place after all those years of having a wife and before that, Mum, who washed and ironed for me in a nice, clean washing machine in a nice house! And I certainly didn't want anyone I knew to see me going into the "Washing Shop" so I made sure I got in there early, as soon as the lady opened up (not Dot Cotton but a nice Salt of the Earth lady that seemed to enjoy her job, handling blokes' nic nacs!). I also wouldn't want to be seen hanging around the place for a couple of hours doing me own washing so I gladly paid the extra £1.50 for Dot to do the Service Wash for me. I popped back in a day or so to pick up my black bag, all washed and neatly folded. Dot seemed to take a little liking to me, don't think she did that for all her customers! It was around this time I discovered the pleasure of shopping in **Iceland**! We'd always shopped in Sainsbury's but now, living on the "minus budget", hand to mouth, it was a case of having to shop frugally and get me bargains! Mind you, the food's pretty good in there and it's so easy to tot up as you go along how much you're spending as pretty much everything's a £1! Then there's Buyology, the local discount store that sells **Everything** really where I got all my cheap cleaning materials and 9 good quality toilet rolls for £1.99! I have now become adept at shopping for bargains in these places even though the Snob in me still scans around while I am in there to see if there's anyone I might know so I can shoot up another aisle to hide!

Then there was Deirdre! . . . Deirdre was the name I gave to the woman whose voice did my talking clock on me old, donkey's old, Nokia! I didn't own a watch that worked so would rely on Deirdre to tell me the time! I am a clock watcher... not in the sense of most people but because my way is to try to fit in as much as I can to my day. Get that trait from my dear old Mum who, even now, in her late eighties, does everything at 100 miles an hour and is always busy and on the go. Me and Mum don't do Doing **Nothing** very easy! Find it hard to relax, only if I plan to Relax and have Earnt my chill time by working for it. As I have said before, it is this instilled ethic that I have that has kept me going through some dark times, not least in those 7/8 months in my bedsit time. So Deirdre became a friend and someone to talk to during my depressed evenings and was there for me when I woke up in the early hours during my many sleep deprived nights. At least I was going to bed Every night with a woman!

BBC 3... was the only channel on my dinosaur of a telly (someone had given me or retrieved from a skip, can't remember now) that properly worked! I had this indoor aerial that wouldn't have looked out of place on an Airport runway and it worked intermittently, sometimes not at all and when the telly just refused to work full stop, even after a kick, it was always BBC3 that miraculously came back on again first when the telly agreed to play ball. This introduced me to lots of fringe comedians, many repeats of very old shows, Family Guy and, of course, Eastenders! Highlight of most of my evenings, watching the repeat of 'Enders at 10.30!

My office from where I ran my little community magazine was just 200 yards from the Bedsit so no commuting! It was above a Computer Shop and directly across the road from this, an Auctions Room had opened up. I got to know Mike, the owner very well and he was keen to advertise his new venture in my magazine. I sorted this for him and got my Designer to give him a good spread. It worked for him and helped to bring in a lot of local people. I gave him "mates rates" and he was getting a good deal but I liked him and his Brother and I was happy to help promote this local Business which the town loved. I went for a beer with him a couple of times, mainly talked business and let him buy the beers as he always owed me for his ads! There was this one night we wandered down the high street to pop into one of the local pubs for a few . . . had quite a few actually and we both staggered our way back up the street after closing time! Me, I was on my way home, the few hundred yards I had to go; I thought he was intending to go home too . . . he lived in a neighbouring village, but a couple of mile walk for him. Instead, though, he invited me into the Auctions Rooms for a night cap. He said he often fell in there after he'd had a few and, in fact, had fallen asleep there a few times! So, I thought sod it, I don't go out much, let's do it! Now, Mike had done a deal on some very BASIC wine (I asked no questions) and had dozens of cases of the stuff at the back of the place, all nice and cold. Italian stuff I think, certainly very cheap stuff, but, as wine goes, it wasn't that bad tasting! I should know as by now Mike had started to "pay me" for his adverts in the stuff! Rather than giving me proper payment, I was given cases of the Red variety to keep me happy. And this is another reason I drank so much, always had boxes of bloody wine in the Bedsit! So he opened a couple of bottles and we carried on drinking into the early hours. So, here I was in this Aladdin's Cave, surrounded by all the lots for Auction, sat on what was like the Queen's palatial throne of a chair, and above my head was one of those stuffed Deer heads hung neatly on the wall! All around me was a huge variety of objects, from porcelain figures, paintings, antique furniture, jewellery to cases of dead butterflies and various other insects etc. etc! A weird and wonderful place, much better than falling into a night club! Bit like a scene from "One Night at the Museum!" . . . And to top it all, Mike had sat down at the seat of a massive Grand Piano that was up for Auction. To my amazement, he just started twiddling with the ivories and belted out a few songs! Mostly common stuff he knew I'd Know and then I started to request a bit of Spandau or Paul Young! Back in me happier, more social days I had been known to belt out a deafening (I made people think I thought I could actually sing though I knew I was tone deaf!) "Through the Barricades" by Spandau. So here I was in the "Cave", pissed but jolly, sat on me throne singing me favourite song! Oblivious to all my problems in the world, what world, what problems? This surreality lasted well into the small hours as we worked through a repertoire covering his and my favs. . . . Ah, the Good old 80's always gives you plenty to sing about! I think I would've just fallen asleep there in my high backed comfy throne but Mike started to veer off into classical shit and "stuff from the shows" . . . boring old crap that didn't relate to the jolliness! I slipped off around 4 ish. I think and left him to it . . . I think he was still playing when I opened up my office later that day! My "Night at the Museum!"

Of course, I saw as much of my boys as I could, even when I was living in the Bedsit. By now, they were starting to come to terms with Dad not coming home and the split up. Tom was 13 and Daniel 19. He was driving and had his own life. I would see him mainly when he played football; he only ever came to my bedsit once, in the early days, probably more out of curiosity but Tom did stay a few times. This was mainly because he played football on a Sunday for the local professional club and that invariably meant a real early start to travel to such places as Swansea, Cheltenham or Oxford. So it was practical to stay with me and get up early. I never had much money to do a lot with Tom but when he stayed I tried to make it comfortable for him and have as much "boys together" fun as I could. We would sometimes have a kick around down the park on a Saturday afternoon, then get a takeaway and eat it on the bed (never had a table . . . or a dining room to put it in!) and watch crap telly (no Sky, X Box or PlayStation like he had at home). But he had me and I gave him my undivided time and attention. Simple times, simple things, time with my Boy. And, despite my lack of money, I am proud to say I did all the running around for his footy. Because he played for a professional club, this involved sometimes 4 training sessions a week and a match on Sundays and, somehow, some way I found the money to get him to all of this! Looking back, I haven't got a clue how I did it but did it I did! He was with that club from 7 to 16 years old and I was there for him every step of the way. Out in all weathers, up and down the motorway, always bought his boots and kit, never let him down. It was hard enough financially and time wise when we were a normal family unit, but how I managed to do it when I was on my own I will never know! I had always been there for Daniel growing up with his footy and everything as he always played football, but Tom's was a little more intense with the professional club slant. But it's unconditional a love for a child and you do whatever you can for them. They were and still are my life and will Always come first. At that time, doing what I could for them meant me living in even more squalor . . . to be able to have a bit of money to do it all, meant me eating beans on toast and lots of pasta! I always paid my maintenance on time, covered Tom's mobile 'phone bill, fed him whenever he was with me and generally contributed wherever I could to his upbringing. At the end of the day, you leave your Wife, NOT YOUR KIDS.

I also broke the landlord's bedsit rules and sneaked Frank in a few times for company. I desperately missed my Kids on a day to day but, also, I missed that dog too! Whilst at the bedsit I started to get into a routine of taking him out weekends for long walks. I was actually allowed a key (yes to my old house) to go around and get him to take out for a walk. Mainly weekends but also the odd time in the week. She and the boys were not giving him the regular exercise and long walks a big Black lab needs. Her added incentive to let me go round was that she knew I would pick up the poos he had done in the garden! I've got to admit, on more than one occasion I let myself into the house when I knew no one was there and, before taking Frank out, would have a sneak around for traces of her having had a bloke in there! I know, it sounds pathetic now but I was still in that mixed up place in my mind and didn't want her to have anyone else. I even went through her lingerie draw a few times and smelt the bed sheets. Sad Man! It was also the chance to look around my house and remember the good times and it always left me with a sense of wanting to go back. If only we could put the past behind us and rebuild again. Who knows, this could be a happy house again? I left that house on so many occasions with tears in my eyes wondering where my life had gone so wrong. How had it come to this? Me living in a shit pit having left all this behind. Poor old Frank had many a dog walk with me in a sad old state . . . but did he care? I still took him out and he was getting away from his Garden prison! I talked to him a lot on those walks ... asked his advice, "how was it all going mate?" Funny how he never gave me any answers ... though I am sure he knew what I was banging on about and picked up on my moods. He gave me those little looks where he was sort of saying, "look we're out, it's lovely fresh air, good exercise, clear your bloody head, forget it all!" ... and "as long as you take me out and let me run and have a good time, I don't give a damn!" ... Cheers Frank, Top Dog! Later down the line I stopped myself going into the house; just opened the back door to let the dog out and locked up and just got out on the walk. It took me a while to wean myself of my sheet and lingerie smelling addiction, but I found some will power and did it eventually. The less time I actually spent in / around that house, the less demons crept in to my head. The less heartache I had to endure. But it was always hard to come away after having dropped Tom or Frank back and go back to that bedsit alone.

The walks with Frank at this time were an absolute tonic for me ... I would say he most definitely became my best mate in this stage as he just loved the time I spent with him and me him. It was just the most simple, uncomplicated thing I had to do or face in my week ... picking him up and just getting out there with him in the open. I began to discover some lovely places to walk him, couldn't go too far, again restricted by money but in this part of the world you are never too far from a great moorland or coastal walk. He had become a superb animal, now creeping towards his 2nd. Birthday, strong, robust and agile. I know from what I have learnt and been told about the breed that you have to keep them as fit and active as possible to maintain their healthiness and endure their life for as long as possible. I was determined to give him as much of this exercise and my time as I could but, obviously, he wasn't living with me predominantly and his day to day care was out of my control. This would be a worry as he got older as, without the correct care and attention as well as diet, they can bloat out and attract health problems. I craved him being in my life more and had made my mind up that, if I could, I would find a place to live next where I could have him back with me permanently. For now, it was just a sheer delight to have him for the quality time I could. I didn't get it properly at the time as my head was all over the place but this Special dog was becoming my saviour, the one permanent thing in my life that was constant and he just remained loyal to me.

When I lived in that bedsit, I started to work out who were my Real, closest friends in life. Because, there is one thing you find out when you're at your lowest, have no money and are pretty screwed up . . . who Really cares, who doesn't judge. That's a True, proper friend, he who doesn't judge! I came to the conclusion I had (and still do have) a handful of good mates who were there for me through thick and thin. As I have said, I had shut a lot of people out, including my family, relying on my pride and independent nature to get me through so my friends didn't know or see everything. But I had George, Al (the Pal), Steve, Danny, Dan, Big Mike, Jase and of course my Friday footy mates. I said a handful! Maybe I am an ogre with more fingers than I thought! These guys dipped in and out of my life as much as I'd let them and as much as their own busy lives would allow. All these guys had relationships, mostly married with kids, with the exception of my mate, Dan. So, they would keep in touch and fit me into their busy lives, offering what worldly wise advice or just listening skills they could or wanted to. They are All different characters and personalities and so each and every one of them gave me a different take on my life. That's what I do with anyone that comes into my life. Speak to them with an open mind, take their views and opinions and advice and process it, using it if I feel it is useful. Of course it works both ways and you give something back to them when they need advice and help. At this time in my life, however, the scales were tipped too far the other way in that when I saw my friends, I tended to bang on about the same old things, to the point where I probably exhausted them with my emotional stress. I didn't allow them in to my deepest, darkest places in my mind but I did allow them to see that I was low and not in a good place mentally. The theme was generally my remorse and confusion over my lingering feelings for what I'd left behind. I was "playing the same old record" every time I saw them and they might've, well I know they did tire of it! . . . I was a contradiction of terms really. "Why did I want it back again? But I still love my Wife (or do I?) and I desperately miss my boys and want my family back again." Of course these thoughts were all fuelled and driven by my loneliness and desperation of living in THAT place but it would take more than my friends chipping in with their chunks of help and advice to sort that stuff out in my warped head! And, obviously, again with the exception of Dan, who never knew my wife, my mates had to stay as impartial as possible because, at that time, she was still on their radar! Steve, for example, well his Wife was my Wife's best friend and she'd already taken her own moral high ground and lodged herself in THAT camp and she wasn't going to be budged! She had me "hung, drawn and quartered" for my wrong doings before I'd had a chance to "present any evidence in my defence!" Women like that and many of that species do see things in black and white don't they? No room for grey or exploration of the mitigating circumstances! Nah . . . you hurt my Best friend, you're a bad, bad man . . . I will forget the fact I have known you, socialised with you and been a friend for 15 odd years . . . you're a Bastard so I don't ever want to speak to you again! So she avoided me like the plague, even crossed the street to avoid me in our little town! This made life difficult for good old Steve to remain my friend! Now he had a decision to make! . . . to be fair, Steve has handled the whole process pretty well really. He kept that impartiality by listening to both sides, continued to keep in touch with me and, though it really pissed off his Wife, he dug in and decided to be my mate, whatever. I also think Steve liked the drama of it all, loved hearing about my 'Enders life script . . . and there was plenty going on at that time to fill a chat over a few beers! Now all these years on, Steve is still a great mate, pops up every now and then for a catch up. Now the dynamic has changed though as my head is in a much better place and we can have a "normal" discussion over our beers and put the world to right, talk footy and women as guys do! . . . But his Wife Still hates me! Al (the Pal) has been brilliant. He lived next door to me in the old house and we had (still have) a great friendship. It was very difficult for him and his

Wife at the time of the split as, obviously, my Ex lived next door and so they naturally saw more of her after I left than they did me on a day to day basis. But Al never ever judged me and parked his "man marries woman, has 2.4 children and stays together" stereotypical view and saw the bigger picture. I had known Al for a long time, 20 odd years of friendship were mounting up there... a strong bond and one hard to break by any life event. Al is a very down to earth, honest, caring, abundantly loyal chap. He and his wife are a lovely couple and their 2 boys, typical lads! Boisterous, exciting and fun kids! Al and Claire had gone many years without wanting kids and, living next door to him all that time with my rowdy two growing up whilst they sought their solitude next door with their cats and rabbits, was a tough act for them! It gave me endless material to banter with him about having kids: "come on Al, pull your finger out mate, why should I have all this noise and mentalness in my life and you get to play with your pussy's!" This was the gist of it, there was plenty of ammunition to goad him into joining the Parents club! Lost count of the times my boys would kick a ball over into his garden! Know that used to get on his nerves and he was probably saying, under his breath, "fucking kids!" They went many years like this but, finally, one day he announced to us she was pregnant! "What the Rabbit?"... "No Claire, you dick!"... His fate was sealed, he had joined the gang and now he could go onto fully empathise with my life! So, Yes, Al was there for me through my troubles... listened to my side and, to be honest, he is the one friend I probably did "let in" more than most. Still not warts and all, still ever so conscious of his predicament with knowing and living next door to her, I gave him my ongoing account of the way things were. Me being a bit like FRANK SPENCER around the house, Al had always been there to put up a shelf or change a light bulb for me! This continued in the bedsit (and everywhere I have lived since!). Hence the name Al the Pal, always reliable, always there with a helping hand and a friendly smile.

George and Big Mike are guys that I play footie with on our pivotal Friday nights. Obviously it's not just us three that play, need a few more than that to play six a side! But these 2 probably are my most prominent friends in that circle and since we've all been playing since the late 'eighties, It's fair to say we are all pretty close! Again, they are both married to those women things! We had all socialised together through the footy connection and had many a momentous dinner party, sometimes "Chinese takeaway nights" at each other's houses over the years. Me and "loud Lorraine", Mike's Wife, would end up on many of those nights together in the corner putting the world to rights or just moaning about our respective lives and partners! Drink has a lot to answer for but me and Lorraine were always truthful, always very opinionated and didn't say anything to each other that we hadn't already said before openly to the gang! But after the split, the girls obviously jumped into the "Girls Camp" and were there for her, as girlies do, through her initial devastation. This caused an obvious rift at the time as the guys had to be there for me but on the other hand had to see their wives' point of view and play that impartial card as best they could . . . even though these guys had known me many years before she came on the scene, they understood my reasons for leaving and knew I had been unhappy for a long time. They are men that have been through divorces themselves (who hasn't) and being, let's say mature men, they could see the bigger picture, weighed up the whole set of circumstances and knew, despite the emotional minefield now unfolding, that Time would do its job and heal all. So these guys played it cool, saw me at footy every week, asked how I was and would've been there for me if I had asked for even more emotional help. To be fair, Mike was very concerned about the welfare of my boys and how it was all affecting them. He was on his 3rd marriage and so was an expert on that aspect! George, as always was and to this day remains my Rock. A very straightforward, stable influence in my life. An accountant by trade, George says it as it is, never loses his consistency in his opinions and is the most reliable, trustworthy friend I have. I would trust George with my life. He is so intelligent and worldly wise, again having been through so much in his life. He can relate to me more than most of my friends as he too has been in Business, therefore self-employed and had those ups and the many downs! Experienced the rollercoaster of that way of life. He has navigated his way through all the crap and come out the other side to make a good life. I respect him intensely. In those early days, his agenda was to make me see things as clearly as possible which was an immense task as I had no idea what was going to jump into my head at any one time or how I was going to react to it! Again, said it many times, you can't legislate for what's in your head and heart and how you're going to deal with it. Indeed only the week before the "day in jail" incident, George had a Man to Man talk with me in which he advised me to get my emotions in check, be careful about my behaviour around the Ex, highlighted I was a "loose cannon" and that if I wasn't careful I could get myself in trouble by saying or doing the wrong thing. He knew I was drinking, lonely and very down and was worried about me. Told me I somehow had to find a way to move on. I took his advice and promised him I would get my act together and stay away from her, only having the necessary contact because of arrangements to see my Sons and Frank. He knew I would find it hard to walk this line and not encroach into the unchartered territory of her new personal life. But little did he know what depths I would go to that following week with my actions that day. He was very disappointed in me and more than a bit let down, having invested time in me to give me his advice. He lost respect for me over that and it has taken a long, long, time to get George's respect for me back. I think, again though he doesn't know everything, he understands I have been through so much and worked my way to a "much better place" in my mind and now conduct myself always in a proper, articulate, responsible way ... I've returned to the guy he knew in the old days as one of his best friends. Now older and wiser!

Jason has been a good mate too. We met when my Son played footy with his at 11 years old so not a longstanding friend but one that came on the scene towards the end of my marriage. It was Jase and his wife, Nicki, who I used to meet down the local on a Friday night to get me out of that shitty bedsit. So grateful to them both for putting up with me on those nights, turning up all bloody emotional and getting even more in a state as the night went on due to the consumption of alcohol. Jase is a bloke's bloke . . . like most guys doesn't really show too much emotion and certainly doesn't wear his heart on his sleeve! Keeps his thoughts and feelings to himself and doesn't discuss stuff like that in public. So I found I would use Jase to get the hard hitting, blokes' take on my situation . . . it was pretty straightforward from Jase: "You were unhappy, you made a decision, you left" . . . "you have to live and die by that decision mate and just get on with it!" At which point, I turned to his Wife, Nicki, to get her take on it and, hopefully some sympathy to cheer me up! BUT, she just gave me the same advice as Jase, though this time, even less flowered up, said it in no uncertain terms . . . Though, as the night went on and more drink was taken in, they both softened up and saw a little of my side . . . I can't deny I pummelled Nicki and others to find out what the Ex was up to. Don't ask me why, just needed to know as many details as possible . . . Self-Torture! As time went on these interrogations dwindled then ceased from me and I realised I had been a pain in the ass even going there but it's something you find yourself doing naturally without thought. NOT my proudest behaviour. Sorry Jason and Nick. As it happened, they too split up about a year later and have gone through the emotional rollercoaster too so I found myself in a bit of a déjà vu situation, offering Jase advice! Well, the life experience and counselling must've done me a bit of good and gleaned some wisdom . . . Suffice to say, Jase handled his split up in a totally different way to me, being a lot more practical. As I said, he is a blokey bloke, is an electrician so works with guys all day and blokes together don't tend to do all that emotional shit do they?

Then of course there was Dan, who I lived with first! Dan kept in touch when I moved out and into the bedsit but I think those first few months away after staying with him were a bit of a respite for him really. He had this new relationship to build with his girlfriend and now had a "breather" from me and all my crap so I think he embraced the time away from me for a while! After all, we had lived in each other's pockets in those early months after me leaving home. To be honest, we probably both needed a break from each other to rekindle our friendship. The dog walks continued, well a couple or so in that year I think, so that gave us quality yapping, catch up time and a chance for Dan to spoil me with his tough love! Now, he has 2 boys of his own and life has changed and evolved for him. We have pretty much reverted back to the odd meet up here and there or a beer now and again to catch up. Still a good mate and our conversations are intense and full of intellect and analysis! Also, can't forget to mention John, Dan's Dad... like, George and Mike, I have played footy with John since those early days and he is just a few years older than me. He's been a constant in my life, a very intelligent man who intelligently plays down his intelligence! For probably at least the first five years or so of our friendship, I had him down as a normal, "salt of the earth" guy, perhaps a factory worker or labourer or something but, in fact, John is a qualified accountant and for many years held down a top job as a Financial Director in a multi-million-pound business. A good family man and strong character, a good soul to have around... and an exceptional Goalkeeper!

I've listed my male mates in no particular order so it has no bearing at all in popularity stakes that I mention (Essex) Danny last in this little break down! I've probably left Danny till last as he is a bit outside the box, the exception to the rule!... Met him not long after my leaving home so Danny has been a mate who only has known me, not my family or anyone really in my circles. He has only met briefly in passing some of the people I have already mentioned in my story but has no affinity or real connection to my old life. This has given him, as a friend, the ability to be totally impartial and neutral in his dealings with me. Also, at the time I met him he was unmarried and had never had kids, despite relationships with women. Though he went onto to have a brief marriage with a lady who already had 3 kids, Danny's advice to me was based mainly on his wisdom, life experiences and his spiritualism. Danny is a lovely guy who has two characters, an ongoing duo of personalities bubbling away. Coming from Essex, he has a strong, positive, very confident nature, backed up by his other side which is gentle, caring and very sensitive. He is a wise old soul and I think would make an excellent counsellor. I've been to enough over the last few years so know my onions on this! Though Danny does try to lecture me occasionally, giving it to me straight, and I resist his directness sometimes, have to say he mostly gets his advice right! It is spooky that he has this bloody intense, almost déjà vu take on life . . . like he has seen all of my life, his and others in a previous one so can advise accordingly! We have had the odd spat over the years over advice he's given me as, sometimes he forgets I have actually lived a bit and do know some of the answers to my own problems. But mostly, Dan's advice on life in general over the years has been spot on and many a time he has stopped me making an idiot of myself by saying or doing the wrong thing in a situation. He has helped me keep a check on my emotions and knocked me into shape! We went out for the odd beer back in the early days but our friendship has never really been a social one . . . more vocal, intense chats, normally on the 'phone or me visiting him at the shop he works at. For the first year or so of our friendship he too was in a "bad place" . . . living alone in a flat and drinking very heavily too. He'd had a failed relationship and was pretty down and depressed and our mutual bond was that we were both a bit miffed about our past; that, underneath it all, we are good guys who had just lost our way in life. I think we both helped each other through that time and since then with all that has happened in both our lives.

So . . . FRIENDS, for every good one I have mentioned here, there was also perhaps a matching number of ones I "lost" in the period after the marital breakdown. I can't really name them for obvious legal reasons(!) here but they know who they are! I do understand some of their reasons for disowning me, in some cases only seeing the one side, the female side but, again, I repeat my old statement of True friends don't judge! It is a shame that there were people I had known for many years, socialised with, confided in, was very close to and then . . . nothing, abandoned due to their opinions on the whole situation. Again though, time sorts out these emotions and feelings towards these fickle people and you learn it is all "part of the process", a flushing out of the bad. No worries, ENOUGH SAID!

Good friends as all the guys were, I can count on my hand... this time only five fingers(!) the amount of times, in total, I had visits from them to my bedsit. This was of course partly because I was embarrassed to let them come round to my one basic room. So, I did see them throughout this period but our meets were very sporadic and pretty strained due to my state of mind. However, there was an old friend that came back into my life now **BECAUSE** of the state of my mind! He was in the "same place" if not more screwed up than me! This was a chap called Paul. He was the Dad of one of Tom's friends, Pat, whom Tom had known since he was 7 or 8. They'd gone through school together and are still mates today. Paul and I met on the touchline of many a footy match a few years before and, this time, we crossed paths again at another match, a School one. We'd lost touch really as my boy had gone on to play for another team and so a different set of parents. Paul is a great guy, another TEACHER (I do attract them don't I?); he is a big guy, built of stone, a chiselled jaw, deep set eyes, a touch scary looking but one of the nicest, gentlest guys you could meet. One of Paul's eyes is a Glass one... had it put in at an early age (he was now late 40's like me) due to some childhood problem so this made him look a bit intimidating at times but was fine when you knew him and you were aware of it. He took all the jokes and banter from it, probably heard it all so many times. "Look at me Paul"... "Oh you ARE, sorry mate!" "Do you take it out and bounce it to see if there's any room on the top of the bus mate?"... Not really funny but an old, ancient really joke! On this day at the match, we shook each other by the hand and had a man hug. It was good to see him and immediately we were chatting like a pair of old women! We found out that we were both in similar circumstances. We had split up from our Wives and were now living alone... sad old gits feeling a bit sorry for ourselves! We swapped our stories, swapped numbers and went onto meet up for a beer in the next week or so. This led to Paul becoming my most frequent visitor to the bedsit, now getting towards the "finishing line" (about 7 months in). We had so much in common at that time it was uncanny. We were totally different characters and in the past, although we'd known each other through our kids, you could never say we were close mates. This period in our lives brought us together and we really helped each other through some bad times, thoughts and events. I thought my stuff was complicated but this guy had a few more cobwebs than me. His Ex Wife and mistress worked in the same school with Paul... so he saw them EVERY day! By the time he'd met me on that touchline, his affair was all but over as this lady had decided to go back to her Husband and kids. So Paul was, like me, in limbo with his life, not knowing which way to turn or how to handle what arrow came in next! We shared our woes, had many tears together. Nothing more funnier... or touching, whatever way you are inclined, than two grown men crying together over their lives but we were just in a mess! We started to spend a lot more time together... we called it "Suicide Watch" as were both conscious of just how low we were. When he was down, I Picked him up and when I had a bad day, he would drag me from the gutter and make me see the bigger picture. We had a mutual respect for each other that developed into a very close affection... we were Gay without the Gayness! Everybody comes into your life for a reason, I believe that and Paul re-entered my life at this time to help drag me out of the deep, dark place my mind was in then. We were good for each other and just wanted the same thing from our lives... peace and happiness...

So, details of how it came about to follow, but I was imminently due another move (the 3rd place I would live in since the split!), initially with my DOG, good old Frank re-joining me... **followed by Paul!**...

Chapter Five

A Life in the Sticks . . . How Life Changes . . . Again!

So, I had lived in the bedsit for about 7 months, around the same amount of time I had been at Dan's. I started to realise (well I think I knew as soon as I stepped in the door the first day!) that I could not live there forever! It had been the "stepping stone" I needed to get me out of Dan's but it was horrible, I hated living there and my sanity and well-being had been affected. But how could I move, where would / could I go? I started to look around and talk to people about my options! Options? What options?

By now there was definitely no going back, to anywhere Really! . . . Not to my Wife and family, certainly not Dan's and these were my options apart from sleeping in the car or YMCA! The big problem I had was money or the lack of it! My little business was bringing in diddlysquat . . . just enough to cover the cost of running it really and a bit over every month to keep up to date with my landlord, pay out my agreed couple of hundred a month for Tom and other bits and bobs like that food stuff you have to eat(!) and the essential odd bottle of wine to top up my free reserves! I WAS JUST SCRAPING BY, "robbing Peter to Pay Paul", living hand to mouth. Somehow, some way though I still managed to do all the running around for my boys' football and get to all the games. This, along with work, was my respite that kept me sane! To this day, it is a great pleasure to see my Sons play footy. They are both good players and have played at a high standard but, that aside, there is a pride in a Dad seeing his Sons' actively involved in sport and all that surrounds it.

Around this time, I got talking to one of my advertiser friends who told me she and her husband lived in a little village on Dartmoor. This lady and her husband owned the cottage two doors down from them that they were willing to let me rent long term as it was currently a Holiday let giving them inconsistent income. Bingo, it all seemed to fit into place! I actually had walked Frank out there on the moors on many occasions and loved the area (for walking a dog, not so sure about living out there!). It is a beautiful part of the country and we are so lucky down here to have that mix of Moors and Coast. As a Surrey / London lad, I have always appreciated the landscape down here and at every opportunity have embraced it. But, this, this was different, the contemplation of living in the sticks was a massive one to get my head around and I did deliberate over my decision for a while. However, it did help that I looked around the cottage in July / August time with the sun still beating down! Gave it a romantic, peaceful aura and left me feeling, yes, I COULD live here; it's another part of the "adventure" I thought and twenty times better than where I was living... there were the practical issues of it being a few miles away from where my business operated, as well as the finance. However, I worked it all out and decided if I reverted to working from home, therefore giving up the office above the shop, even with petrol etc., what Vanessa and Rob were charging me (mates rates), I could manage... just. So I agreed a deal with them, I started to clear out my office and bedsit of any unnecessary junk to make the move easier and all was arranged for me to move to the third place I would live in since the split! Another flushing out of the old, onto the new!

I was to become a Country BOY! Go out and live with the Wurzels in t' sticks! They had a Summer Holiday let booking to fulfil and a bit of work to do on the place so we pencilled in September for the move. This for me was fine as it gave me a couple of months to get things sorted, give notice on the flat, few trips to the dump with excess office stuff preparing for working from a tiny spare bedroom and so on.

Of course, the other **major** part of my decision to totally change my lifestyle was that I now had a place I could have Frank FULL-TIME! Yep, I could have my dog back, how good was that? Vanessa and Rob had a dog and cats . . . and horses and totally welcomed the fact I had Frank. The Ex and the kids didn't take much persuading to let me have him back to live with me as they were not really looking after him properly, they didn't really get the "dog thing" and they knew he would love living in the country with me. After all, any decent walks or attention he was getting came from me on my regular trips back to the old house . . . by now the knicker smelling well and truly in the past! I will concede they cuddled him a lot which, on his return to me he didn't get quite so much, as I made him into a Man's dog but he was never short of love and attention and from the moment we moved into the cottage, his (and my) exercise rations went up tenfold!

Psychologically this gave me a massive boost to be getting Frank back . . . it gave me a purpose in my life, something (a being) to focus on and be responsible for Every day again, another reason to get out of bed in the morning, a positive influence. And an INSTANT cure to the loneliness. I loved that dog so much, I can't thank him enough for what he brought to my life . . . from the day he came back to me and we moved into the cottage, I realised the reason we had got him a couple of years back. Yes, initially, he was a family dog but, perhaps, this was the Real reason FRANK had come into our lives, my Life . . . to Save me, to give me my sanity back. Obviously back on that November day when we bought him, I didn't know that I would be leaving him behind in the family home not even a year after, going off to my life of singledom.

So here was Frank . . . coming home I felt . . . coming to live with me on the moors! Don't get me wrong, I was never really a doggy or animal (in fact I am allergic to cats) person. I can't whistle to save my life and I don't like screaming out orders to a dog, not that I had to with Frank as I had him well trained. In fact, most of the time, I avoided the hardened doggy lovers . . . instead I embraced my time with MY dog, savoured my privacy, enjoyed the being outdoors and the exercise. I was a "social" dog walker when I chose to be and only when I was in the mood to talk to others. It was mine and Frank's time . . . he always made the most of it by running and exploring as much as he could. Never too far from me and always looking back to see where I was and that he wasn't over-stepping the mark. If I gave him 15 minutes in the morning, he made the most of his 15 minutes; if I gave him 2 hours he never stopped running and looking around for excitement. He was a vibrant dog, full of beans and personality.

After realising his great love for being in water, he developed this "party trick" of swimming out into the water and just diving down to the bottom, his back legs coming up as if he was doing a hand-stand! He would be under the water for ages before resurfacing with the biggest stone he could muster from the bottom! Got it in his mouth, brought it into shore then shook himself off, then straight back in to do it again, until he had a collection of slabs that could build a bloody house! He had people in fits on the side, kept them well entertained, or shitting it that my dog was drowning! But I assured them he was extremely strong and just enjoying himself. The deeper the water, the more he enjoyed the challenge. 12 seconds under water was his record! Sometimes he'd dive off the river bank, almost like a belly flop. Amazing dog! . . . MY DOG, only one Frank! Personally I have never had a dog or seen another dog do what he did in the water . . . I was easily pleased and it cost NOTHING! After my initial shock of seeing him do this, it went onto become something I was proud to see him do and it never ceased to amaze me just how he managed it! Whatever the weather, even in sub-zero conditions in the Winter, you just couldn't keep him out of the water. I never worried about him as he was just so robust and agile. Labs also have their 2 coats, an inner protective one almost like a wetsuit! and the external short haired one to keep them warm. Truly hardy, REAL dogs! Over the years, I was to collect an array of stones he dredged up from the bottom of rivers, lakes, ponds or the sea, from massive boulders to pebbles. I have a collection that could probably make a fantastic looking (very large) rockery! And I believe there are many people around who have vivid recollections of the "incredible swimming / diving dog!"

When he'd mastered this amazing party trick, it inspired me to look back on the history of labs. Please indulge me here . . .

From all accounts Labs originated in Newfoundland. The name assignment may have resulted from a geographical association since Labrador is situated just north-west of Newfoundland and the sub-arctic waters of the Labrador Current flow down the east coast of insular Newfoundland. The name may also be explained by the origin of the word labrador, Portuguese for yeoman or labourer and the Spanish word for workmen, labradores. A related connection could be the village in northern Portugal called Castro Laboreiro where the dogs that guard livestock bear a striking resemblance to Labrador Retrievers.

There is a bit of mystery about the ancestors of the Labrador, appropriate perhaps given the amazing versatility of the breed. After all, how could one dog be so adept at such a wide variety of jobs, be capable of working under very harsh conditions and also have one of the friendliest personalities around? From the men who began to use the Newfoundland region for fishing in the mid to late 15th. century, a rough and often seedy sort, to the aristocratic English gentlemen who refined and preserved the breed in the 19th. century, the people responsible for the development of the Lab were themselves a remarkably diverse group!

The fishermen used dogs to retrieve fish that fell off hooks and to help haul in swimming lines or fishing nets. These dogs needed to be eager to please, strong swimmers and small enough to haul in and out of the two man "Dory" type boats. They needed to have short, water repellent dense coats that could withstand very cold water and wouldn't ball up with ice or bring excess water onboard. This would explain Frank's passion for swimming . . . in ALL weathers! Onshore, as temporary settlements gave way to more permanent ones, a retrieving dog would have been a very useful hunting companion. The St. John's area of

Newfoundland was settled predominantly by Englishmen who brought these working dogs to England through Poole Harbour, Dorset, the hub of the Newfoundland fishing trade. These St. John's dogs became the most prized sporting dogs for the gentry who could afford to maintain kennels for controlled breeding.

There are no written records from the earliest days to detail which dogs came from where and to whom they were bred, so there is only speculation about the ancestors of these St. John's dogs. The black St. Hubert's hound from France, working water dogs from Portugal, old European pointer breeds and dogs belonging to the native Indians have all been suggested as possible predecessors. Certainly some mixture of these or others is logical since tradesmen from around the world frequented Newfoundland for several centuries, plenty of time to develop breeds with the desired working traits. Two distinctly different breeds resulted, the larger longer haired dog used for hauling that became the Newfoundland we know today and the smaller, shorter coated retriever that led to our present day labs.

History lesson over! . . . That said, I am eternally grateful to those guys all those years ago for throwing their dogs into the icy waters to get their fish. Without them, I would not have my memories of Frank's diving . . . or my rockery!

SO I moved in to the little, stone-walled, basic, but quaint cottage in the first week or so of October that year. It was, at that time, still fairly mild . . . the last dregs of a fairly average Summer. It actually seemed, at first, quite idyllic, in me little pad with me little garden, with an Even bigger "garden" surrounding it . . . **the Moors**! I looked out of the windows and there were miles of Moorland. I opened my front door and a sheep or several sheep walked by, sometimes a horse or a few horses, occasionally a cow or two! Arghhhhhhh! How nice I thought, isn't that lovely? . . . That emotion soon went after a few weeks, then they became those "shitty sheep, horrendous horses and crazy cows!" Stepping in dung the minute you leave the house, sometimes with a Suit on, rushing to a meeting, brought home to me the "joys" of living in the country! Those bloody horses . . . they are the worst! Like lots of people,

I guess, I had seen them on the Moors many times before and thought how sweet they were, even felt sorry for them living out in the open all the time, running wild, living off the sparse land. Out in all weathers . . . shame, poor little horses. Sod all that, totally changed my perception off them when I was living out there! I would walk Frank out on the moors sometimes and occasionally wander along with my lunch in hand, just a sarnie and perhaps some crisps or a choccie bar. Well, those bloody 'orses are like Seagulls . . . scavengers they are! The minute they smelt the food they were there, sniffing around you. Once I had taken out a few scraps of left-over food to feed them (this was really early on in my tenure) as Ness (Vanessa my landlady) had said that is what all the villagers did to do their bit to look after them. Well, I don't think I had got 100 yards into my walk that day, certainly hadn't even opened the carrier bag my scraps were in (and we are only talking potato peelings, onion ends and fatty leftovers) before around a dozen bloody horses had descended on me and Frank . . . stampeded towards us when they whiffed the food. Bloody frightening seeing all these big beasts hurtling my way! Frank just ran a mile, bloody dog! leaving me to erratically scatter the contents of my bag all over the place whilst running scared behind a rock! Never took food out again with me! But another time, I was cooking, forgetting I'd left the front door open for Frank to pop in and out when I turned around to see Shergar in me Kitchen! Bloody big brown scruffy 'orse had wandered in and was just about to shove his big nose into the Wok on the stove when I shooed him out! It was like a scene from a pantomime and I was the villain! . . .

What a huge transition and adaptation from where and how I'd been living before. From being alone in a shitty bedsit to now being Doctor Dolittle! But, joking aside, having Frank back, being surrounded by animals . . . and having Ness and Rob around now and again (mainly to light the fire for the central heating cos I was never a Boy Scout!), went a long way to curing any loneliness. Still had, let's say, interesting, neighbours though! In fact, soon learnt there are a lot of weird and scatty people live in these little villages. The guy next door was called Robbie, a funny looking little man in his 40's, Fred West look-a-like! I imagined he'd inherited the house from his Mum and Dad whom he'd probably killed and buried under the patio! Robbie was a Bee-Keeper, made his own honey and sold it at the local markets. Didn't have much to say apart from "Alright Boy" and "Looks like rain again" . . . in his broad West country accent. I would say "Hi Robbie, you ok?" and try to be pleasant and keep in with the neighbours, conscious they all knew each other from their years of interbreeding! but I also valued my privacy and kept myself to myself. The guy the other side of me also lived alone . . . he'd had a sad life in that his son had died in a motor bike crash in his 20's I think. Had a couple of dogs so we said hallo from time to time. Both these guys never knew my name! The pleasantries never went to that level! Found out all the gossip from my landlords who'd lived out there for many years. But, as I say, despite my knowledge and minimal research, I just did my own thing, ran my little mag from the spare room, walked me dog and, as ever, drank red wine!

Having Frank back full time also allowed me to get him properly back into a routine . . . dogs love routine and Labs thrive on it, as well as pleasing their Master. But I had a bit of a confused dog here initially as he didn't really know who he had to answer to, who was calling the shots. But it didn't take me long to "remind" him that I was the guy who came round to take him out for what was then a treat of a walk, long ones, sometimes here on the moors. "Frank, remember me, mate, and remember those great treks we had? . . . well, now, you're gonna get those walks a lot, lot more and . . . look, mate, you now LIVE on the moors, the moors is YOUR BACK GARDEN! . . . That's where you do your poos, no more shitting on your own doorstep!" He soon adapted, excelled in it and got into the routine of a very well trained dog. His reward was loads of clear, healthy, country air, endless exercise and discovering some fantastic new places to walk. Brilliant! . . .

Around this time, me and Frank discovered Gables, a local Cats & Dogs Home. The magazine had done a few features and advertising for them so this evolved into an ongoing Special relationship with the lovely, caring people that ran it. In particular, we got to know Ruth, the Deputy Manager up there. She was a very kind lady who just loved Frank and All animals! It was a very inspirational place all round to visit, which me and Frank did on a regular basis. Ruth checked Frank out for me and reminded me how we'd done well to keep him through the marriage split up. She showed me a lot of the dogs that they had taken in and a great number of them were from homes where the relationships had broken down and the owners could no longer keep their pets. Financially and / or emotionally they could not cope any longer with the dog or cat so Gables stepped in to re-home these animals. Frank was one of the lucky ones and she could see how much I loved him and she was grateful that he had not, through our circumstances, become another one of their residents at the sanctuary. Though, I am certain she would've loved him and cared for him . . . also, I doubt if it would've taken long to re-home him with loving new owners. But the thought NEVER crossed my mind to put him into Gables, at any stage of the process. However, I did take the opportunity when we visited Ruth to point out to Franky Boy how lucky he was! I would turn his head into the direction of the cages where the dogs were housed . . . "Take a look mate, look at those doggies . . . could be worse than living with me mate, you could be in one of those (cages) . . .." I think he knew what I was talking about!

My mind was still in a bad place and I was still not sure about what was coming next in my personal life or how to handle it. I was still confused about my feelings. Still craved and missed my family life. So still screwed up but at least now I was living in a nicer environment with bundles of fresh air to help clear my mind! Me and Frank soon got into a 2 or 3 times a day walking routine which gave me loads of thinking time. Time to try and work it all out at least. The counselling was ongoing but I wasn't dependant on it and the deep, dark depression had lifted. But it was starting to get colder . . . Winter was looming and the reality was this was a stone built cottage, very cold and the heating around the house was fed by the back-boiler in the kitchen, a very old unit that was bloody hard to keep going . . . for me anyway. It meant having to light a coal fire all the time and all that goes with that dirty old task. Coal is black did you know? . . . dirty, dusty, smelly and **Black**! First month or so didn't bother me as it wasn't really *That* cold but as November went on, the spare quilt started making an appearance to bung on top of the main one! And I started wearing layers IN the house as well as out! . . . But Never resorted to taking Frank to bed; never ever got into that habit, despite needing a cuddle to keep warm! I have only ever done that a couple of times and they were both at Dan's house when he let me keep Frank overnight. But the bloody hairs on my bed to hoover off in the morning were a nightmare. No, Frank had his bed in the kitchen. Black Labs are hard anyway . . . they have Canadian ancestry and, as I knew, Frank would bung himself into freezing cold rivers and streams in the middle of Winter, no worries! He was a Real Dog, not like these "hand-bag" accessory efforts! With the temperatures dropping though, it was becoming ever so apparent that I was not really a "Country Boy" . . . give me proper central heating any day, carpets on the floor and plastered walls! I am a Switch man; having to light a coal fire to keep warm is for Campers, Girl Guides and Scouts. As much as I tried to master it, I just couldn't light the stupid thing. And who has the time to clean it out Every morning, go and get more coal in then go through the whole fire-lighting malarkey . . . put on your kindle wood, shove in some paper in between and beg it, talk to it nicely, practically caress and cajole it into burning! Bastard fire . . . soon as I saw a flame, teased it with a bit of coal. "Please, please little fire, keep burning" . . . but alas, Couldn't do it, it didn't happen. Just as soon as it was started, it was all over, burnt out . . . reminded me of my bloody sex life really! Grrrrr . . . so it became the "FUCKIN' FIRE" and the bane of my life. Every time I saw Vanessa and Rob (poor them, they must've dreaded seeing me), I moaned at them about it! Ness used to walk past the cottage every morning early to clean out her horses and stuff; I am sure some mornings she would duck down under the window so I didn't see her to have my verbal blast! It wasn't their fault I wasn't indoctrinated into the ways of the Country and had been spoilt on the finer, simple things you take for granted like heat and water! They were country bumpkins, accustomed to the bleakness and raw aspects of living on t' moor. They were, however, very helpful (at the beginning) and empathised enough to pop in some evenings when they saw me blue in the face from working in this igloo all day, to light my fire for me! They seemed to share out fire lighting duties and the few times Rob popped in, I always rewarded him with a nice glass of Red and some boy's talk!

It did start to get me down coping with my fire phobia. It was starting to get even colder and I had been warned that Winter on the moors was not a pleasant experience. Oh for those June / July days walking the dog out there. No problem back then.

I was still grabbing a beer or two with Paul, my teacher mate. Extending our newly found bond, we would swap stories and put the world to rights. We shared a lot of our inner thoughts and feelings around that time and, because we had so much in common, talked about things in depth on an equal level. Again, I have said before, people come into your life for a reason and Paul had re-entered mine at a time when, yes, I needed an ally, a male friend in my camp to help me with my emotions . . . AND to light the FUCKIN' FIRE! He visited me at the Cottage a lot, shared dog walks with me or just fell in there after we'd had a few beers at the local. Now, he said to me he had lived in the country as a boy and the fire was no problem to him. Well, although he had a few problems with it at first, he did succeed with it where I couldn't . . . That WAS IT! He had the job . . . "Paul, fuck it, it makes sense mate; you're living in that shitty ROOM (even worse than my bedsit) above a noisy pub; you hate it, you're lonely, I'm lonely; we get on great . . . do you want to move in here with me? . . . Not in a Gay way, just to light the FUCKIN' FIRE!" Well we had a Man hug, job done, why not, it did make sense and I was too cold to think of bigger pictures, potential problems of living with someone, money all that shit. I just needed him to help me get warm again!

So, 3rd dwelling since the split, 2nd guy I had lived with . . . AND NO I AM NOT GAY! . . . And another teacher to boot. Cleared it with Ness and Rob, a couple of van loads later, Paul was in within the week. It was all a bit make-shift but we got by. For instance, I had already claimed the double bedroom with my own bed but that meant Paul, as my sort of sub tenant, had second best . . . he was in the "kids room" . . . don't forget it was really a Holiday cottage and in here there were already Bunk beds in situ. Ness didn't really want us to dismantle these so he opted to use the Top Bunk and when Pat, his boy stayed over, he slept in the bottom one! Tom in with me. All sorted . . .

We soon adapted to living together and I found out his bad habits almost immediately! He was a Real bloke, I guess, or my perception of what That is . . . left his pubes in the bath after a shower, toilet seat up, coughed n' burped loudly, spat in the sink and washed it down, put his dirty shoes on the side of the sink to do his laces up . . . all that sort of stuff and ALL the things *I don't do*! I took on the mantle of cleaner and housekeeper. It was partly because I worked from home and had Frank that I did the majority of the hoovering and dusting but also because that is Me; I am a cleaning freak and Ness was more than delighted her little abode was being looked after, even after Paul had moved in with me. She knew I would take care of it and treat it as my own . . . she had seen how clean and tidy my old office was above the shop and that was enough for her to let me have the cottage. Paul, to be fair, chipped in with the house-work and cooking (he was a much better cook than me). Although a bit messy and untidy, he did keep the majority of his bedlam to his own room. Whereas I am meticulous and organised and Very tidy, Paul had stuff all over the place, books, paper, empty bottles, wrappers, you name it! I can't live like that but most blokes do . . . apparently.

The negatives of sharing were far outweighed by the positives. All the things we had discussed before like our friendship, our close bond, our common thoughts and feelings as two disconsolate Divorcee's! We actually got closer and our friendship deepened and we helped each other through some very black moments in those times in the Cottage. We were just 2 emotive, sensitive guys that had been and were still going through a lot and found a way of fuelling all this into a very dependable, healthy male to male relationship. Ok, we were aware how it looked to the outside world, especially to all those people that knew us. Here were two guys, in their forties, both left their Wives and now living together with No girlfriends, just them two . . . in a little cottage on the Moors away from everyone, how sweet! Of course, this started the gossip train going and before long the rumours circling around our families and friends were that we had to be Gay! In fact, Tom, the little Sod and Pat, Paul's Son, chucked it on Faceache that their "Dads had moved in together so they MUST be Gay!" . . . Took me so long to live that one down and convince people I wasn't! We didn't help ourselves really by practically doing everything together, spending most of our free time in each other's company and, as I say, getting very close. We also fed the rumours by giving each other Man Hugs in public and sitting together at Parents' Evening instead of with our Exes! All the Parents thought it now! Even on our regular trips to the local pub, just a short walk away, we'd sit together on a cosy leather settee and chat over our beer! So, yes, it must've looked a bit strange but we were just two guys at the same place in our lives and we were just helping each other through things with a lot of laughs, tears and chats.

It was a base for our Sons to come around and stay. Paul has two boys like me. It was now more fun for Tom to come round to mine now as Pat was there too most times. Much more of an incentive than the bedsit. Our elder Sons just popped in when it suited them, being that bit older. We had some momentous evenings in the "Igloo", cooking for our boys while they ran amuck just trying to keep warm! We would have X-Factor and Take Me Out nights, proper Boys stuff, all boys together . . . who needs women? Sometimes we'd get the cards out or play Monopoly . . . simple stuff, simple fun. How different was this now to drinking myself stupid in a depressed state alone in that Bedshit? It was great and I have to say I felt like I was rebuilding the relationship with my Sons again, especially Tom. He often talks about those fun nights in the Cottage, our aborted attempts to light the **FF**, Paul drinking his Cider and nodding off mid Monopoly and me on the Red stuff. The boys, Tom and Pat, got closer too; after all, they had their situations, dysfunctional families and Gay Dads in common!

Paul and I shared many a dog walk together. We just loved getting out in that fresh air . . . and, with our layers on and walking briskly, it was warmer out there than in that blimmin' igloo! We explored a few new walks on the Moors and found some interesting places. It was in this time, I discovered a very Special place to me which became close to my heart and I subsequently visited many times with Frank. It was perhaps a mile or so walk from our cottage and is quite simply at the top of a disused / partly still working China Clay site. Just the sheer beauty of the view up there at that spot is awesome. You look for miles and take in the sight of the formed lakes from the mining, the colour of the water changing as per the weather or the season . . . it is at its best when you're up there in the Summer and the water appears a beautiful tourquoise blue with the Sun's rays beating down on it. Stunning. I think when I die, if it can't be arranged to scatter my ashes at Stamford Bridge, the Home of Football(!), I would be happy to be bunged up there to roam Free!

I found many places of interest to walk either with Paul or alone and I would often reflect how nice it would've been to have shared these walks and experiences with a Special Lady . . .

My Demons were still in my head but I was starting to cope with them. The loneliness, as I said, had definitely been eradicated, despite no lady in my life and the fact I still worked alone and, therefore spent a lot of time with Me! But life, again was to take Another twist which I had not anticipated or in my wildest dreams ever thought would happen. Back at the house, my old family home, we still had the problem that hardly anything was being paid towards the mortgage. She only had a part-time job and a few benefits coming in and was not getting any help towards the mortgage as it was still solely in my name. Even if hers had been on it, they still wouldn't help much as on paper I was still liable. We should've sold it when we'd agree to, which, by now was about 15 months previous. I had pleaded with her many times to let it go, that I just physically could not afford to scrape by where I was living, pay her money for my Son and do all I did for him . . . AND pay the mortgage and all the bills! I am an entrepreneur but I aint no Simon Cowell! I had kept in touch (on a monthly basis) with the mortgage company, 'phoning or writing to them without fail regularly. Just keeping them abreast of the situation and begging them to let my family stay in that house, always asking for more time in case my luck changed, perhaps I came into some big money (yeah right, not in my lifetime, don't have that kinda luck!), but, never ever ignoring the debt that was compounding by the day. I did pay them something and she did what she could here and there, even managed to get them to do interest free for a few months but, ultimately, they were not getting full whack and their patience ran thin. My 'phone calls to them went from tolerance and patience at the beginning to anger and frustration. Allow me a rant here . . . after what I have experienced in my life and especially what I went through after the split, ONE fact I now know is that Mortgage companies, financial institutions per say, do **Not** want to help you when you're down. Quick to do a deal and take yer money when you've got it, but when you aint got none . . . purely through life changing circumstances, they just don't help at all, are not empathetic and just lay on the penalty charges and clauses to make you even more in debt, then bung you in Court . . . **FACT, FACT, FACT** . . . Rant still not over, Sorry! One day, if ever I get a few bob(!), I am going to take these bastards on and fight that corner for all of us poor sods whose life just went off track temporarily . . . Rant nearly over! . . . I would have these conversations with these faceless idiots in the Call Centres and, after getting through 20 minutes of "security" questions and switching of departments, I would eventually talk to some poor sod, who, I am sorry if you were one of those that drew the short straw with me, got my monthly ear-bashing. The general theme of the monthly script was them going through (for the 1000th time) my income / expenditure or lack of it and then eventually, after an hour or so, saying they couldn't help me and they'd be starting "proceedings" to take the house. I always asked if the conversation was being recorded because I WANTED IT TO BE RECORDED FOR POSTERITY! . . . "Mr Call Centre Man" who doesn't know me from Adam (whoever the fuck he is? . . . no, I NEVER swore at CC Man or Lady . . . well, perhaps once or twice when they put That 'orrible waiting room music on) . . . "Let me just say, officially, for the record and if you are not recording it, please write it on my notes and put in My file, how many times did you speak to me in the first 18 years of paying this mortgage? . . . ANSWER – NEVER . . . How many times have you spoken to me in the last 2 Years . . . ANSWER -Every (fucking . . . I never said it, I thought it!) MONTH! . . . And in those last 2/3 years I have lost a Business and am going through a Divorce so Mr CC Man, yeah you could say I have hit bad times and need your help now and need you to look at the fact I was once, only recently, a VERY good (fucking . . . I'm losing the plot now in me head) CUSTOMER of yours whom you threw re-mortgage after re-mortgage offers at . . ." Of course I was wasting my time and energy because Call Centre Man or Lady just quoted the book, the book of Financial Fuckwits to me and read me out the small print . . . that bit you see on their ads "If you fall behind with your repayments . . . blah, fucking blah", Twats, cretins the lot of them. So, after nearly 2 years of under payment, the arrears had reached a point where they completely lost their patience and could not / would not help us. They actually bunged us in Court that year, twice in fact . . . with repossession proceedings. Gave them a chance to put us through more stress and misery and bung some more costs and penalties onto the debt! The first time I went with my Ex Wife and we managed to get the Judge to show some lenience and ask the mortgage company for more time to review our situation. The second time, I actually had Paul with me for moral back up as she couldn't attend. This time they threw the book at us. There was no more time and they wanted their money . . . the situation had gone on long enough and they were actually right. I was not going to be able to magic the arrears payments out of a hat, we were never going to resume our marriage, me move back to pull together on this and she was not going to earn any more than she did. So, I had to break the news to her that she would be getting an official repossession notice and Bailiff's date to be evicted! It was a sad day after all the years we'd lived in that house and worked so hard to keep it and brought our family up there. Though I understood the Court's decision, I was still fuming at the Mortgage company who had just not helped us one little bit . . . they say they do but they have absolutely no policies in place to help once good, regular paying customers when their lives hit crisis times like lots of people. This part of my story in all this I am certain is one bit that lots and lots of people can relate to.

So, my family were being evicted and nobody, me or anybody could prevent it. Of course, it was another opportunity for the world to jump on the "it's Malc's fault" bandwagon. Get that baseball bat out and beat me up again. As much as I tried to empathise with this notion and was so sad that despite her efforts to not let the split up affect the kids' lifestyle too much, I still knew that I had tried my best too to avoid this happening. It was not what I wanted either . . . for her and the kids to have to uproot and now find another house, obviously rented, to live in. I outwardly sympathised and shared the sadness but, have to admit, inside was very angry that it had come to this.

I simply could not afford to keep that house and live somewhere else . . . a common situation in these circumstances. I was losing the house that I had worked so hard for all those years, blood sweat and tears, through thick and thin. Somehow, some way we had kept it going all that time and brought our kids up there. There were a lot of good memories from that house and we had good times over the years, despite our recent troubles.

The reality WAS very sad and emotional. My family was now looking for somewhere else to live. At this juncture, I would have been delighted if Tom and even Daniel had turned round and said they'd like to come to live with me. Really hoped that might happen but they wanted to stay with their Mum and saw that as home and wherever she moved onto. That hurt, still hurts but they make their own decisions and they saw their place was with their Mum. They looked at a few places. Of course, now she was officially being evicted and legally separated, the good old Social Security would **now** jump in and help her to fund a new home with 2 dependant kids in tow . . . Daniel was still a full time

Student. Well her search didn't take long! It was a beautiful, converted Barn,3 bedrooms over 2 floors, en suite etc., modern décor and posh flooring. But do you know where it was? . . . Only half a mile from where I was living on the Moors! She was going to be in the next bloody village! What the hell is that all about? Out of all the places she could've gone to she chooses a house a dog's walk away from me, and in the Country . . . like me, she was not a Country bumpkin, a proper Townie. But she had REAL CENTRAL HEATING in her new abode . . . Not a "fucking fire!" I know she was sad at having to get out of the family home but I think it's safe to say her impending move to Beckingham Palace on the Moor did soften the blow somewhat!

They then had a month or so to prepare to move out before the Bailiff's came in and her move date was set to go to her new abode. She started to have a clear out of junk and prepare herself mentally for the move. It was an emotional time for all of us and a horrible exercise going through years of stuff including photos, memories, the kids' old toys and clothes . . . everything. Very upsetting. But do you know what? She didn't include me in any of that exercise! I got to hear from her that she was upset doing it and how much hard work it was for her sorting it all but she never allowed me to help her with it, go through any stuff I might want from the house at that juncture. Nothing. No, she just shut me out of all that. I already had nothing from the split up; I left that day with a few clothes, she added to that with a chosen pile a little later on but I had never taken anything more than that from my marriage or the house. In a way, I am proud that I have survived since with the bare minimum and got by with possessions begged, given or borrowed from friends but, at this time, it did dawn on me how much material investment I had put in over the years to our relationship. And I had none of it . . . not even any of the decent photos of the kids from our extensive collection. Part of letting her keep everything was still down to my guilt that I had destroyed the family and by her keeping all the lovely stuff we had bought or accumulated, the expensive sofa, table & chairs, tellies, beds etc. etc., somehow allowed her to not have something Else to have a go at me about. It also gave the kids a little bit of stability in keeping their familiar things. They had been through enough and I didn't want them to be upset anymore by Dad taking stuff they lived with. But, for Christ's sake, all I really wanted were a few bits and bobs, mainly personal stuff, mementoes, at most some pictures and maybe some chosen CD's! But she had the control over this situation . . . The final straw was the DAY she actually moved all her stuff out and moved into the new place. She assembled a "team" of around a dozen friends and family (they used to be my friends and family!) and got them all around that day to help with the move. Of course, I WAS NOT THERE . . . NO "invite" for me obviously. No, I was the leper, the curse, the Bastard that had caused all this hassle and stress. Moving is a stressful thing at the best of times and, of course, there was the emotional attachment to the house in this equation. But, as I said before, **I also** was losing the house I'd had for years . . . it was mine before she even came on the scene for Christ's sake! BUT EVERYBODY FORGOT that on this day; I tried to block it out of my mind by doing my normal Saturday stuff, work for a couple of hours, chores and housework and a long walk with Frank but it was very difficult to switch off from what was happening that day. As I wasn't there I only have a Third Party account of what happened but I was told that the front window of the house had to be taken out to facilitate getting all the stuff out . . . no way was she going to leave the £3k leather sofa suite! All these people pitched in to help her get it all done in a day, cars and vans turning up like Spaghetti Junction! They must've looked like ants scurrying around to collect stuff up for their nest. She supervised her little helpers including the boys' friends too and got it all done, mission accomplished. Then, at the end of that day, I finally got a call from her to say they had finished, she was at the new house and (finally some acknowledgement) "would I like to pop round and see her and the kids and share a Chinese" in her new abode as she knew it must've been "a hard day for me too" I had to ponder on this for a minute or two as did I really want to get involved at this point of the day? An after- thought, still lots of emotions flying around. But she got me with "well it's up to you but the boys would like to show you their new rooms" . . . not quite emotional black-mail but whenever the boys are mentioned I melt. So, after due thought, I psyched myself up and drove the very short journey round to her new abode. Though it only took me less than 5 minutes, I still had time to think "what the hell is she doing moving into the country and secondly, so bloody Near to me!" Anyway, got there and went in to be "greeted" by her in triumphant mode that she had achieved her objective that day in moving out / moving in, in the ONE day! She was on the wine by now and had that horrible gloating expression on her face I hated . . . Her Sting in the Tail look! Our friends, Jason and his wife Nicki, were there . . . the last of her elves she'd assembled that day, and the boys, of course. The whole dynamic was a weird one for me . . . a HUGE mix of emotions and thoughts. Here I was in her new palace, the boys by now were in excitement mode sorting out their new rooms, she was on her new throne and, to cap it all, I was now faced with the added anger of facing my friends who had helped her dismantle my old house! I might've got it all wrong, but it just seemed that any sadness that anyone should've had about what had really happened that day, losing the family home, was overlooked by all of them because now they were living in the house from NEXT! She had ordered Chinese for us all and gave me a glass of wine. I was shown around . . . by Nicki, goodness knows why. Then I saw it . . . HER New bedroom . . . already steeped in silk bedclothes and all her perfumes, make-up, CD Player, candles . . . not all in their correct places yet but ready to be maneuvered into place . . . in time for her inevitable nights of passion in that pad. To top it all, she had an en suite with a lovely WALK IN Shower . . . That's where I imagined, well, whatever . . . That was IT . . . **My demons had returned**; I couldn't handle it, made my apologies, hurtled up the stairs crying and fled that scene well before the Chinese turned up! I was angry, sad, very confused and just another moment in all this where I questioned what it had all come to.

I had an opportunity in the next few days to go back to the old house. They'd moved out before the Bailiffs were due to do their bit and hand over the keys to the Estate Agents trying to sell the house for the Mortgage company. So I did it . . . I went back round there to see the old house for what I thought would be the last time. It was probably a bad move but I did it all the same. What I faced though was so upsetting, I was almost physically sick. It felt like my heart had been ripped out. Well, she had not only cleared out all our stuff but in addition to that, had her little elves rip out the integrated bedroom units and worse still, the built in freezer and other stuff from the kitchen. There was rubbish strewn around most rooms and the whole place felt dirty, damp and uncared for . . . AND EMPTY! Grass up to my knees in the garden, it was like squatters had left there. This was My house, my family home, not anymore, desecrated. I cried (again) . . . please let's pause at this juncture and touch base on this crying stuff! In my lifetime before this split up I think I cried on maybe three or four occasions . . . certainly cried buckets when my dear Dad died far too young (58), when I was a mere 23, another time when the Ex suffered a Stillbirth and lost our baby girl, Megan, before Tom came along. Then, I am struggling to think of other times; oh I did mention the rabbit's passing! . . . So I am not a serial crier, I shed more tears in the 6/7 years after the business/marriage breakdowns than the whole of my life!

She had left, in the middle of the bare front room, ONE box of photos, memories . . . ONE box and that was the remnants of all our stuff . . . she had cherry picked all the good photos, pictures etc. There was some junk up in the attic that she couldn't be bothered to take but that was that. I just looked around in bewilderment that it had come to this, an empty, dishevelled house that was once full of vibrancy and MY family. I remember I 'phoned my mate, Dan, teacher Dan and shared this moment with him. Don't know specifically why I chose Dan out of all my friends to make that pivotal call but maybe because I knew he had not been involved in this part of the process . . . he certainly hadn't been party to the moving day debacle and didn't really know where we were with everything so I guess I needed to tap into his temporary neutrality of the situation at that moment. Yes it was a NEEDY moment and I needed to 'phone a friend for a few empathetic words. This time Dan didn't give me Tough love but was very kind to me and sensed my deep level of sadness at this moment, the extent of my loss. As well, he knew on a pure practical level how bloody hard I had worked to keep that house and make it a nice place to live in . . . he was already on that property ladder and was starting to understand how tough life can be and what you have to put in to achieve the house stuff. But at that moment, that bit was irrelevant . . . this was a time to reflect and realise that that WAS IT . . . No house, no Wife, no family, no possessions . . . I'd lost the lot . . . **STARK REALITY.**

MY FAMILY now living on the moors and less than a mile from me totally changed the whole dynamic of things in this navigation of the emotional process. If I had been getting somewhere with entangling the demons, anxiety and horrible stuff that had gone on in my head, this just pushed me back another ten steps. No amount of "head clearing" dog walks in the fresh, cold Moors air were going to quickly fix this one! Yes, I saw more of the boys, Tom especially but it also meant I saw more of my Ex Wife too! At the beginning especially, she had me jumping through the "guilt rings" it seemed as often as it suited her . . . sometimes "fire" on those hoops! But I was jumping through **all of them** at this time. Because of the logistical closeness, I seemed to be doing EVEN MORE running around for Tom, school runs, football etc., dropping water around to her when her pipes froze in the Winter, picking bits up from the shop, general chores, that kind of stuff. All to help her ease herself into country life! I did all this and more because I felt guilty at what I'd done . . . it was All My Fault that my poor family had to vacate their home and move, to this beautiful (properly heated!) country residence. And, of course, at this time, I still wanted her back . . . mainly because HE had her! Should've been over that by now but it was just thrusted upon me that she was still with him on the many nights I dropped Tom back to hers and her car wasn't there because while I was doing All the running around for Tom's footy and after school stuff, she was out. If her car wasn't there, she HAD to be with him didn't she? And even if she wasn't, the demons in my head just made up what she was doing with him at that moment. Because she lived so close, there was the odd occasion when I couldn't sleep when I would drive out in the early hours in pitch darkness down her lane to see if another car was in her driveway . . . these were nights when either Tom was sleeping at mine or I knew he was at Nan and Grandad's house. Because I knew, at this juncture, she would not have had a man back while the kids were in the house and we trusted each other on that one. There was only once I did see another car there as well as hers and, again, it was a heart-wrenching moment . . . but I never repeated my antics of my day in JAIL, just drove off crying my eyes out. It turned out it was a girl friend of hers that had stayed over. But it didn't stop me carrying out more spying missions either in the car or when walking the dog, conveniently in the area of her house! You can't get arrested for walking a dog on the Moors, only if he eats a sheep and Frank's not partial to lamb!

So my behaviour around her and generally had gone back a peg or two and it was back to the Docs, then more counselling to sort my head out. I had started to sink again into that black place in my mind. Not to the depths of depression or suicidal inclinations but just black, confused moments and irrational thoughts. Still sensibly running my little magazine business from the tiny spare room, still busy running around most of the week for my Son, walking the dog and living with Paul . . . which was a full-time job in itself! No, I don't mean that horribly because me and Paul were good for each other but we both said we were "Time Bandits", meaning our seemingly endless, intense chats lasted for ages and stole our time! But as I have already said, Paul and I had obviously come together at this time for a reason . . . I think if I had chucked loneliness into this period as well, on top of my mind games, It may well have taken me back to THAT DEEP, DARK place and the hose-pipe! So as nuts as the whole living situation was, the insanity perhaps kept me Sane if you see what I mean! As a teacher, and someone who had been through divorce and the whole dysfunctional thing, Paul was able to guide me a lot on how to get my relationship right with the boys. The biggest thing he made me aware of at this time was to be careful what I said and did around my sons in relation to my thoughts about her. He advised me not to be asking Tom if his Mum was out with him, or anyone for that matter and, generally, Paul pummelled into me that it was vital that whatever I said or did around Tom at his vulnerable age, would stay with him forever and go some way to establishing how he would conduct himself in relationships and generally in his adult life. Because of Paul and this advice I THINK (I hope) I got it right most of the time but I am also aware that because of my angry state of mind at that time, I did "slip off the wagon" on a few occasions and asked Tom what was happening in his Mum's life. There was this one Saturday night when the boys were around (Tom and Paul's boy Pat) and we'd cooked a nice meal and settled to watch our Saturday night telly, but I just couldn't get the thought out of my head of her being with him, Rambo. I was the only one that called him Rambo. Just my "pet" name to avoid using his Real name, which of course in my mind made him a Real person which I ***still*** didn't want to deal with! Bloody demons. I tried to hide my despair and emotions from Tom, stiff upper lip and all that. Although, that said, I also was honest with Tom when I was in a bad mood or down, even if I didn't let him know the details, therefore giving him a sound realisation that life isn't always a bed of roses. But on this night, with a couple of wines inside me, I couldn't keep it in and just blurted out "bet your Mum is out Again tonight, having a great time, always out these days . . . I think she's happy and over things don't you?" . . . I continued my verbal tirade till I was done. WHEN I came up for air, I realised all of Paul's good advice had gone out of the window in that moment and it was not the way to speak to my 14-year-old Son at this time, not ever. A complete lack of respect for his feelings, everybody's and just totally out of order . . . but all down to where I was in my head and a blatant, public display of irrationality. Tom just "escaped" upstairs and played with Paul's Son and I think Pat, who'd probably seen his Dad have the odd blast over the years, had a word with him to appease the situation. I was wrong though and spent most of the next day apologising to my Son with some carefully chosen "make up" words advised by Paul. I just tried to explain that life isn't always happy and adults do lose it sometimes caused by events going on in their lives and sometimes just can't explain how that manifests itself into behaviour such as mine the night before. I was so sorry and said that I obviously still cared about his Mum and would dearly love it if everything could be "put back together" and that's probably why I had said what I did. I was hurt and upset she had found someone else. A 14-year-old doesn't really want to hear all that from his Dad and doesn't really get the bigger picture. His reply was just an angry: "but YOU left US so why should you be upset Dad?" . . . and this retaliation was his parting shot as he was getting out of my car to go into his house so I had no chance to counter that one! But what would I have said to this anyway? That was his juvenile, naive perception of the whole situation. He lived in his Mum's camp and his main loyalty in all this was to her. She was the victim, you are the Bastard Dad, now leave me alone as I am off to play on X-Box! Another sad day, another day it became clear to me that it would take a lot of time, maybe years, maybe never (?) to get to a point where we ALL had worked through the aftermath of the split up. At that point I felt so much guilt for everything I HAD DONE. It was ALL my fault; I had thrown a hand grenade into this family by leaving and caused so much havoc, it was unbearable. From then on, I tried so hard to not involve my boys in the tangle of the split. I had left their Mum, not the kids and I had to keep reminding myself of that fact. It was difficult though as it was such an easy slip of the tongue to ask Tom "what was Mum up to tonight or this weekend?" . . . He just looked at me with disdain and confusion as to why I was even bothered. On the odd occasion Daniel popped into my life, I too chipped away at him asking about his Mum. In his case, he was bumping into her down the town when he was out on a lads' night with his mates and she was "out there" with the girls . . . I can only say sorry to my boys for my erratic behaviour at this time and for trying to get information out of them which was so unfair of me. Again, it was just the "place" I was in then, so confused. It just felt that I was swimming with my feet tied down by bricks and I was desperately battling to overcome my handicap. I had tried to "move on" when I had gone out to the cottage on the Moors, a new life, a new beginning, but then here she was, always around me, just down the road, always in my face and what I didn't know or find out about what she was up to in that place or where or who she was with, I made up in my imagination!

As I have said, I was trying, desperately trying to move on with my life, put the past behind me and just find some peace and happiness. Pretty hard when your Ex Wife is now just living a kite flight away! Add to all that being skint and living in an Igloo away from the REAL World and what chance did I have of meeting anyone special? Only one thing for it, go back on the Internet dating site! I re- wrote my Profile on there. I think the first time I had gone on there when I was living in the bedsit, I had perhaps been a little TOO honest in presenting myself as this down and out, fallen on hard times kind of chap. Though I'd had some success that time in pulling the ladies, I think this time I was in a slightly better place in my life to come across let's say "half sorted!" My profile this time seemed to get across that, ok I was going through a Divorce and was not quite as well off in body, mind AND wallet as the good old days but I was still a positive, articulate, hopefully still fairly attractive guy? At the end of the day on this site, at our sort of age, most of the people on there, men and women were in similar circumstances to me after their life experiences. But, by the pure nature of the thing, you have to "sell yourself" a little bit on there as you are looking for a date after all aren't you! Aren't you? Paul, again, was around to give me his input on this and together we concocted a half decent resume' of ME to present to potential dates! This time, after my first dip in the pond, I also had the experience of it to now be a bit more selective. Not answer EVERY blimmin' message that came in, have a look at them first before . . . mostly pressing DELETE! I had learnt from my first go at it that it is not to be taken personally (either way) if you didn't respond to every contact made. This is a bit like going into the pub and either reciprocating an eye or body contact . . . OR NOT! In other words, you either fancied them or you didn't, or they you! With Internet dating it is a "fast track" to getting to know them with dialogue as soon as you forget that instant attraction from their picture and look of their profile. But it still NEVER beats the Real thing of actually meeting and talking in person. So I set about going on the odd date this time and that's all it was really, 2 or 3 in about the same amount of months . . . My heart was not really in it and this time it took a lot of talking online before I ventured out into the Dating scene. I met a lovely lady called Sue. She'd had a much troubled childhood in that her Dad had committed suicide and, though I never told her about my fumbled attempts, our chats about this made me realise just how it Had affected her throughout her whole life. It was obviously a terrible event to have dealt with as a child. Her Brother had remained totally screwed up by it all his life and turned to drink and drugs to blot it out. She, on the other hand, coped with the devastation by (outwardly) remaining a very positive, happy go lucky, cup half full kinda girl. I am sure she had her moments of depression over it throughout the years but I had ultimate respect for the way she handled her life and had brought up her Son, now about 19 I think, with a strong, determined, mental attitude, encouraging him and supporting him in his goals and dreams. We had this very much in common as this is what I try to do with both my boys, despite all the shit (nothing as bad as hers) that has happened to me. We met several times but it never quite went to that next level. We would just meet up for a quiet drink in a nice pub somewhere, talk till we were blue in the face and then kiss politely and go our separate ways. It Never went to the bedroom stage or even visits to each other's houses. None of that, just a mutual respectful liking of each other's company, two lost souls I guess. We kept in touch a long time after our last meeting, just by text really but it fizzled out eventually. A Really nice lady.

Then there was TINKERBELL! That was a pseudonym she used until she was interested enough in you to tell you her Real name! In Linda's case, her pet name for herself was so apt! She was up there with the bloody fairies! EVEN in her ramblings to me on

Tinternet, she had talked in complete riddles! But I have to say she transfixed me, intrigued me with her stories, her laid back take on life and what came through was a supremely intelligent, witty and charming lady ... and, wow, was she gorgeous too! So, I turned up for this one, my latest victim, quite excited but not really knowing what to expect ... Hey, in for a penny I thought. She was very attractive in the flesh, quite short (I knew that she would be of course from her profile), blonde, well groomed ... and Scottish! She hadn't told me that bit! Nothing against the Scots but I didn't understand a word that came out of her mouth! ... As her internet ramblings, she seemed to be talking in rhymes, almost an endless tirade of poetry and these were hard enough to understand the meaning or context of, let alone chucking in a broad Scottish accent to contend with too! We had a couple of, let's say, interesting evenings out but, again, never went anywhere with it. I think we fancied each other but there was no spark between us and, I have to say, she was put off a lot by my emotional confusion at that time. She identified very early on that I was not really ready to move on properly and questioned why I was even on a dating site? I constantly asked myself that one!

Paul used to call me "Task orientated" and observed that I "fitted in" my dates and Online correspondence around my work and chores. I am a doer and constantly on the go. If I was not working, I was cleaning the house, doing the washing, getting the chores done, or running around for my kids. ... oh and walking the dog! I was the COMPLETE opposite of him as he was very laid back, just let everything Hit him before prompting himself to react and get his ass in gear. Not in a lazy way at all or procrastinating, just never really worrying about things until they needed to be worried about! I so wished I could be like him and he thought the same about me! They say opposites attract ... !

He was scatty was Paul. For a hugely intelligent, articulate guy, he meandered his way through life in a very disorganised, mad, extremely casual way! We were totally up front about how different we were and often he would say how it was a miracle he'd survived in the cauldron of a high pressure teaching job for so many years! He was always being chased by the Admin. department for a report or something that should've been in 3 weeks or so ago! He was constantly losing his keys, credit card, wallet or 'phone . . . things I NEVER did in my ultra-organised existence. There was this one time he'd been out in his little fishing boat he owned, nothing special but a lovely little vessel he'd picked up years earlier. It was his respite, his escape from the world, to just disappear into the ocean for a few hours, a whole day sometimes. He'd got it back into its mooring, about 200 yards from the shore, then proceeded to row in towards the bank in a lot smaller tender boat he had, a rubber dinghy. He 'phoned me in a panic at this point to say that just as he was getting out of the dinghy and onto the bank, he had dropped his car keys into the water! The tide was in so it was about perhaps 4 or 5 feet of water. He said he could see the shiny keys glimmering at him at the bottom so he was going to wait there for the tide to go out, rather than getting wet by wading in! So I had this vision of this burly, happy go lucky soul, sitting on the side of the river bank staring profusely at these keys for hours until the water went down to a sufficient level for him to retrieve his keys! This was the kind of nuts thing that was an everyday event in scatty Paul's life, a terrible time keeper too, always chasing his tail for no apparent reason! But a Super guy, heart of Gold and a terrific friend and confidante.

Well, overall it was a weird, surreal tenure in the Igloo. There was the adapting to living in the sticks and coping with country living, co-habiting with Teacher Paul AND the constant onslaught of emotions living so close to the Enemy EX. Then, to top it all, we had to vacate the property for the 2 whole weeks before and after Christmas!Ness and Rob had mentioned (back in Julyish time) that they had a booking in the Diary for the Christmas period for a couple and their 2 children. Apparently, they were from Derby and had stayed in the cottage a few times before, regulars and always for Christmas, to visit relatives down here. Though, when Ness agreed to let me have the cottage, they said they would try and get the family to stay somewhere else and find them alternative accommodation close by. However, a few weeks before Christmas,

Ness told us that she was sorry, she and Rob had been unsuccessful in persuading the people to go elsewhere. They were staunch lovers of their Christmas break in the Cottage on the moors and weren't budging. So, it fell upon me and Paul to find SOMEWHERE else to spend our Christmas! We now didn't have a lot of time to prepare for this temporary eviction and there wasn't a lot of options open to us. Ness and Rob's contacts had hit a brick wall and both Paul and I were busy as normal and certainly didn't have much time to shop around for cheap (it had to be) accommodation at bloody Christmas! By this time, family and friends had made their arrangements for the festivities and putting up one or two miserable old codgers was not in their plans or desires! At a push we both could've forced ourselves on someone we knew but we both didn't want to do that really, not fair. Besides, as I have said, I was in this place with my family where I wanted to keep them out of my life and my problems. In the end, the good old Tinternet did its job and we came across an inexpensive HOLIDAY CHALET with 3 bedrooms on the outskirts of . . . Newquay! This meant it was big enough for me, Paul and the boys if they wanted to come and spend at least a bit of Christmas with us, though it would be hard logistically. We also had Frank and this place was dog friendly. The biggest problem we had was that we had to physically pack up ALL our belongings and take Everything we had in the house away to Newquay! They did let us store some of our stuff in the locked cupboard under the stairs but, even though I had flushed out a lot of stuff in my 2 moves thus far, it is amazing how much you realise you have in belongings when you have to carry out an exercise like this! It worked two ways . . . the family coming in to stay were expecting a vacant cottage, just furniture etc. and basic kitchen and bedding stuff supplied by our Landlords . . . and, secondly, me and Paul didn't want strangers using any of our personal possessions. So, after a few weeks of intermittent packing in readiness, it was a couple of days before Christmas Eve that we actually MOVED OUT! I remember that day with huge anger and bewilderment. One of those "can't believe this is really happening" days! It was snowing, yes 3 or 4 inches of bloody snow had fallen over the Moor. This meant we couldn't get our cars up the little road to park outside the house to make it easier to load up. So, with utter disdain, sheer frustration and lots of snarling and swearing, we began to carry all of our belongings, mostly in big black bags, in shifts to the cars. This meant a walk of around 200 metres or so, slipping all over the place in the snow and ice. The first 3 or 4 trips were funny but then, several falls later, tiredness and stress creeping in, we began to lose all humour. It didn't help that EVERY journey we carried out, we passed Vanessa and Robert's (see what I did there? . . . no longer lovely Ness and Rob!) cottage on the corner and could see them inside, in the warm (cos they COULD light their fucking fire), sat all around their cosy dining room table eating a lovely, HOT meal! Grrrrrrrrrrrrrrr! I was like Mr. Grinch and scowled at them every time I went past. When we were finished, finally, a couple of hours later, they popped into the cottage to have an inspection to see if we'd cleared out sufficiently! I couldn't resist: "Have a Fucking Lovely Fucking Christmas you two with your family in your lovely Fucking warm cottage spending your dosh from your lucrative Fucking Christmas holiday booking, while we are holed up in some cheap, probably cold and damp wooden chalet in FUCKING NEWQUAY grrrrrrrrrrrrrr!" . . . I blasted out. It sounds worse than it reads as I had built Ness and Rob up for this sarcastic, funny parting gesture in the weeks leading up to this pivotal day. I did finish it off with a hug for Ness and a shake (around the throat . . . no!) of the hand to Rob and they did apologise again for the inconvenience in between their giggles! . . . And, besides, they had given us a huge credit on the Rent to compensate!

We drove, carefully, out of the village, both cars full to the brim with our Tat! To be fair, on arrival in Newquay the chalet was not that bad really. Fairly modern . . . with heating you switched on with a SWITCH! Heaven, no Scout duties for us for 2 weeks, yippee! It was a basic Holiday abode, with everything we needed to get us through Christmas, albeit wasn't Home . . . but either of us had not had a proper home for a while now, let alone a proper family Christmas. We unloaded the cars, more trekking from the car park which was 100 or so metres from the chalet . . . good job we were fit old buggars! Finally got everything in and just sat there looking at each other with a couple of beers in hand and laughed and laughed and laughed at the surreality of Life, our lives anyway!

We Decided it was one of those situations in life where we had to make the best of it. Another challenge . . . hey, that course in Character building had given us some practical work to test us again! Although we didn't go the full hog of putting up Christmas decs. (bah, humbug), we did do a Festive shop and got in some drink, choccie, sweets and general food goodies to at least make it feel like Christmas! Of course we'd brought the Monopoly and cards . . . wow, we were gonna have a whale of a time! Two lonely, sad old gits, drinking our sorrows away in a place where we had no family or friends . . . Just like the Igloo then really! I suppose you could look at this from the outside and point out that we were two single men, in Newquay and it was Christmas after all . . . and, therefore, surmise that all we should've been doing was going out to the local bars and clubs and having a great time where nobody knew us! Perhaps even pulling a couple of those female creatures and bringing them back to our plush pad! . . . well, nothing could be further from our minds or plans. For me, I was still in a darkish place in my head, now even more down at being away from the boys even further at Christmas and I was still very short of money. THIS WAS NO HOLIDAY . . . It was merely an inconvenience, a pain in the ass interruption of our everyday lives. I had done the whole clubbing scene and, yes, in Newquay many, many years before; bought that tee-shirt and I had no intention or the means to repeat that fiasco on this trip. Paul, though he had more money than me, felt the same way and we had discussed this before coming. With his income from teaching, though not flush with money (and don't forget he was going through Divorce number 2 now), he probably could've used the 2 weeks to book himself into a nice hotel nearer Plymouth to have a good break from everything, including me and Frank! Then he would've been closer to his two sons which would've made sense. But we decided we were in this together, the two Musketeers and we wanted to help each other through this Christmas as we had done the emotional turmoil of that year . . . a True Friend he is and always will have a soft spot for Paul from that time . . . The plan was we'd get through the first week down there on our own then we would drive up to bring our Sons back (well at least the younger ones, as the older ones had their own plans) to spend the 2nd week with us and at least see in the New Year. As it happened, because Paul had that bit more money than me, he did actually pop back a couple of times that first week to see his boys and sort out some stuff. This meant I spent the majority of that first week alone (used to that!) and just got out with Frank and walked along a few beaches which, actually, was ok really . . . one of my most favourite places, the beach. As a family, we had always loved Cornwall and spent many special times in Newquay not only with the kids but also Romantic weekends away, predominantly in our really Special place, the Headland Hotel on Fistral beach, the famous surfing venue. Indeed, it was on the first time I took her there (a complete surprise to her) that I proposed on the cliff edge! The wind was howling and rain bleating down but I still carried out my plan and she said YES before we both got blown away! Happy Memories of better times. We fell in love with Cornwall and always said that would be the place we retired to one day . . . ahh, best laid plans and all that! So it was again with an array of emotions that I walked Frank on the beaches of Newquay this Christmastime. In fact, Paul and I spent Christmas Day morning on Watergate Bay with Frank. Whilst Frank was having a great time in and out of the water, Paul and I 'phoned our boys and wished them Happy Christmas. Two grown men sharing the solitude of a near empty beach in a beautiful part of the world on Christmas Day but without our family or a woman between us! Sad bastards! Watergate that day also evoked memories of another Christmas I had visited there. It was a few years ago when the kids were small. Back in the September (I think) of that year, we'd invited our friends, Ken and Tracie around for a meal and drinks, nothing unusual in that, a regular nice social occurrence. Ken was like the man on the BLACK MAGIC adverts on telly (now I am showing me age!) . . . for those too young to know what I'm talking about, this was a man who skied, swam, abseiled, whatever he had to do to get through the elements to safely deliver a bloody box of Black Magic chocolates to his intended sexual partner for that night! Do they even still make BLACK MAGIC, I wonder? Ken did it all, a territorial SAS man for all seasons, very fit and active. Well on this night, after a few glasses of Red, drunkenly I agreed with Ken to go body boarding (he did the proper surfing stuff) on Christmas Day in Watergate Bay! Of course when I sobered up the next day, I realised what I had said and for the next few months was dreading fulfilling my promise but a promise it was and a gentleman's agreement was in place! On Christmas Day that year, sure enough we all met up at Watergate. Ken, Tracie and their kids in their car and us in ours. We parked up and as soon as I got out of the car, I realised when the freezing cold wind hit me nearly off my feet, just what I'd bloody well let myself in for! . . . All I remember from that day is that I had a Summer Shorty wet suit and a Santa Claus hat on . . . Ken, of course, had ALL THE GEAR . . . proper Winter wet suit, gloves, surfy balaclava, all the finite trimmings! But I did it . . . I braved it, went into the murky . . . AND VERY COLD . . . sea for at least a full half hour or so. Needless to say, Black Magic MAN was still out surfing the waves for another hour or so, going out much further than I'd dare to even on a perfect Summer's Day! I swear I spent the rest of that Christmas with hypothermia, but I had fulfilled my promise, a Man of my word! I will NEVER forget that Christmas!

So it was to be the Second Christmas running fundamentally on my own as, after our morning walk, Paul carried out his plan to drive back for the rest of the day and see his boys and family and friends. It was a case of stiff upper lip; cooked myself a Chicken Roast dinner with all the trimmings, treated Frank to some rare left-overs and washed it all down with a bottle of Red, me not Frank! Okay, I admit it was a moment in time to feel a little sorry for myself . . . Christmas does that doesn't it? The emotions just stir up into a frenzy and come and bite you on the bum when you're a little down. But I got through it, added another distinction merit to my ongoing . . . (never-ending!) Character Building Course and just said to myself . . . "it could be Worse!" Starving kids in Africa, people in hospital, people dying, the disabled, the troops in the Services away from their families wherever . . . they were all in a worse place than me this Christmas . . . bet they'd all swap their fates for a damp, basic, holiday chalet in a quiet Newquay Holiday Camp! Perhaps? Paul actually did return that night to "finish off Christmas" with me . . . quite thoughtful of him really as I had expected him to stay over but I think he had done his bit with his kids that he was allowed to do amongst their family plans. He then made the decision to drive back down to make sure I was ok. We had a Man Hug, swapped our stories from the day and retreated to the lounge to watch crap Christmas telly and drink and chat into the early hours. We got through it. It WAS DONE, Christmas ticked off the list.

I spent a lot of my time down there completing my Tax Return, great way to spend the festive holiday eh? But it was a psychological plan to do this just to take my mind off my demons and in a warped way, try to enjoy the "holiday" as best I could. THIS and walking the dog were 2 Free things I could do as what little money I had I was determined to keep for week two when Tom and Pat were coming down to see the New Year in with us. Paul had planned to bring them both down and I was really looking forward to seeing my boy so prayed he wouldn't change his mind!

New Year's Eve came and sure enough, the boys joined us in our little abode. We made it as special as we could for them, let them have the run of the place and showed them no sign of our unhappiness at being there or the state of our lives in general. With kids, they just add a whole different dynamic to your life, it is an unconditional love and it was just great fun to have them both with us to see the New Year in. We played some golf in the day (I am no golfer so played very badly) just for fun on the camp's half size course. Tom stretched that unconditional love I just mentioned by, albeit inadvertently, hitting my ankle with a bloody golf ball with a drive from the tee that went way off course! Little bugger. I was rolling across the wet ground in absolute agony, shouting and balling at him. But, despite it being a crap shot, I should've known better than to stand where I did, especially when he's playing! I milked that one for the rest of the day, ribbing him he had played like Happy Gilmour so that became his pet name for the rest of the stay. We went out into Newquay in the evening to grab a pub meal and sample the atmosphere of New Year's Eve though we decided not to be on the streets too late as the drunken (probably drug fuelled as well) tension was already in the air. So back to the Chalet for a big game of Monopoly and eats and drinks . . . simple stuff! We had a surprise visit from my friend Jason and his son, CJ, a footy friend of Tom's . . . another 2 for Monopoly! . . . so 6 of us at our New Year's Eve "PARTY" now! . . . I reflected that this was so much better than last year alone in that Hotel room with me wine and wine gums!

When our festive vacation had ended(!) it was back to reality and the Igloo. We returned to a pile of post duly collected in by Ness and Rob in our absence. In with this was a couple of letters from my Solicitor, basically bringing me up to date with the proceedings, or lack of them, on the house (my old family home). He requested I call him asap in the New Year to discuss the situation. I didn't think much of it really as that was a chapter I had closed behind me; a box ticked off the list I thought. So I procrastinated on this for a couple of weeks and got on with just keeping warm in that igloo with Paul throughout Winter! We Still couldn't light that stupid fire and found ourselves either chucking 2 or 3 duvets over us while watching the telly or just going to bed at 7 p.m.! Ok, there were a couple of times we got chatting (we talked incessantly like a couple of old women) and couldn't be bothered to be shouting rather than talking so he came into my bedroom and just laid on the bed with the quilt over him . . . I had a Telly in my room and he didn't in his! He'd have a cider and me with my wine. I'd be yapping away and then, when I came up for air, turned to see him just dozing off . . . bloody old man! Of course I had to wake him and shove him back to his Bunk Bed . . . I SWEAR, honest truth . . . HE DID NOT SLEEP with me, we are NOT gay!

January was meandering its way to a slow cessation . . . as it always seems to do. Our Christmas debacle seemed a distant memory now and we were just getting on with life and all its reality and turmoil. No New Year's Resolutions for us two old gits, we were too long in the tooth for all that shit! He was busy back at work and juggling his feelings for his two exes. ME . . . I too was back at work and . . . juggling my feelings, demons and hang ups! I always kept busy and tried to let errands, chores, work, people, stuff fill my day but the emotions were never too far from the surface.

It was, I think, around this time I acquired the **Bean Tin**! . . . Let me expand on that . . . I had a nice but old BMW at the time but it was starting to play up and the Winter on the moors had perhaps taken its toll on it. I couldn't really afford to spend a lot on it but had to put it into a friend's garage; they worked on it for me at a heavy discount so it wasn't a priority job for them. Whilst in there, Paul leant me his old (15-year-old) Corsa. He'd been driving this around till recently as his main car . . . the Scatty teacher buzzing around in his little jalopy! On his Teacher's salary, I always wondered why he hadn't bought himself a decent car! But he'd had this one for a few years, actually looked after it quite well and it wasn't in bad nick really. However, his elderly Mum had died recently and left him, amongst other possessions, her fairly new Fiesta . . . so his life had been materially elevated to a man with two cars! He had no problem lending me the Bean Tin, as I affectionately christened it . . . reference to the fact its colour was exactly that turquoise blue on the Heinz baked beans tins! It was a fun little car and perfect for whizzing around the country lanes on the moors, avoiding the sheep, horses and cows! Frank loved it, loved jumping up into the hatch-back or, if he was lucky, I would let him sit on the passenger seat next to me and stare out the window as if he owned the car and I was his chauffeur! He was never allowed to sit in the BM like that! . . . So Frank's Bean Tin was indoctrinated into my life and was to become an important factor in the years ahead . . . I actually bought it off Paul for £600 at £50 quid a month! Best few hundred quid I had spent in years!

Probably only second to the £450 we had paid for that incredible dog.

So there was this Solicitor to contact to follow up on **that** letter... I did finally get to it around mid-January; we set up a meeting for the following week I think. I just assumed it would be a little catch up, procedural kind of stuff, the normal bollocks, nothing major or controversial... but what followed as a result of that pivotal meeting was to change my life (again) dramatically.

I was going to be on the move again... this time I was going "Home!"

Chapter Six

We "Go Home!" ... Sort of ...

I met up with my Solicitor and it turned into a very interesting meeting. Basically, Jon told me that the Estate Agent who had been in charge of selling the house on behalf of the Mortgage company had not, thus far, been successful. They'd had several viewings but no one had made a concrete offer. One young couple had shown more interest than most but were still deliberating on buying it, being put off somewhat by the amount of work needed to make it properly inhabitable again! This meant it probably would now go to an open Auction and the mortgage company would have to accept selling it at a hugely deflated price therefore losing a lot of money. We talked in depth about my current situation and my finances or lack of them! However, he was an optimist and suggested that it wouldn't be beyond the realms of possibility for me to take the house back on. We discussed the pros and cons and he left me with a lot to think about after that meeting. He advised me to get in touch with the mortgage company and discuss my options with them. But did I really want to? Did I really want the hassle? Was I happier staying in the igloo and just trying to get on with my life? Why the hell would I want to go back to a house that I had left nearly 2 years ago, left it and closed that chapter. Or Had I? I was so indecisive about it all, didn't know what to do. It was back to Paul and a long chat over a beer.

We talked through all the positives and negatives and, as two pretty intelligent guys, jotted down on paper all of this, the old fashioned way of one column for plusses, the other for "don't be a twat!" Whatever we wrote down, I just seemed to keep coming back to the thought that this was just such a ludicrous notion to be Even considering. In those next few weeks there was a lot of soul searching, deliberating, further chats with Paul, close friends, the Solicitor and the Mortgage Company. There were so many ways to look at this decision, so much to consider. But, in the end, what sealed it was that in actual fact, all talking aside, it was a no brainer as my solicitor reminded me that IF they sold it at auction and there was a huge loss (which was very likely), the mortgage company would forever chase ME for the short-fall, which at this time was a logical estimate in the region of £20,000! YES, ME . . . NOT HER . . . it was my name on the Mortgage and they'd hound me for it. I had no choice but to try and get back in there and chip away at the colossal problem. The mortgage company took some convincing I could do it and insisted that IF I were to go back, I needed to give them a couple of months' payments at least up front to show my ability and intention to pay as, to be fair, they'd not had a payment per say by now for bloody ages! I sat down again with my mate Paul and he came up trumps. He assured me he would help me with this practically, emotionally AND financially. He didn't fail on any of these counts and, financially, we knew it would be tight but we worked out if we put into the mortgage what we were paying for the igloo and a little bit on top (saved by not having to spend so much on fuel . . . I mean PETROL AND BLOODY COAL!), we could together just about scrape up each month what they needed. Additionally, Paul, leant me the 2 or 3 months up front to hand over to the blood suckers and it was all in place (I still owe him to this day for the majority of that!). The Solicitor did his bit and we planned to move in end of Feb/March. Yes, **ANOTHER** move . . . now my fourth abode in less than 2 years . . . AND I WAS GOING HOME! What the hell is that all about? The finances were worked out, still a major worry as to whether I could afford it but I had my buddy to support me . . .

The weeks leading up to the move were very stressful. I kept revisiting my thought process and questioned what I was doing. With the financial and legal side sort of ticked off, this left the emotional challenge to overcome. I was going back (they say never do it don't they?) to my old family home for Christ's sake, to a cauldron of memories, lots of good but also many bad. And I had left hadn't I, I had left that "home" because in the end it was not a happy home. What the hell was I thinking of, going back. However, I have to admit, part of my thinking, part of my incentive to make that incredibly brave decision was that if I went back and turned around the mortgage arrears, worked hard to sort everything out and, maybe get it properly liveable again, maybe . . . JUST MAYBE, my family, Wife and kids might come back too? Yes, I know, sounds so ridiculous and irrational but, again, that's "where I was" in my mind and, looking back, it was a little bit of that old conditioning creeping back in again. In a stupid, pathetic way I guess I felt I had to go back to being the bread winner again . . . Doesn't even make sense when I write it!

We explained to Ness and Rob what was happening. They were delighted for me to be honest that I was getting my house back. They were also probably a bit relieved to be getting rid of the two grumpy old men who couldn't light the Fucking Fire! But I have remained good friends with them. Paul borrowed a van from School and over a week or so and several van loads later, we had moved all our tat back to the old house. Paul had not realised until our first van load trip back, just how much the house had been let go. He'd not seen the state it had been left in, with grass grown like in a jungle, kitchen and bedroom units ripped out, rubbish and dust everywhere and the damp situation out of control. Now, we were faced with an even worse situation as, since then, the house had been left vacant for around 6 months so the damp and fustiness was unbearable. Between us we had very little furniture as we had been in rented. So this was a mountain we had taken on to climb! We pledged to rise to this challenge and get it all sorted. Such a great mate, I had every confidence in him that he would come through on all those three counts we had painstakingly discussed in the preceding weeks . . . I was depending on it as I was in a vulnerable state here. When he was out for a couple of hours, I took my first proper look around on my own and looked at the dog who looked back at me as if to say: "What the hell are we doing back here?" . . . "I aint gotta a damn clue Frank, not a bloody clue mate . . . ! But Don't worry, you aint going to be shitting in That garden, we have our routine now and you will bloody stick to it ok!" As stupid as it sounds, that was a pivotal conversation as its significance was that in lots of ways my life had moved on in bounds with new routines and my way of doing things were different from the last time I had lived in this house. So I could bring this strength to the situation I was now in but IT WAS STILL my old house and adapting to actually living in it day to day would take a long, long time.

As well as living with Paul and having him to support me, moving back also meant living next door again to me old mate, Al the Pal! . . . and of course his lovely Wife, Claire and two little boys, Ash and Charlie. Al had been a good friend throughout my stuff going on these last couple of years and popped in and out of my life as and when he could, the odd beer and chat here and there. But this was great to actually be back living next door to him and have him there a little more often. He came round, met Paul and surveyed the "damage" to be repaired on the house to make it habitual. Me and Paul were about as good as each other at DIY . . . i.e. CRAP! . . . So good old Al the Pal who is great with all that kind of normal Man stuff, stepped in and did all our immediate, pressing jobs to get us in there. The biggest job of all was sorting out where all the leaks were coming from and there were lots of them! The Bathroom floor was rotten right through with damp from an ongoing leak that had not been tended to . . . how she'd not gone through the ceiling in her regular evening bath astounded all of us as the floor was so weak with water damage. That is not saying she was big because she had a lovely figure but hers and the bath waters weight together should have taken her hurtling through that ceiling to end up sat in the kitchen! Al took up the whole floor and replaced it for me. He re-plastered a few other bits after filling in damp damage and generally went around the house and made tidy for us. He couldn't mend the boiler which had seized up in the time it had been stagnant so I had to call in a proper plumber for that job. All these jobs to be done were mounting up in cost just to get us back in there, as well as a couple of utility bill arrears I had to take on as well to allow them to supply us. All in all, the whole Project, if you could call it that, was turning into an absolute nightmare which . . . of course, I knew it would be but had not anticipated JUST how big a job it would be in reality!

Al and Claire pretty much knew the story behind me returning but still couldn't believe I was back! They had seen me leave nearly 2 years before and, as close friends, obviously knew why. Then they had subsequently lived next door to the family in the aftermath of the split so knew her side and a bit about where she was with everything. To be fair, these lovely people remained friends with us both, never judged, never got too involved and stayed as impartial as possible. Good, genuine friends. But, never in a month of Sundays did they expect to see me back in That house as their neighbour again! The other neighbours and people who lived in the street were happy to see me back but as periphery people in my life didn't really know or need to know the circumstances. But you know what people are like! . . . They probably made up their own stories from what they saw and perceived. I had left my Wife 2 years back and now returned with big, butch, Glass Eyed Paul! No women or kids in tow, you can imagine I was the talk of the street for a while but very soon Yesterday's News!

We got into a kind of routine as soon as possible . . . that is I got into a routine and Paul went along with it! Same as the country experience, I took up the mantle of Chief Cook and bottle washer, constantly cleaning and tidying as I do! But this was a little different; this was MY house, not someone else's, not Paul's and not rented. The whole dynamic had changed completely and it was evident to me from the first day that this was all going to be very hard to deal with. Despite the mess it had been left in and, perhaps, in spite of the mess, I had an added pride in that house and a further incentive to get it clean, tidy and back to being a Home again. I had done my couple of years living in places that were NOT HOME. Obviously the situation was vastly different and I am aware People make a home, not things or cleanliness but, as I said earlier, I think sub consciously I was perhaps thinking if I could turn this now shit pit back into the lovely abode it once was, maybe those people I cared about would come back and make it into a Home again and we'd all live Happy Ever After!

Once again in my life, I had set myself a massive challenge and putting ticks into all the boxes thrown up by this situation looked almost impossible! Let's see:

> **Moving Back to my old house – emotions and memories.**
> **Cleaning, repairing and maintaining it to make it liveable.**
> **Living with Paul . . . in MY house!**
> **Re-acquainting myself with the neighbours – how much DID they know?**
> **Adjusting to working from home in the office in the Garage.**
> **Explaining to my Sons why I was back in the house!**
> **Finding more money! This was the biggest BOX . . . this was all going to cost lots of dosh!**

Well we got stuck in to the task in hand. Emotionally, I just couldn't get my head around sleeping back in the old marital bedroom so opted to give Paul that room and I went into what had been Daniel's old room. I looked into that room that had been mine and my Wife's and it was a weird feeling to think back to the days when we had shared a bed in there. I wondered how many men she had slept with since I had left in that room but, in all honesty, I don't actually think she'd brought **any** guys back in that time, to be fair to her and if she did, certainly not for THAT. She was good like that around the boys. I then tried to make Tom's old room, the 3rd bedroom, as comfortable as possible for when he came to stay. Again, my thoughts were Tom would now stay with me more as, after all, this was his old home and his School and all his mates were nearer. But now, Dad was back in town and if he stayed with me more, logistically if nothing else, life would be easier for him. His school and friends were within a mile of the old house whereas his Mum was still back out in the sticks, it seemed a million miles from civilization . . . couldn't easily and don't think he ever did have his mates round out there for tea or a sleepover! The reality was, however, that he still only stayed with me when it suited him or he had to, mainly for his footy arrangements. He had no problem with Dad taking on the old house again; in fact, he was really happy about it but I think the main problem for him was that he had by now acclimatised his little life to living with Mum on the moors in their lovely house and he had all his home comforts out there. I still think If I could've had the money at this point to stick in a flat screen telly, DVD player, X-Box and whatever else he had out there, he would then have come round a bit more to mine. But I couldn't do it, really could not afford all that stuff on top of the massive burden I had already taken on. This hurt me at first that he didn't want to stay as much as I wanted him to but, again, was a reminder of where I was in this process and the bigger picture is that my kids valued their material things, perhaps more than what really counts, love, affection and quality time. Isn't this partly why I no longer lived with them all? So why did I want them all to move back in with me then? Confused. com! They'll get it one day . . . I hope, the Real things that matter in life. Daniel popped in the odd time but never stayed really . . . don't think he really got why I'd moved back and it was still hard to tie him down to a Man to Man chat. As much as the boys loved me as their Dad, I was always aware from the start that for the majority of their time they lived with her, therefore heard and saw her side to all of this. Obviously, at this moment, it was still fairly raw for them that they had seen themselves have to move out of that house and relocate to the moors! They'd been there for the build up to Moving Out Day and seen that day unfold.

The word now going round was "I had planned all this to get the house back" therefore re opening the "Malc is a bastard" box again. Excuse me, I feel another rant coming on! . . . Planned THIS? What, I really had the stupidity to PLAN to leave home 2 years ago, live in a fucking bedsit and other places, be lonely, skint, miserable and depressed . . . AND NOW move back in, take on a mountain of debt and jobs to do as well as the emotional turmoil of living here again . . . PLANNED ALL THAT? I don't think so; nobody could possibly have chosen to do all that. All of that was like a script from Eastenders! Paul and I knew the truth though and the few friends who I still had knew what had happened here and Why I was back in that house again.

In the first few weeks there was so much to sort out as you can imagine . . . getting through all those boxes I listed! Paul's way of living in organised chaos naturally seemed to suit this enforced bedlam! Indeed, his room (our old marital bedroom) was like a bomb site and so different to how tidy it had been in the old days. For now, also, it had temporary, make shift curtains just strung up on a pole as we'd had to take down the really damp, black old blinds. I just couldn't afford to replace everything straight away and Paul understood this and was fine about it all. I had Promised him, as a thank-you for all his help, a brand new double bed for his room. Also to make him feel a bit better about the whole move thing, especially as he had just slept in a Bunk Bed for months! I did a deal with my advertiser chap again and ordered Paul a new bed as promised! Meanwhile, he just put down on the floor for now a couple of old single mattresses we had, surrounded by all his crap just chucked in the room and, as I said, these shit "curtains" that were actually old sheets I think! He was happy living in this cave like existence, nothing bothered Paul! But, to my amazement, well before the new bed turned up, he had brought back to the house the first woman to cross the threshold in this, our new chapter! This was the guy that had lived pretty much like a hermit in the igloo for the past few months, hardly ever going out and only drinking the odd beer or cider on occasion. No party animal at all. But here, back at my old house, he seemed to almost immediately have a personality change and he was out socialising on the town with his friends from the Rugby fraternity. And on one of these drunken nights, he met this woman in a club and brought her back in the early hours to his Cave! Now . . . yet another change of dynamic. This was a scary sight to see at breakfast in my kitchen . . . A **woman** in the House! I put it down as a one off but Paul then went on to see her quite often after that and, very quickly, began to have feelings (he said) for her! She had left her husband and was kipping rough at her friend's house and they were all part of Paul's rugby crowd. Hence the meet in the Club that night. It was none of my business really and it was up to him what he did in his social life and who with but it was just a shock that for months he had done nothing socially and, now, almost overnight it seemed, he had fallen lock, stock and barrel for this lady who had lots of baggage, far too much for Paul to handle in his present mental state! He had just changed into a party animal and wanted to be out drinking, clubbing and shagging . . . not the same guy I had just lived with for all those months! Of course, all he was actually doing was living like a normal Batchelor I guess which he had somewhat curtailed in the igloo! But for me, this whole dynamic didn't work. I am no angel myself and, for sure, as a Man I was happy he was finally sowing his wild oats after so long! But from my point of view, at this particular time, it was hugely insensitive of him, this early in our move back, to have brought a woman back to the house. We had a Man to Man about it and I reminded him of our in depth chats about me needing him to support me on those three counts, especially emotionally. For CHRIST SAKE, that was the bedroom me and the wife used to share for all those years and here he was, not even before he had a proper bed in there, shagging some stranger in there on the floor! I just said to him, "Paul, understand you have your needs mate but do me a favour! Just give me a bit of time to get my head around being back in this memory bubble, exercise a few demons before you totally change the dynamic! You knew, we talked about it enough, that it would take me time to adjust to being here again and you knew I needed your help with that. It's only been a couple of weeks, there is so much to do and sort out and I need the Paul I lived with on the moors, my rock, my support, not a serial shagger and party animal!" Further to that we discussed as adults the implication of Tom seeing a woman in the house at breakfast time or whenever! He hadn't yet but the chances are, if Paul carried on seeing this or other women, Tom would do and, again, I reminded Paul it was hard enough for me coping with the move back but I also had to make this a stable, secure abode for the boys so they could see it as somewhere they could visit whenever they liked, thus easing their need to adapt to Dad moving back to Their old house. Paul, as a Dad himself, got this line of thought and totally understood, using the comparison of if the tables were turned and I was HIM moving back to HIS old family home in the same circumstances. He got it. Now the rational, thoughtful bloke I had got to know in the last year had returned. This was temporary though and restricted to just that specific chat in the kitchen! He was smitten with this lady, fallen like a brick for her and this caused him to get on this 1000 mile an hour rollercoaster with her which meant embracing her Circus of a life . . . and we already had enough of a Circus going on with our stuff thanks very much! This was a "spanner in the works" and yes, caused a rift between me and Paul. It probably would all have been fine if this had happened in the Igloo as that was Ness's house but this was MY house and the rules had changed. It just seemed to me he had obliterated from his mind the intense chats we'd had in preparation for this colossal move and the whole emotional substance of it all. Our Bond was gone and our mutual empathy for each other had taken a nose dive. There was a huge crack in our relationship. Maybe I am not explaining it right but both me and Paul knew that the Power of a Woman had come between us. Those bloody powerful, conniving and clever things they call FEMALES . . . How dare they use their tricks to come between me and my mate? It had happened though . . . once they get into your heart, your trousers and then your head . . . You are fucked, fucked up that is! This lady took his time and all his thoughts and Paul and I agreed, after another Man to Man in that kitchen(!) he had to move on into Singledom land . . . his current antics, behaviour and erraticness inspired by said lady, coupled with his already confirmed scattiness, laid back (ness!) and all round confusion of mind, was now not conducive to the situation I was in with this move. Therefore, we agreed, his staying with me had become untenable and he had to move on to pastures new. So literally weeks after he'd moved in with me, ticked the Practical and Financial boxes, he'd let me down on the emotional front! He moved out within days, packing up what he Wanted to take, not a lot really; he moved in temporarily with another mate, a colleague from School and picked up his new found lifestyle. Luckily for me, he left behind some old white goods and a sofa that he'd not wanted to take and I have added these to the bill I owe him! I DID pay him off in full for the little car. The Bean Tin or POD (N643 **POD**) became and still is a great "family friend", the butt of many jokes aimed at me, how the "mighty have fallen and all that" . . . but it was and remains, the most reliable car I've ever owned and, like women, I've had a few in my time! . . . In recent times, it has now become my second car but is a great back up. I taught Tom to drive in it (proud of that) and leant it out to a few people including the Enemy Ex (see I don't hate her!) when hers was off the road. They all moaned about no power steering and crappy gears but get a life! What got me talking about that? . . . Good old Paul, that was it . . . the Bean Tin is a reminder of the simplicity, reliability, honesty and consistency that guy brought into my life. The little blip at the end was just that, a blip . . . a natural end to the tenure of our intense relationship. We have gone on to remain great friends and always will be and we have to see each other now and again anyway cos I owe him money!

So Paul had moved out and taken his life down another road. The stark reality of this now was . . . FUCK! . . . I was now on my own in a run-down, three-bedroom home with a £1000 plus a month mortgage to find! FUCK, FUCK, FUCKETY FUCK! Bloody hell, what the hell was happening here? Bitten my nose off to spite my face? Whatever, the Paul thing didn't work anymore and I had to Man up and deal with this. More Character Building! Obviously, the sensible thing would have been to go out and get another lodger in but, I think I had been tainted by the whole living with people thing and just wanted to try this alone now! TWAT, Idiot, Wanker . . . a few of the expletives cast at me by my opinionated friends trying to give me best Advice! Of course they were right because it was clear, on my limited income I could NOT afford this exercise of living at this house as well as maintaining it, decorating it and putting food on the table! But I'd been called worse before and my stubbornness and determination took over now and I just dug in and went it alone. Quite apart from anything else, THIS WAS MY HOME, my castle, I was back . . . I COULD do this and when I DID IT, my family would come back wouldn't they? I just had to somehow work EVEN harder, pay my way, get it all sorted. I was determined; I HAD been through worse, hadn't I?

So I dug in, head down, worked hard. It was, at the end of the day, All I knew how to do in such a situation. However, what followed this tumultuous decision was two years of, to be honest, doom and gloom. Was that bloody Karma playing her part again, it certainly felt like it. Every penny I earnt and some I didn't(!) was ploughed into that house and surviving . . . just as soon as the business had an amount of money in the account, I took it out and made sure the mortgage and bills were paid before anything or anybody else. I began to learn the "art" of just existing. Again, I was entering a period in my life that was to be very black and confusing.

Body Clock . . . woke me up in the morning at 5 ish, no matter how much I'd drunk the night before, or what time my demons had allowed me to eventually get off to sleep! "Malc this is ridiculous; you can't get up at 5" . . . went through my head; but as soon as I was semi-conscious, immediately all the worries, stresses, bad thoughts, horrible demons and insecurities went flashing through my head, coming at me like bullets . . . hundreds of horrible things that I had to contend with That day or whenever . . . it was horrible, like being in a War Zone. I tried to doze again by "chucking" something NICE into my head to make me sleep for a bit longer? Anything, just not a worry, not a demon . . . anything . . . I FOUND something . . . a nice memory, a good thought, a morsel, something; I half slept for a little while but then they came back, like they'd had a rest and now wanted to pummel me some more. I lay there, thinking can't do anything about all these problems just lying here; got up and at it . . . take on the Fucking World and all it was gonna throw at me that day. Up the field with Frank by 6.30 ish . . . shower etc., start work in the cold garage by 7.30 ish . . . punish, punish, fight myself . . . got to be done; I DESERVE this; it was ALL MY FAULT. Work for as long as I was able, 8 hours, 10 hours, sometimes more in that cold, dismal garage . . . ok it was lovely in the Summer! but still a GARAGE! . . . It Just didn't matter how hard I pushed myself, how hard I Worked. The business I was in . . . advertising and print, simply wasn't making much money anymore.

It didn't take long living like this for the good old Depression to come back. I was determined though not to go back to the doctors and just to fight it alone this time. I HAD made this decision to come back and I was going to live or die by that decision and nobody could help me. No one really understood why I had gone back anyway so how was anyone going to help me with this? No, I was alone and on a ONE MAN MISSION to prove everybody I was right and they were wrong! TWAT, Idiot, WANKER!

This was a weird loneliness; an emotion I had not encountered before. Back in that house, day after day, night after night, living there alone, working alone in THAT house where so much of my life had taken place. My mind began to play all kinds of tricks . . . There were days I was working away in that office and I would "see" little Tom come running in from School excitedly . . . "Hi Dad, look at this drawing I did today" or "Dad, I was good today, I got a Gold Star" . . . These were the things I missed from the marriage, simple little instances, quality moments of time with my kids and here I was, back in the place **they had all happened!** . . . On my Own! What the fuck was this all about? TWAT, idiot, WANKER!

I began very quickly to retreat into a shell, an almost Hermit like existence. Living and working there was not healthy. It was so difficult, because, aside from my weekly outing to play football on a Friday night, I was not and could not really afford to do much socially. There was the odd beer or catch up with a mate or two, as well as the increased contact with Al the Pal next door. But, even he had his busy life to sort with his Wife, kids and work so didn't get to see him as much as I'd like. When you shut your door at night, everybody does the same thing and just gets on with their lives. I was very conscious not to invade his privacy too much and not make myself a burden on him and Claire. We did talk over the garden fence when the Sun came out but it was just normal neighbourly stuff. My work got me out sometimes during the day, but running a local, community magazine on a shoe string doesn't exactly take you to the far corners of the globe or anywhere too exciting! Tom, as I said, didn't stay with me much, only when it suited him or it tied in with the Ex's social plans. So this existence was weird, a strange kind of life . . . me in an empty three-bedroom house, living with the Ghosts from the past all around me. I still couldn't go back to sleeping in **That** room, the marital bedroom, even after Paul had gone. It took me around a year before I finally plucked up the courage to make the switch and, even then, with great trepidation. This loneliness was worse than I had encountered in the bedsit even, as there was so much space around me, devoid of possessions and people! Weekends were the worst! That's when it really hit me . . . time to think even more, especially in the Summer when the boys weren't playing football. If Tom didn't stay with me there were some weekends (many) where from Friday night after footy right through till Monday morning, I didn't see or speak to a soul! . . . with the exception of me dear old Mum who I do tend to call at the weekends on the 'phone. Her half hour call aside, I spent whole weekends on my own with the dog, sad Man, sad existence! I would use the mobile to call the landline number or e-mail myself just to make sure it was all still working!

It was around this time I discovered **Loose Women!** Another fantastic pastime to add to my repertoire! I fell into a bit of a routine of up early, get my morning's work done in the office, then cut off nicely in time for Loose Women at 12.30 with me sandwich and crisps! My excuse is . . . Everyone has to eat and you can't work ALL day long; everyone needs a break and mine just coincided with when those lovely ladies were on the box spouting out their opinions and comments on current events but, mainly, life in general. They talked candidly about Divorce, split ups, stress and anxiety amongst many other subjects. It was almost like having 4 counsellors in the room with me but invariably, all these women had their own, different views on the subject they were covering that particular day. And, it has to be said, with the exception of Janet Street Porter who is definitely very dominant with her forthright views, a woman who has lived a full life, I was tapping into the **female** take on life and all it has thrown at me and them! I loved JSP as she made no apology for her life decisions, good or bad ones and just lived with a positive attitude for today. I think she was five marriages in and had admitted to cheating on pretty much all of her partners! Her only regret was, in her words, that she "got caught!" Loose Women stirred many emotions in me ... Wow! Interesting note ... my favourite on there was Lisa Maxwell, the little, attractive blonde, intelligent, funny and strong minded, independent lady ... Do I have a "type" who knows! But thanks to you Loose ladies for keeping me company on many a lunchtime ... not EVERY day you know, just 5 days a week (you aint on weekends!)

A few months in to my tenure back at the house, a horrible letter dropped through the post. I had known it was coming but the timing just couldn't have been worse ... whenever is there a good time to receive your Divorce papers? This was just another nail in the coffin; already feeling down with no money, no company, eating beans on toast, this was just another Statement of where I was with all this. She had rushed through the Divorce as soon as she could, so she could Move on, she said. I get that after all we'd been through and, at this stage, we weren't exactly friends but it was just like she'd said Right, forget that 16 years, meant nothing, put a line under and move onto the next chapter. Thing is, looking back NOW, she was so right to do this; she'd lost her house and her husband and she was now making a new life for herself out on the moors and with her new found friends. She had reinvented herself and moved in different circles now. Despite the fact it was ME who had done the leaving in the first place, it was now ME that COULD'NT move on! WHICH was why the

Divorce hit me so much; I hadn't wanted it at that juncture and, everything aside, I couldn't actually afford to divorce her! She had got Legal Aid and just pursued it on the grounds of "unreasonable behaviour" . . . roughly translated means she thought I was a CRAP Husband and in these 'papers were listed all the reasons why so the Solicitor could have their "grounds." It does hit you when you process the thought that my loving Wife(!) who I'd lived with for 16 odd years can sit in front of a stranger and say her Husband was moody, always stressed about work, money problems and was "never happy with anything!" She therefore found ME intolerable to live with! . . . (I Wasn't intolerable when the money was rolling in and I couldn't possibly have been unhappy ALL the time or else we wouldn't have had such great memories, two well balanced and great boys or have lasted as long as we did!) . . . But I didn't contest it or go back with any specific retorts. There was no point; I had lost the will to fight all this at this stage. And I couldn't really deny any of it could I? These things are so clinically documented that there is no room for rhyme and reasons to counter the statements and, at that time, my mind was just full of remorse that it had got to this stage, not really the reasons why. That mode of thought only falls into place years down the line when you have chance to reflect and write a book about it! So the Divorce papers coming through really hit me for six and just added to my current woes. The stress of moving back in, my blip with Paul, him moving out, adapting to living back there, having no money, living like a pauper and just generally feeling down, that week I just cracked I think under the pressure of it all. I just needed to get away from everything and everyone! Just escape for a little while . . . though I spent the majority of my life alone, I JUST felt the need to do this loneliness somewhere else . . . and not on the Moors with a hose-pipe! No, I needed to go to somewhere different, but cheap! So, with the help of Tinternet, I found a cheap (very cheap) weekend away in a caravan in Looe, out of season, "bums on seats" promotional last minute, cancellation. Whatever, it was cheap, not a million miles away from home and I was allowed to take the dog. My intention was to just bugger off for the weekend and not tell anyone, a real proper escape! It was a weekend I wasn't due to have Tom to stay as it happened, so there was no need to tell him, so that was that. Just slip away I thought with Frank. However, thought I had better tell someone, just one mate, just in case anything happened, you never know do you! So I mentioned it to (Essex) Dan, who reacted by insisting he came with me! He said he needed the break too and, being genuinely worried about me, thought we'd be better off going down there together. So off to Looe we went, two men and a dog. Which pretty much doubled the amount of people staying at the camp that weekend! It was a strange weekend full of drinking, walking and, for me, just reflecting. Dan was good company; he is a very spiritual guy and has deep, intensive thoughts about life and gave me a totally different insight to my troubles. He always gets me to realise that anything we go through in life is part of a bigger picture and that Everything happens for a reason. Not quite the solitude I had planned but, all the same, an entertaining weekend that still achieved to help me sort of escape!

Escaping is ok for 48 hours but it is short lived and you still have to come back to reality and face everything. I was slipping back into a deep depression and, though I could see the signs from my first visit to that black hole when I was in the Bedsit, I still couldn't prevent it happening. Every day just seemed to be a slog, an endless battle to just survive financially as well as fight off those horrible demons and insecurities going on in my head. I decided I had to try and beat it this time and not let this bout take me back to the counsellor's chair, especially that bloody Cracker guy who scared the life out of me! No, I was never going back to that place! Instead, I found some strength and a morsel of confidence I had stashed away for a rainy day, bunged on me suit and went out and got a job! Al the Pal had actually put a word in for me at his company and got me an interview. Took a while for me AND the company to decide if we'd be a fit after my many years of being self-employed but I needed a stable income and they needed someone with my experience. So I got it! But from Day One, I hated it . . . I had been my own boss for around ten years and now I was working for a company that dictated (or they tried) to me the time when I could go to the canteen to make a cup of tea! I tried, I really tried but I just found it so hard to adhere to working for someone, to being employed by a large company with all their petty rules, policies, politics and back-biting. It was a massive open office filled with people . . . I called it the Bingo Hall! I had gone from being a man that worked alone in a quiet garage to now sharing my day with 20 odd staff in what was tantamount to a Call Centre . . . noisy was an understatement. The noise though was manageable; it was the bitchiness and back-biting from the two faced staff that I found unbearable. I was glad to get out of there most days and be "on the road" selling. However, in truth, the job was never really me . . . I worked hard as always to meet my targets and manage my little Sales team. But I hated every minute of it, selling a product I didn't really know, learning complicated computer systems and working to all those rules. I did it, I got through and gave it my best shot but in the end, the monthly "fight" to get paid my commission just wore me down. Everyone in there had the same problem and moral was low; a couple of fellow managers left before me then I finally decided, after realising I was now earning less than when I was self-employed(!) to leave too. My venture into the jungle was over! This experience could've and I was hoping would've been the making of me but sadly backfired. So it was back to the cold, old garage and working . . . and living alone and scraping by on the sporadicity of self-employment.

I did have a little respite from everything that first year when I took a week out to watch Tom play in a footy tournament in Northern Ireland . . . scraped up the pennies to go on the cheap just to make sure I was there for my boy to support him and watch him make a memory. He travelled separately, as was normal, with the team and the coaches and stayed in a separate hotel in Coleraine. The trip for me was another realisation that I was totally single and on my own in this world! The parents of the other boys, though I'd known them for years, all travelled in their couples, mostly married, "normal" Mum and Dads! At training back home, us Dads were normally the ones that stood together and just a sprinkling of Mums but training was always predominantly a

DAD thing! So there was male bonding on those nights. However, Ireland and a tournament was a different ball game altogether. In fact, the ladies had taken it on themselves to organise their own respective holidays and booked their flights in unison. So there was a definite clique culture developing for this trip. Partly because of this and also because I couldn't commit myself to much after they'd all got organised (for money reasons), we ended up on different flights out! The clan of couples, I called them the Swingers(!) flew out all together on an earlier flight than me and I rolled up to the hotel later in the evening (via a flight that took me to Edinburgh first where I just sat around for 2 hours; things you have to do to get a cheaper deal!).By the time I got there, they'd all eaten and were already ensconced in their clique brigade . . . I felt like I had gate-crashed a party, though you'd probably have a few mates in tow when you do that! So the theme of the week was set on that first night. These people that I had spent 1000's of hours with on many football touchlines over the years, watching our Kids Grow up, literally, now seemed like Complete and utter strangers to me. I felt like I had the plague or something in their company. That's the joy of being Single! As the week went on, sure, we watched the matches (one a day) and stood together on the touchline to show our unity to support our boys, but even then the couples and their chosen couple friends seemed to be together and I had to force a "mingle" to get their attention. It sounds like I was being paranoid but really I wasn't; I was an alien, a leper, didn't fit into the groove anymore . . . the guy that used to have a Wife and "normal" family like all of them (yeh right!) was now a dishevelled, skint, depressed AND SINGLE bloke who now didn't have anything in common with this crowd of, to put it into perspective, periphery friends. I sought solace in that fact that had these people been TRUE friends they would've included me a bit more, not judged, but empathised . . . remembered the guy that, when he was "one of them" with 2 point 4 children they liked and had time for. I used to be the one who was confident, positive, joined in and quite often led the humour, the natural banter that ensues the social side of this footy scene. Now I was half that bloke, pummelled and affected by life's recent events. This situation felt relative to the dealings with the Mortgage company in that I really wanted to rant at these people when they were all collected together in the bar of an evening and give them a similar sermon that preached the fact that things change when you split up, divorce and go through the stuff I had been through. Along the lines of what I'd said to Mr. Mortgage Call Centre Man where I ranted that they only speak to me when I am down and out, well the opposite applied here! If I was brave enough and thought it would do any good, I would've stood on a table and said : "You bunch of judgemental, patronising and, actually, hypocrites with your perfect marriages and lives (?) . . . none of you have a Scooby doo what I've been through these last couple of years and cannot and should not be treating me any differently than the Man that you thought was leading the same life as you back then; get off your high horses and let me back in the gang" . . . but I didn't air my thoughts which probably in all honesty were a bit over the top and too analytical but this was how I was feeling and it all just left a bad taste in my mouth. Instead, I retreated into my shell, relied on my Degree in Hermitness! I found myself avoiding the times they all went down for meals and I ate alone and, although there were a couple of times we all had a few drinks together, in the main I stuck to my own company and got up to my room alone of an evening. Then there were the pre-match build ups . . . We always got to the daily matches early, sometimes a couple of hours before Kick-off. After all, that's the main reason we were all there wasn't it! To see our boys play footy. But I decided I couldn't spend those couple of hours fighting to break down the barriers of their cliques so I would disappear on me own and find another way of killing that waiting time . . . that's when I bought a note-book and started jotting down my thoughts and feelings at that time, which . . . ultimately became the infrastructure for this book! One of the places I found to hole myself away was by the beach, can't remember exactly which one but somewhere in the Coleraine region of Northern Ireland! Love the beach and what a perfect place to share my earliest scribbles and doodlings towards the book! So it was a strange old week in Ireland, a learning curve, a realisation of how people react when they discover that species, the "lesser spotted Single Man!" Above all though, I was there for my boy and he had no inkling of my predicament with the Swingers! As far as he was concerned, I was his Dad and his Dad was there to support him along with the other Parents . . .

The first Christmas back in the old house was always going to be a difficult one. Part of me wanted to do the whole escape act again but the other half was urging me to Man Up for Christ's Sake and come to terms with it all. Besides, it's bloody expensive to escape at Christmas isn't it! I was determined to use this Christmas as a catalyst to get strong, put the past behind me and just try and come to terms with the situation I found myself in. Though I was pretty low and my life was again in a shitty place, I was Not going back to "that place" I had been in when at my lowest. I was NOT going back to Cracker! The main thing I did this Christmas was get myself back into the old bedroom. It was a challenge, a Demon I had to overcome. Paul had that bedroom for that first month or so but since he moved out I had still carried on sleeping in the back bedroom, now around 10 months or so!

I would only go in there to clean it, hoover and dust, open the windows but that was it. Just couldn't face actually sleeping in there. But I had to sort this; this was stupid . . . I hadn't even replaced the make-shift "curtains" Paul had bunged up there . . . the sheets on poles! And, the new bed I had got Paul was Still there, mattress still in the polythene cover and all, not used! Even if I couldn't haul myself back in there to sleep, these practical things needed putting in place and the whole room properly spring cleaned. So this was my Christmas Task to myself! Whilst everyone else was out shopping for the festivities, getting all excited, partying and all caught up in the commercialism of Christmas, I was painting the bedroom a totally different colour . . . Fresh purple, hanging up new blinds (I'd done a deal on!), scrubbing, cleaning and placing strategically in the room the very few clothes and personal bits n' bobs I had. By Christmas it was ready but Was I? . . . I began by tentatively laying on the bed with all my clothes on and just seeing what "jumped" into my head at that moment in that room. Surprisingly and refreshingly it was not as bad as I'd thought . . . yes, there were a few memories of times in that room in our old bed (I still had to have the new bed in the same position, just because of the size and formation of the room) but, in the main, my mind was full of positivity, a sense of having to do this, having to fight this demon, get it done and bloody move on. So, I persevered; I slept in there and, despite the odd sleepless night with a million and one things jumping into my head, I did it, I was there to stay . . . and the memory foam mattress was the clincher! Seriously though, my bigger, more pressing problems were happening Outside that bedroom now . . . that's where my bigger worries were, just keeping on top of everything and somehow, some way affording to stay in that house. I had sort of let my family back in a little bit that Christmas . . . just went out for a meal with them, my dear old Mum, who was down from Surrey, Sister and Nephew. They insisted on me being there and, conscious of the fact I had not seen them now properly for years, I did go and spend the 2 main days of Christmas in the bosom of my family. It was part of my strategy to be strong that Christmas, overcome, move on, show mental strength far above what I was feeling inside. In a sense it was an escape from the mundaneness and near on poverty stricken life I was leading. Mum, Sis and my Nephew did pop back to my house for a cuppa after the meal as Mum actually stayed with me Christmas Day night so I "let them in" a little to the way I was living. My pride would not allow me to totally confide in them the struggle it was and certainly, at this juncture, I was not going to disclose my overall plight from the previous few years. But they only had to see the sparsity of the house, the damp on the walls I couldn't afford to do anything about and the sheer lack of attention to outside and inside of a house that, the last time they had been there, had been a vibrant, fun filled, family home full of pretty posh furniture and trimmings. Now everything in there was begged for, stolen or borrowed, very basic and didn't colour co-ordinate! . . . couldn't worry about those things anymore! Sis and nephew left after their cuppa, I think in a state of shock at my demise and I settled down for the evening with my lovely old Mum. I tried to make her as comfortable as possible; I EVEN turned the heating on that night! We'd had a nice meal that day which she'd paid for(!) so we didn't need to eat much fortunately but we had a few drinkies and I did open up to her a bit . . . still being guarded enough not to let her in completely. If she had known where I really was at that time in my head, she might've whisked me back up to Surrey with her and tied me to the chair in her little Council bungalow to keep an eye on me! Or even had me sectioned herself! So we had a pleasant evening under the circumstances and the next day I dropped her to my Niece's where she was staying so this, again, meant seeing family I had shut out, parked for years now. Small talk and pleasantries in these situations are great though; I hate them but they have their place in life's rich tapestry and this Christmas of "putting my toe back into the family pond" was a necessary time to get them out of my "tool box." They knew I was down but not out and I left them all that Christmas not worrying too much about me; aware that I was not living a great life but not overly concerned because I'd shown them that I still had a strength and determination (which they'd always seen in me) to overcome my situation.

However, Christmas out the way, the natural doom and gloom of January soon stepped in . . . as I know it does for everyone! I had put on the Stage paint for Christmas and risen to my role in front of the family but the stark reality of living in that house in the Winter months was dire. It just seemed that I had stepped out of my War Zone over the festive week or so and raised my head above the trenches to experience another world out there. That's just how my life felt at this time . . . that everyone else was leading a normal life, ok and happy but I was leading this hermit like, very lonely and skint existence, fighting my own battle of survival. God that sounds so needy just writing it and, for Christ's sake, I know everyone has problems in their life but I just could see no end to mine and had no answers. I lived in a damp, under maintained house, too big for just me and the dog, broke, cold and fucking lonely. On top of everything else, I was starting to let slip my pride and dignity and let myself go. This is something I had never done . . . at Dan's, in the Bedsit or out in the sticks, or NEVER in my life, no matter how bad things had ever got. No matter what, I had Always showered, shaved and taken care of myself; looked the best I possibly could whether in or out of the house. Now, I was starting to fall into bad, unhygienic habits . . . still would get up early to walk the dog and tend to him (and still wouldn't let him poo in the garden!) but I found myself not bothering to shower or shave for days on end, not even cleaning my teeth. Just sorting the dog, bit of brekkie and go up to the garage to work in 2 or 3 layers of clothes. Still grind out a day's work for a bloody pittance (if anything) and then sleek back into the house to hole myself in for the cold evenings. I was eating beans on toast, pasta, all basic, cheap stuff . . . easy to live like a Student when you're in this boat . . . cook up a lasagne, pasta dish or cottage pie and eek it out for the whole week! Still works to this day! Of course, I would still make sure I saw the boys when they needed or wanted me and the football thing continued but these were brief respites in the course of my week. Tom, in fact, had started to lose a bit of interest in the football and was not as committed as he once was.

I just started to feel a deep, dark depression creep up on me . . . it is like walking into a big cloud of black smoke, where you really are blinded, don't know how to get yourself out and you just get overwhelmed by the intensity of it all. I swore to myself I could be stronger. I was done with counsellors and didn't need them to pull me through this latest blip . . . that's all it was surely? So I refused myself the thought of going to the Docs, or of asking anyone for help. **Family or friends**. I had put myself back in this position of struggle and I alone would get bloody well through it by whatever means. It was all part of my Karma, my punishment for leaving and hurting my family; I had to suffer this and not moan, get on with it Malc. Even Al and Claire next door didn't really know how low I was or how I was living. As I have said before, as good a friends as they were, they had their own busy little lives with their kids, work and their cats! Once the doors were closed at night, you were in hibernation in your own house. Hardly saw them or anybody really . . . had the very rare beer with

Al and he knew from my body language and limited outpourings of my problems that I wasn't in the best of places but didn't get the true extent.

Going up to that garage office to work every day meant me passing by a pile of junk I had left in the corner. Well, to be precise, it was a tidy box and a little pile of things as I am the tidiest guy in the world! In this pile, was a tow rope for the car which I'd had for years and years. Well everyone has one don't they? Don't think I'd ever used it to tow a car! but I had recently used it to tie something to the top of the car to go to the tip. So it was in sight Every day I went up to that garage . . . just sitting there, heavy duty, blue though slightly frayed from use, filling me with thoughts of: "if only I had been in the Scouts and knew how to tie a strong knot, leaving a loop just big enough for my neck to fit into . . ." These thoughts became serious thoughts and more regular with my moods controlled by depression, stress, anger and sheer frustration. Sometimes I was just a zombie going up to that garage, going through the motions, working as I'd always known how but seemingly just "hitting my head against a brick wall" . . . not literally you understand! I just wasn't making any head way with money; anything I earnt just seemed to get swallowed up in the outgoings of keeping that house. I was living hand to mouth and this WAS literally! If I did a good deal with the business, had a rare Good day, any extra I made just went into the pot, as it were, constant, relentless catch up . . . keeping the Mortgage people happy and off my back. This meant my business cash-flow was being affected as I was committing the cardinal sin in business of using that to bail out my personal issues . . . resulting in a build-up of debt and once you are on that train, you aint getting off quick. It was just a huge Catch 22 and, through previous experience, though I knew the signs, I just couldn't do anything about it. Walk Dog, Work hard, eat beans on toast and go to bed early or freeze . . . that pretty much seemed to sum up how the majority of my life was being lived at this time . . . and look at the blue rope EVERY DAY. I went as far as actually tying the bloody thing, leaving a loop for my head to go in. There was also a very wide steel girder in that garage that runs the whole length of it in the roof . . . I think those DIY guys call it a Joist! I just called it my HMD or "HANGING ME DEVICE!" I climbed up on a table and tied the rope to it, allowing it to dangle . . . I'd done it! I'd made my Suicide vehicle. Now to practice . . . and I actually worked out that if I stood on the table, put my head through the noose bit, then kicked the table away, I would probably dangle with about 20 inches of space below my feet, not being able to touch the floor . . . job done, that would do it. Twice . . . only twice (not enough to warrant a trip back to the Docs I told myself) did I SERIOUSLY consider it; 2 very very bad days, can't even remember what jumped into my head on those days or what specific stress or demons triggered my desire to actually do it . . . I walked into the garage as usual, cup of tea in hand, closed behind me the big garage door. This of course meant nobody really knew I was in there . . . I was alone totally, never even took the dog up with me; he was busy and happy with himself in the garden, having had his morning walk and breakfast. Unusually, on these 2 occasions, I also locked the garage door. If I was going to do this, I didn't want anybody being able to get to me too soon as this wasn't about being found; this was about just ending it. I really had had enough of the continual slog that was my life, sick and tired of it all. Surely there was more to life than this fucking shit existence? I cried, I paused, I thought, I got on That table, I held the rope . . . I was shaking, panicking, just so confused that I was here, in a cold garage ending my life. This was real. I hated myself at that moment and felt a complete failure; what had become of my life, what had become of Me? Then, almost by fate, I heard the next door neighbours, Al and Claire and, most importantly, the chirpy little voices of their two little boys, Ash and Charlie, getting in the car to go off to school and work. Ash, in particular, reminded me so much of Tom when he was that age, 4 /5 ish . . . not so much in looks (he actually looked like Daniel did as a boy!) but in his ways, a boisterous, fun, into anything, NOT naughty just exuberant little boy. That was it, enough for me to pause longer, take in the background sound outside that garage of those 2 lovely little kids just innocently and excitedly going about their normal day's events. This inspired the immediate thought of my two boys and how they had left from that house, in their little school uniforms and gone off to school . . . I was not ALWAYS around to see that as was probably at work by then but at this moment, I had enough memories of the days I **did** see that simple event in a family household to stop me kicking the table away. So close, yet on reflection, it wasn't my Time, this was no way to go . . . not there, not then. As I said, twice this happened. The second time I avoided the School Run time for obvious reasons but I still couldn't go through with it, even of an evening, as I couldn't leave behind my boys. One other time, I did get that old black hose out, the thin, cheap B & Q one I had used on the moors that time and, very early one morning, after walking Frank, I "connected" it up to my little Corsa's exhaust in the drive-way and actually fed it into the car via the window, sat there in the driver's seat and switched on the engine for a couple of minutes. But this really was NOT a serious bid at Suicide I remember . . . just probably a curious attempt at making sure everything worked, just in case I ever felt like doing it That way . . . a What If scenario. If I was going to do it that way, certainly would Not carry it out in that drive way for Christ Sake, for Al, Claire and, above all, THOSE sweet little boys to come home and possibly see me there, dead in my car NEXT DOOR! I couldn't have lived with That guilt . . . excuse the pun!

So, really, did I really want to kill myself? Probably not, but I know that sometimes you can just get so bloody down with it all and feel Everything is impossible, then these crazy, black, horrible thoughts Do enter your head. I DID not go back to the Doctor, mainly through fear I would be catapulted back to the counselling high-way, or worse still, perhaps THIS time she would just section me immediately and by-pass all the "niceties!" Or at least insist I take drugs to zombie me out and get over it. No, bugger all that for a game of cherries, I wasn't having any of That malarkey. I could cope on my own, I could get through this . . . I took a long, hard look at myself and talked incessantly to Me in front of a Mirror . . . "Malc, this IS SHIT, yes, this is a fucking crap, futile existence, a Nothing Life. But, it can't possibly ALWAYS be like this, it hasn't always been like this. Think what made you happy, think what made you the confident, articulate go getter you used to be . . . Think about That guy. . . . THINK POSITIVE!" After all, I had been through enough by now and experienced enough counselling to make a bit of sense of it all. It was a case of dusting myself down, pulling myself together and giving Me a huge bloody kick up the backside.

So with positive thoughts and an inner strength I had summoned from my Self lectures, I steamed through this period. Just worked EVEN harder if that was possible, refused to let the black thoughts take over my mind, just punched them out and replaced them with happy thoughts! Most importantly, I just concentrated and focused on the things I COULD do something about rather than worry about things out of my control. Gradually, slow but sure I worked my way out of this latest bout of depression and simply just got on with life, counting my blessings and just trying to make the most of a bad job.

If thoughts of my Ex entered my mind, I just knew these would make me unhappy or angry so as soon as I saw her face in my head I started to think of nice things, simple things that made me happy like walking Frank . . . the simplest "task" I had in my life . . . except it was never a task taking Frank out, a pure pleasure. More and more it dawned on me how important this dog had become to me and my life. He had become my saviour, a being that depended on me to be responsible and be there for him. I cherished my time with him and our adventures. His swimming exploits were an immense pleasure to me and many other people that saw him do his diving trick! I began to learn how to make my walks with Frank my complete "switch off" to the depression and my problems. Though being out for hours with him gave me a clear mind to think and mull it all over, I just somehow taught myself to use this time to think positive, embrace the moment, enjoy the good. Be thankful I was still here and in good health to enjoy keeping up with this amazing creature . . . though I couldn't keep up when he sprinted off to try and catch squirrels! Now

THAT is another funny sight, seeing this big, strong, athletic dog beaten in a race by a rat with a tail! Saying that, if Frank could've climbed trees like those little pests, he WOULD'VE caught the little sods!

Though I had been on the odd date and met women here and there, nothing really had lasted nor was I in the right frame of mind to put energies into this side of my life. Also, how could I take a woman out without any money? But I conceded I was bloody lonely and perhaps needed some female company so there was no other option but to get back on Tinternet! I re-posted my Profile, being as honest as I could be about my current plight without trying to scare them off! Think I just went along the lines of "I aint got no money but don't want Yours . . . just understand I aint gone none!" I was trying to attract those ladies that would genuinely be interested in Me, just me, the person . . . that's all I could offer; a guy that was not happy with where he was in life at this stage but one that understood his mistakes, had learnt so much from life's lessons and just wanted to meet someone for company, simple stuff, dog walks, chats, share a bottle of wine. If they were looking for Theatre trips, wining and dining, holidays, they had the wrong man! My well was now dry; Sorry Ladies! This time around, I was also VERY selective in who I answered or messaged myself. I didn't have the time, energy or Money to get involved with any timewasters, any freaks or nutters or simply anybody I wasn't a little bit attracted to from their profile at least. As I have said before, Internet dating is a bit of a lottery and you are taking your chances but I really had no choice at this juncture . . . my social life was extinct and I wasn't going to meet many ladies in that garage or my odd trips out to the bank or Iceland! The dog had let me down as I hadn't seen Amanda Holden whilst out on my walks with him! This time, I ended up talking to quite a few nice ladies online. I was keen to fact find a bit more intently before committing to a date and also wanted to make sure they knew as much as I felt secure enough to tell them about me and my life. I went on a couple of dates (dog walks) which came to nothing but, then, when I was just about to give up again, I met Julie who I really liked the sound of! She came across as very intelligent, articulate, funny . . . and, yes, I fancied her! Our online dating evolved into e-mails then text messages. As we found out more and more about each other, we realised we had an awful lot in common. After sufficient fact finding, we agreed to meet for a drink. We met at a nice pub in town that I wouldn't normally go to but just felt I had to make an effort to spruce up and be in a nice ambience for this one, my latest victim! Turned out she was very natural, down to earth, unassuming and yes, I did FANCY her! She was a petite, dark haired (I had moved away from blondes!) lady with an immediate genuineness I found endearing. We agreed to meet again a few days later and, again, we got on well and opened up a little bit more. Finally, I had found someone whom I could feel at ease with and, for the first time in a long, long time, actually wanted to see again! 3rd "date" lined up was a milestone for me on this Tinternet dating . . . didn't normally get to that stage! We never went anywhere near the intimate stage until a few weeks down the line but did clarify at the end of date 2 that we were compatible in the kissing Department, thank God! Julie understood my current predicament and empathised. She was more than happy to do the simple things I did, dog walking, staying in, cooking for each other, drinking wine. She was not a big socialiser and didn't need to go out all the time. Perfect! . . . a lady that wanted me the person, not the wallet! Yessss! A massive thing we really had in common was that we had both been through counselling. Indeed, when we met, she had just finished a course specifically for anxiety, stress and panic attacks and I was about half way through a Sex counselling course, a weekly hour with a great guy called John. This was something I **had** decided to sign up for as I had been concerned about my, let's say, lack of performance "down there!" This, in fact, turned out to be the final bit of counselling I would receive (to date!). I had gone to the Doctors a couple of months previously to discuss my concerns over the state of affairs in my genitals section! It was not because I was seeing anyone but a bloke knows if he has a problem down there because things were just not "looking up" and hadn't been for a long time! I could not seem to perform and was very conscious of it. Again, I swallowed my pride and went to see the Doc to talk about it. I did not share with her my suicide thoughts of that year, knew where that line would take me didn't I? No, I was there for a catch up with her and, "oh by the way Doc, I haven't been able to get an erection since I can't remember when" . . . Now what I didn't know was that this statement also opens a can of medical worms. Say you're suicidal and they send you to Cracker; talk non erection and you're off to the STD clinic! . . . Their line of thought is process of elimination; she was certain that my problem was stress related, caused by the stuff I had been through thus far, all in my head . . . and the brain was saying to my penis "you aint up to this sex stuff old chap, just hang fire till you get yourself sorted." But, the Doc has to do her job and before she can 100% confirm this synopsis she had to get me checked out for any other possible symptoms like STD's. Wow, I was on my way to a Sex Clinic . . . first time ever in my whole life. Ok, I have not been an Angel in my life and yes, I've had a bit of that sex stuff in my time but, even in the promiscuous 80's, I never ever had one of those diseases, Never! Not even an itch or rash to boast! Like a good boy though, I did what the Doc demanded and turned up at the Clinic, complete with me urine sample in a bottle, carefully wrapped into an Iceland carrier bag. It is situated in a weird place in the main Hospital . . . just down the corridor from the Maternity Unit! The last time I had been in that part of the hospital was when we'd had Tom! The signs take you down the corridor as if you're going to the Babies but then, almost by default, at the last minute detour you to the STD Dept.! Rather than the obscure sign showing me the way, they should've had a tannoy announcement at that point in my quest to find it with Chris Tarrant's "Millionaire" voice saying: "We don't want you to have one of those (babies), here's what you're getting (an STD)!" "Turn Right." I checked myself in at the reception which, to be fair, is quite private and confidential. WELL, it is shielded by a glass partition so fellow "defendants" can see you but can't hear you giving your name to the Receptionist. Luckily for me, I looked around and there was no one I knew in that waiting room. Phew! There was a diverse mix of people there; young, old, fat, thin, various ethnic origins . . . but I DID stand out, though I say it myself, as the smartest. I HAD shaved, dressed in my suit and tie as if I was going to a professional meeting. Call me old fashioned but this was me; I was fulfilling an appointment and my pride wouldn't allow me to be late or look untidy. In contrast, most of the reprobates in that room looked like they had just fallen in there from the Night Club after a skinful of drink (and probably drugs) the previous night. Probably a regular event for them . . . have a One night stand and just pop in to get checked out for the pure hell of it! After what seemed like an eternity in that hell hole, my number came up and I was beckoned in to a side room where this little guy with long, scraggy hair and a rough beard was waiting for me. He had a white coat on so he must've worked there! He didn't hang around . . . cut straight to the chase and asked me a bundle of questions. He had my Doctor's notes in front of him so knew I had erectile dysfunction and explained to me that this was common in guys of my age "so probably was nothing to worry about." I think he sensed my uneasiness and reluctance to being in this place and was trying to comfort me. He could see that I wasn't his normal, everyday patient; He'd NEVER seen me before unlike his regulars out there in the waiting room. His job was to give me the "physical" i.e. have a feel of my balls and penis for any lumps or anything untoward, I assume like rashes or stuff. I assume . . . well I hope he wasn't just touching me up! All clear and the physical done, I was ushered into another room to see a Nurse, a lady of about my age who, again, was extremely sympathetic to my uneasiness. She took my blood sample and we had a chat. I explained to her that this was the first time in my Whole life I had been in a place like this and she was bloody brilliant at her job, telling me there was no shame in being there; it was a part of today's life and the Doc was only doing her job sending me there. I thanked her for her kind words and her time and I was out of there. I had been longer in the waiting room than in the examination / blood taking! That was it, shame over, a dent only in my pride and no embarrassment of seeing anyone I knew! The way it works these days is they

TEXT you a couple of days later if your results are negative and you don't have one of those nasties! Sure enough, I got THE TEXT and I was all clear . . . I'd never suspected anything other. So it was back to the Docs a week later as booked, to discuss PLAN B to sort out me droopy penis. NOW, as we'd confirmed it wasn't a physical thing, my head needed to be sorted. Consequently, she fixed me up with John, an extensively qualified (and old) guy for a minimum six-week exploration of my mind with specific reference to sex! I must admit, when I FIRST met John it was like meeting my Grandad and for the first ten minutes I had to work at overcoming my reservations of telling my Grandad all about my sex life. But John, again, was bloody good at his job and settled me very quickly with his knowledge and very calm, relaxed nature. The first couple of sessions were him getting lots of background on me and also involved him giving me a revision in Human Biology and how it all works down there! I thought that after that, I would go in for the 3rd week and he'd have All the answers for me, wave a magic wand and Pete the Penis would be working perfectly again, maybe with a big jar of Viagra in hand! But, no, there was no quick fix to my problem and this careful, considerate and very quietly spoken man had a deliberate course of action planned out for me that was to strategically take as long as he deemed it necessary (it actually lasted about 7 / 8 weeks in total of hourly sessions). This guy, perhaps more so than any of the counsellors, and probably because he was searching deeply for the answers to what in my brain was affecting the lack lustre performance of my sexual organs, delved into very specific instances and people from my past. He explored my views on sex and women and, by the end of our time together, gave me a complete understanding of ME, with particular reference to THAT box in my life . . . again, excuse the pun here! We discussed in great depth my experiences which enlightened my inner cravings for a beautiful, loving, affectionate and tactile relationship. He clarified that this was what I had always wanted above all, just a natural, genuine meeting of minds with a lady and that I had not, thus far, achieved that level of compatibility in my life. This guy was brilliant; it was like he had a vision into my Soul and knew me inside out. He looked back into my childhood, again in huge depth and got me to open up about my Catholic upbringing and my relationships with my Parents and Siblings, especially my Brother. John made me realise, as I had always done, that my Mum and Dad were absolutely fantastic parents and I cannot complain about any lack of love or affection in my childhood . . . but, maybe, they shielded us all a little from the realities of Life. We were never allowed to see them argue in front of us and, though we knew we weren't the richest family in the street, we didn't find out till Adult life just how much money troubles they had and the massive fight to put food on the table for 4 kids. Perhaps if we'd been "let in" a bit more we would've been able to deal better with the imperfections of life as an adult. The Catholic thing was huge as well; Mum was a staunch Church goer when we were kids and, though I don't think my old Dad was in complete agreement, we were all dressed up and dragged to Church every Sunday. Went for Catholic lessons on the Saturday too! Always remember the old, Irish Priest at our local Church, Father O'Flanaghan, coming up to me Every Sunday and giving me a big welcoming hug and a few kind words about my fluffy, brown, very warm jacket! Catholic priests, eh . . . let's not go there! The whole religion thing was a big part of our lives and only faded out when we moved away from Surrey as the years went on. But those early years of having it drummed into us had a lasting effect . . . still say three Hail Mary's to myself when I do something wrong! "I have sinned Father" . . . "Spank me" . . . No I don't say that bit! Probably because of this ordainment, sex was not a word banded about in our household and was shunned every time a glimmer of it came on the telly or radio! So with regard to sex, John could see that my Catholicism had held me back a bit and made me very naïve and somewhat innocent to what it was all about. Then he found out something else about me that I didn't know myself till then, which also affected my early thoughts and perceptions of sex . . . He exposed my Brother as a bully. Honestly, I never had thought about the impact of my Brother's relationship with me until this counselling nor had I ever really discussed this aspect of my childhood properly with **anyone, till then.** In a three-bedroom council house with Mum, Dad and four kids, there wasn't the luxury of having your own bedroom. So, right up until the day my Brother moved out to get married at around 20 I think, I shared a room with him. As small kids me, my two sisters and brother had all been pretty close, brought up by loving parents. Not much money in the pot, but they worked hard and gave us everything they could. Simple things, small presents and very low budget holidays, second hand cars... they did their best and treated us all equally, also in terms of love and affection. But there was always something different about my Brother than the rest of us siblings, perhaps the Black Sheep of the family; never happy and always a little angry with his lot, troubled I think is the way to describe him. As I shared a room with him, I probably noticed this more than the others and took his back-lash as a result. He started going out drinking with his mates from an early age. John reminded me of how I felt when he would come home at the end of an evening to our shared bedroom. There are 6 years between us so if he was say 17, 18 I'd have been 11,12... He would stagger in drunk late at night or early hours of the morning, mostly unbeknown to my parents and my Sisters who were sound asleep by now. He'd come in, stinking of drink, bedraggled and quite frankly, I was a little (a lot actually) intimidated, perhaps a bit scared of him in this state. If he just wanted to get to bed, he would clamber on to the top bunk (yes we had bunk beds as we had the "little room!") and flake out. He'd obviously woken me up but I always pretended to be asleep and had a sigh of relief that he'd opted to do the same. That's if I was lucky but invariably he wanted to finish off his night by telling his little brother all about his drunken escapades that evening. He would nudge me with a stiff poke to my ribs or a heavy ruffle of my hair and make sure I WAS awake... Then, not missing out any of the details he would tell me how he'd "shagged this girl senseless" or done this or that with a girl or girls, how his mates had sometimes watched or joined in, whatever... urghh, grotesque. I know he went into far more intimate (wrong choice of word as there was nothing intimate about my Brother's behaviour) detail than I am prepared to revisit and write here. Needless to say, John advised me that these early perceptions of love-making, thrust upon me by my older (should have been more responsible) Brother, coupled with my extreme lack of Knowledge due to my Catholicism, led me to believe from this early age that when I started to engage in sexual activities with a lady, it was all about Performance... as My Brother had explained to me, you would have to do it 3 or 4 times in a night, always be erect and make sure they satisfied you more than you satisfied them though that had to be done too to show you were a REAL Man. I have cleaned that up as the sordidity of my brother's sexual exploits still to this day appals and upsets me and, I couldn't believe he could share that, actually force his little Brother to hear all that stuff. After he was finished telling me all his crap, he then would always say to me: "When I SAY turn the light out, you can turn the light out"... I would wait, shaking, for his command, he'd start to say something and I thought that was enough to do as he'd ordered so I flicked the switch as I was nearest to the light from my bottom bunk. But then he would bellow in anger: "I didn't fucking say turn the light out!"... sometimes this was followed up with a brisk slap around the head with his dangling hand coming down with force from the top bunk. So I'd quickly put it back on until his full sentence was completed: "Now you can turn the light out"... this charade was a regular occurrence in our house, in That bedroom. I lived in fear of my Brother coming home from his nights out but Never ever told Mum and Dad, I guess thinking this is what all older brothers did... Bullying was not a common word in those days; it has a lot more publicity now; so that didn't even cross my mind back then. John, however, made me realise that my Brother had bullied me into a thought process, an expectation of what sex and relations with girls was all about. I had taken this through into my adult life, thinking if I didn't "perform" I was less of a Man. In my adult relationships, I had never achieved what I REALLY craved, as everyone if they are honest does, true love and affection. The idea that love making was ultimately about performance had never been eradicated from my mind.

John explored and made me realise the importance of kissing, touching, taking time to explore each other's bodies, massage, caressing and generally talking to each other about likes and dislikes, finding common ground, SHARING pure intimacy. Because of the conditioning I had suffered, all these qualities had somehow by-passed me in adult life. Add stress, depression and anxiety into the equation, as well as the fact that, bloody hell, I was a man in his late forties(!) . . . these were all contributing factors to my poor little tool having no chance of rising to the occasion at this time! I joke but this was a serious matter and any bloke would have hang ups in the same circumstances. John worked through all this with me and basically had to re-educate me on the true meaning of Sex . . . I mean of course the art of love making. Through John's patience with me and the careful way he deliberated his teachings, I hoped that one day I wouldn't be sat in this counsellor's room but would be fulfilled, happy and a guy very much in love.

Julie, as I said earlier, met me a few weeks into my sessions with John. Because of her experience of anxiety counselling, she totally understood what I was going through and was very interested to share this with me. At one point, she was going to come to a session with me but I decided to keep going alone. Though, we openly discussed my discoveries from John's brilliant navigation and she was more than happy for me to talk to John about our relationship . . . and our love making. Because of all this openness and honesty, I became very close to her very quickly and was so pleased to have met her at this time. I guess I started to fall for her a bit and let my guard down and "let her in." She was good for me and, in fact, me for her. It was all so simple and our love making was NOT about performance. Indeed, we could go to bed sometimes and just cuddle each other all night and still be satisfied we'd had a lovely night. This made the sex so much better that the pressure was off. It seemed all the things Mike was teaching or re-educating me, were happening naturally with her and it was like fate had brought her to me to run side by side with the counselling on this part of my journey. In turn I tried to help Julie with her anxieties, other hang ups she had in her mind. One of those was an insecurity about being stable. In a financial way. She raised this with me very early on, citing her little bit of panic about the fact I was self-employed, a risk taker, no guaranteed income. It wasn't that she needed a guy to keep her; God no, she was an independent lady who had worked hard for this, bought out her ex-husband and brought up her 2 kids alone through sheer hard work. She had her own house, car and enough material things. And it wasn't about me having little or any money to do the whole wining and dining thing . . . she knew that about me from Day One, even from our Tinternet conversations. No, it was more for her that our working lives, cultures and outlooks were so vastly different. She worked as a Civil Servant and had done for over 30 years since leaving school, in a very straightforward, safe, "clock on, clock off" job. Regular salary, pension, health plan all that stuff . . . like the majority of people our age! I, of course, was the complete opposite, totally dependent on my next deal being a good one, then reliant on people to pay me to get paid myself! Yes, a different world altogether. It was WEEK TWO we discussed this in great detail before any of the intimate stuff kicked in. She'd cooked me a meal at her house and we looked each other totally in the eye to get this out in the open honestly and without missing any detail. I just said to her that yes this is what I was and could not change my ethics on this. I had tried to work for a company but it had not been successful . . . I am an entrepreneur and a bit of a maverick perhaps. But I had and always will work my hardest to survive and live up to my responsibilities. I understood that this makes me financially unstable but assured her I was 100% independent, didn't want or need her money and, though I was struggling at this time, I would always get by. I reminded her of my profile on the dating site and my honesty about this from the start and if this was going to be an issue for her that gave her anxiety, panic attacks or cause her to be unhappy, we should end this NOW as friends and go our separate ways. We talked and talked that night and, eventually, she decided that she was 100% certain she wanted me in her life and she could overcome her uncertainties and anxiety about my lifestyle. The positives of our relationship far outweighed the negatives and she wanted ME, the person. I was satisfied that night she was happy to continue with Us and that this issue was now buried.

So our little relationship flourished and we shared some lovely, simple, uncomplicated times together. We stayed at each other's houses, cooked, drank wine, walked and talked a lot! It was evolving into what John labelled an "adult kind of love!" A slow but sure build-up of feelings . . . not the fireworks, the spontaneity you experience as a teenager or even when you are in your slightly more mature twenties. No, just the comfort and ease of being in a like-minded person's company and sharing intimacy. Companionship seems far too old fashioned to say but this was probably a good word to describe it. Running parallel to the counselling all was ticking along nicely. Then, it was around the time the counselling was fizzling out to a natural end, not that I think that is relevant, Julie finished with me! It was I think Week 8 and we were going out for a dog walk on the Moors. I picked her up and just sensed as she got in the car that something was amiss. I hadn't seen her for a couple of days and her texts and communication with me had been unusually vague. She was quiet on the way to the moor but let me drive all the way out there, about a 5-mile trip. I turned to her and asked what was wrong and she hit me with the fact she'd been agonising over our Week 2 discussion about lifestyles and said she'd started to have panic attacks and anxiety again about it! I couldn't believe it as I thought we'd moved on from all that, got it out in the open and she had accepted it. But there was no budging her . . . she was so sorry as she loved all the rest of our relationship but just could not overlook her worries and concerns about that bit! I was flabbergasted as I had let my barriers down with this lady and would've understood more if it was some other problem we had but to cite something that we'd already parked early doors was a little confusing to say the least. There was nobody else involved; it was purely her insecurity about the difference in our views. THAT was that! In complete silence, as I didn't want to vent my anger and say something that would

Spoil EVERYTHING we had, I drove her home and dropped her off. We spoke a few days later to put a line under things but it was very sad that something so nice had to end. Looking back though, as sad as it was, perhaps we had run our course and got out of each other as much as that relationship was going to give us. We helped each other through our mutual insecurities but there just wasn't enough substance there to take it to another level.

Christmas No. 2 in the old house was creeping towards me. Still very skint and, despite my brief bit of happiness with Julie, the year had been full of turmoil and I was really wondering if this struggle to keep this house was ever going to get easier? . . . And would I ever have a LIFE again! This just existing to pay a mortgage and bills, this FUTILITY had to end . . . This CHRISTMAS I was to make more MAJOR decisions about the way ahead and then something I hadn't seen coming at all . . .

I was going to be living with a Man again! . . .

Chapter Seven

This Has to End ... Decisions, Decisions

Christmas was another gloomy one, sprinkled with the brief "letting in" of the family, as the previous year really. However, my second year in That house had pummelled me, beaten me up emotionally, drained me to the extent I was rapidly losing my will to fight, to go on. Something had to change, had to give ... I reflected that Christmas. Though ordinarily I spent a lot of time alone and had a bit of time to think about things, in the main on a week to week, there was still a lot to fit in just fighting the fight ... Business, my boys, the dog, house, just as most people do, spinning those plates of life! So the couple of weeks over Christmas was a good time to have some SOLID thinking without most of the mundane distractions. A time to Review and regather. For me, it was a time to decide to take a totally different approach to this pathetic situation and way of life I was leading ... Quite simply I decided to Throw in the Towel! It sounds like such an easy thing to say and quite a flippant way of dealing with things but I assure you this was no easy decision, a huge amount of thought and soul searching went into this one. I am a lot of things but I am No quitter; always put heart and soul into everything and even more into the things in my life I totally believe in, jobs, relationships whatever it is. I **don't** quit things but, on the flip side, my character also recognises when enough is enough, when it just isn't working anymore and there is no point going on with it and, again, this applies to anything in my life. I was just getting nowhere with this house situ; I couldn't afford it, I had got into huge debt just to keep it, it had affected my sanity and wellbeing and another year of this drudgery I felt would only take me to even further depths of depression I did not want to go to. It was time to get out of the Game, leave the playground, close down the Circus. I was going to give up EVERYTHING, everything I had worked towards all my life . . . an Englishman's home is his castle and all that shit. It was just time, time to get real and tell myself that, no matter what, I could be paying this house off till the day I die . . . and not having any money to do it up or live. No, it was time to Throw that towel in. The irony was I had all but caught up with the arrears situ I had taken on 2 years back, but the killer was the mortgage itself that still had over 20 years to run and they still weren't letting me swing over to Interest only, the bastards! What would I do and where would I go? At that point in the decision making process, I really didn't know! All I knew was I had to go Bankrupt, close down my business and allow the house to be repossessed. Two massive things to do but it was damage limitation time . . . a few suppliers in the business would be affected but we aren't talking Barings Bank figures here and I aint no Nick Leeson! In reality, it was a few thousand spread amongst 3 or 4 suppliers, all smallish amounts that would not have closed their businesses down. Probably insured against bad debt anyway, certainly tax deductible and better to do this now than let the figures just get worse. Again, no flippancy here on my part; writing off monies I owed . . . to anybody, whether 50p or £2000 never sits comfortably with me but, as I say, it could've been a lot worse if I let this situation snowball for another year. It is Business, not personal and I had the experience of my previous business going down years before to confirm this. Back then it had been mainly the Banks that had lost money in my downfall but I think they have been helped out enough by the Government over the years to compensate don't you? No sleep lost there . . . The suppliers that I were (and still am) close to, I had meetings with prior to lodging the Bankruptcy and explained to them face to face my predicament. They agreed with me entirely that this could not go on anymore and totally understood the reason for losing money on me and that it was not intentional. Like everyone, I had just tried to keep a roof above my head. Those Friends in business have remained friends to this day despite their business' losses from me. Indeed, I have subsequently tried to put work their way to compensate a bit and they have been hugely grateful for my honesty and integrity. The Mortgage company . . . well, they are a different animal altogether. Totally changed their tack when I 'phoned them to inform them of my decision to throw them the towel . . . God, if I could've actually thrown at them a real heavy, water laden, stained, messy, perhaps one of Frank's old towels . . . I would've done at that point, straight in their proverbial face so it splattered them with crap! Instead, when I made THE CALL . . . they were actually trying to be nice to me now and discuss my options! But, in fact, I knew and They knew my options were no different . . . they tried to go around the houses, excuse another pun, but we just kept coming back to the fact that they couldn't do anything to help: no mortgage "holiday", no interest only payment plan, no end to charges, penalties and interest should I now get into arrears again. In other words, NO FUCKING HELP FOR PEOPLE LIKE ME THAT HAD JUST TRIED TO DO THEIR BEST IN VERY DIFFICULT LIFE CIRCUMSTANCES . . . Bunch of fuckwits . . . "your home could be repossessed if . . ." Sorry they had me on a Rant again. They DID acknowledge my recent track record i.e. the last couple of years had been infinitely better than the previous couple in that I was bloody well up to date and had made the regular monthly payments . . . but it was those couple of years or so prior that had crippled my "track record" and any hope, therefore, of help. How many more times did I have to state the obvious that for over 20 years, apart from those couple, I had done the right thing, not slipped off the ice, paid my way, no trouble to them . . . oh, it was pointless, at this juncture, actually needless to have the conversation. They are a waste of space, all of them. So, change of tact and attitude, stay calm Malc . . . Mr. Mortgage Man in Glass house in India, China or wherever you are . . . I am out of the game, I am not playing your game anymore, you aint getting another penny out of me, I am done, do your worst! . . . I just informed them that I had filed for Bankruptcy and stopped All my direct debits including theirs and, in a minute, my "estate" would be in the hands of the Official Receiver. I took advice, obviously . . . and knew from the minute they stopped getting a payment, their clock to get me out of that house would be ticking. I figured that I had a few more months there by the time they got their act together and all the legal stuff and admin had been processed. I was right . . . I went Bankrupt in the January and didn't get eviction papers through till end of May. This gave me a bit of time to try and get my head around what was happening here!

It also meant I had to think about what the hell was I going to do now for an income! It was time for a complete reinvention of myself (if that was possible) and make some New Goals. How the bloody hell do you do that when you are a "Dinosaur!" . . . Also, where was I going to live?

This was a massive, massive decision to give IT ALL UP . . . I think I took all the December and Christmas to work through all the connotations of it. As I said, I had sought legal advice and shared some of the process with very close family and friends but, ultimately, it was my OWN, purely my decision. After all, it was me and only Me that was going to be affected by it all . . . **well and Frank!** But, let's be frank . . . he had already had a couple of adaptations to make in his little life so far because of my journey and had come through those admirably. So, I guessed, wherever we ended up living, he was going to be alright with it! Do you know what? . . . It is a funny thing because here I was going to be losing everything, skint and, who knows, possibly homeless but at no point did it come into my mind that I would give Frank away. Obviously, people in this situation normally have to give the pets up . . . probably the first thing to go. But I had a word with him and told him I would do my utmost to work through this situation and "Boy, you are on this journey with me now. You are my Best mate, Frank and together we'll support each other along the way." Of course the reality of that promise was that ultimately I'd have to find somewhere to live that would accept a dog! Never an easy option! A Tent, perhaps?

However, from the moment I made the decision, I knew it was the only one I could really make, the fight was over and it in fact allowed me some relief, a cloud lifted. I began immediately the task of "falling out of love" with that house. To distance myself from any emotion in this decision so that the day I eventually and, now inevitably, had to leave, it would not be a huge wrench . . . Yeh, that's easier said than done! Though, I think these last two years of struggle in that house had drained any love or affection I had for it . . . I think the fact I have consistently in this chapter called it **that house** or **the house** rather than **home** is pivotal.

Decision made, plans in place to wind down my business by the end of the month and lots of paperwork to do for the Bankruptcy, my mind now had to be focused on trying to sort this mess out properly and get myself and my future sorted . . . with no money or income stream! However, my life was to take another, very unexpected twist on the day before New Year's Eve.

David was an ex colleague from that ill-fated, very brief toe back into the "pond of employment." We had kept in touch tentatively since we both left that company, him first then me a few months later. When we worked for that company, what brought us together to forge a friendship was the fact that we were now working for a company when once we had both had (and lost) good businesses. We shared the common empathy that we hated working for this company with all its petty rules, politics and egos and spent all our time there moaning about it and trying to plot our "Escape Route!" A tall man, with a bald head, or little slithers of hair above his ears as a token gesture, David was a sad looking man, as if he had the world on his shoulders all the time. He had lost a lot of weight through his personal troubles and his once proud looking, expensive suits just didn't seem to look right anymore. Like me, he was living on his pride and dignity and "going on stage" to get through the day. Though David had recently gone through a lot of what I'd gone through, losing his business, Divorce and depression, we used to relate that our stories were parallel but his story had a few more £000's on the end of it! In other words, he had lost a lot more in monetary terms as he'd had a lot more than me. He'd fallen off the Top Shelf with a huge thud; I'd jumped from the middle shelf to the Bargain Basement. But we were totally in the same boat when it came to all the emotional stuff, being very sensitive, caring, open and honest guys. We had seen each other perhaps only a handful of times since leaving the company but, in the build up to Christmas, he had sort of appeared a little bit more in my life . . . a McDonalds here, a coffee there . . . both of us pretty skint, NEVER lunch! I told him a little about my plight and sought his neutral advice, based on my knowledge that he had lost his house the year before after his business going bust. So he knew a bit about the process I was just about to let myself in for. He, in turn, openly told me how things had taken a turn for the worse for him. Since leaving the company, another job had come and gone and, though he'd tried to start up another business in the same field, this had failed. He was back in debt to people, was just about to be evicted from a rented house he'd been allowed to live in by a friend and was also losing his hire car. Shit, I was going through hell but this guy seemed at the end of the road and . . . this was to be a huge mistake . . . I felt sorry for him! I have no doubt he was going through all this doom which I knew a bit about from our previous contact, but I had no idea it had sunk that low for him. Adamantly, though I sympathised and wanted to be there for him, I also said I had my own problems and that, at that time, there was not a lot I could do to help him. My hands were tied, I had little or no money, was going Bankrupt and losing my house in the New Year! . . . But there's where I was vulnerable . . . he knew I had a three-bedroom house and only a dog to share it with, though he also knew Tom came to stay whenever he wanted and, in fact, Daniel from time to time. So in our chats, the conversation seemed to always end up with him stating how he didn't know where he was going to live or get by . . . he was hinting that he was going to be homeless. He was working his way into my good nature. I think there was once and once only in those conversations where I let my guard down and did say that if, and only **if** he became desperate for somewhere to live then I would not see him homeless. But I remember when I said it, I never thought he wouldn't be able to sort out his own problems and work things out. At the end of the day, he was a periphery friend, an associate only. We had lots of common problems but even after opening up to each other with these sporadic chats, I Always went away from them with the feeling that David would pull through and he had far more people in his life, family and friends to whom he could turn to before relying on me for help. We kept in touch over Christmas though didn't see each other ... until that day before New Year's Eve when I got a frantic call from him saying he was "at the end of his tether, didn't know who else to turn to." He'd had the argument of all arguments with his landlord / friend who had given him a day to move out and, on top of that, he was losing his car too the next day! So I had this guy telling me that night he was either going to sleep in the car or the YMCA ... or even worse? He had no money and actually **was** thinking of ending it all. What do you do faced with that dilemma when you DO have a three bedroom house to yourself and a bit of food in the cupboard? I couldn't see him out on the streets (and he knew I wouldn't do that) as I saw where he was in his mind and I had been that low too before. So, I said he could come and stay with me ... for the short term "until he got somewhere else to stay." I was crazy, absolutely crazy ... there I was in the house, about to go bankrupt within weeks, going to lose the house too AND very little money or food for me and Tom when he was around and I am taking in a Stray Lodger ... one with less money than me and a very fragile, emotionally disturbed one to boot. Like I hadn't got enough of my own problems! But I stand by the fact that, no matter what the circumstances were, it would have taken a very ruthless, hard, emotionless person to not do what I did that day. I would never have forgiven myself if I had read in the local paper the next day or seen it on the news that "Prominent Businessman KILLS himself due to depression." The day he came to me, I remember he had also run out of petrol so I went out to him in the Bean Tin with a tank of petrol and got him back to my place. He looked dishevelled, had been crying and, yes, I thought he could be suicidal... he had very few personal belongings. Said he'd only been given time to collect together what he could and had to make an arrangement with the landlord to go back and get the rest of the stuff at a later time. That first night was surreal... I was in a very black place myself, had got myself through Christmas and made this momentous decision to change my whole life somehow some way and then here I was, living with this, I have to say, strange guy who I didn't really know as a person. There he was in My house, eating my food, drinking my wine and sleeping under my roof. Weird, surreal, couldn't believe what I had done. He literally had no money, nothing and only had the clothes he was in and a few other bits in some bags. I was on the bare bones of my ass and I was feeding another person! Most of the food I had in was leftovers from Christmas and, it pains me to admit it, handouts from family and friends. My dear old Mum, for instance, had insisted on giving me a couple of bob for food, as did my Sister. Also my wonderful Nephew, Darren, had visited me over the break (pre. David) and brought me in a couple of big bags of basic food items. I also had a lady friend, just a friend, who gave me a hamper of food, wine and beer. I hated taking it and this was the huge downside of "letting people in" to where I was but without these lovely acts of kindness I wouldn't of eaten that Christmas, well not anything decent anyway. With this and some money I had been given for Christmas, I had enough to get me, and as it turned out, David too, through the gloomy January. My family and friends were not happy that I had taken him in but they also knew that my good nature could not have done anything other. It's who I am and how I have been brought up... and HE knew that. As he chipped away at my unstinting kindness... and my food and drink! without any mention of contribution (how could he contribute... he had nothing!), we did share a lot more empathy about our current situation. To be a bit fair to him, we did help each other emotionally through our respective crises. After all, he had lost everything like I had, or was about to. There were many times when we confided in each other and, with hindsight, I regret telling him some of the stuff about my personal life, past and present. I just got the feeling he was using it, as, in my opinion a leech does. If you look up the definition of **leech** the dictionary says: "a **leech** is one who benefits, usually deliberately, from others' information or effort but does not offer anything in return" . . . I might've been wrong, but This was how I was starting to feel about this strange man in my house? I was working out very quickly that this guy, who I hardly knew, was, in fact cleverly manipulating me, with no humility for the situation I was in and had and consistently used his emotions to steer himself into a position where he could take from me. Our only saving grace, the only thing that stopped me throwing him out after a few weeks when the penny dropped, was that between us, in our mutual jobless state, we had come up with a Business Idea! Strip it all bear and you still had two rather intelligent, articulate . . . once successful entrepreneurial businessmen, living together! I will give credit where it's due, David had researched this idea which was working in the States and he presented it to me for my opinion. He had done a fair bit of work on it but needed my experience of the print & design business to put it all together and get it to business plan stage . . . of course, without any resources of his own, he also needed the use of My computer, phone, electricity and the . . . cold (it was very cold as we were now in mid-winter) office in the garage! But an office it WAS. It was a bizarre situation really. On the one hand I had this guy living with me who was like a parasite, eating all my food, using my car, living totally rent free and gnawing away at my kindness. But, then, when we put our business heads on, we would go out to that office in our layers of clothes to keep warm as I definitely couldn't afford any heating out there (hardly had it on in the house then either!); we would dig into our professional skills and park our personal differences and put in a 10 hour, sometimes longer shift to try to launch a new business in the only way we both knew how . . . with pure hard work, effort and positive thoughts! Of course we both had our doubts about it all and, yes, sometimes the personal conflicts we had about our living conditions would overflow into the working day but, by nook and cranny we overcame all and actually got a viable product launched. We would put these stupid hours in, congratulate ourselves on how we'd got through another day and how motivating it was to see a flicker of the once top guys we used to be and then we'd go into the house and have an argument about how he'd still got no money and there I was cooking for us again using my food, my money! Weird, totally mad situation. I did retain a morsel of the emotion of feeling sorry for him that I'd had at the outset of this, but, as the weeks crept on ... and it soon became a couple of months, my resentment for his selfishness, lack of humility and downright blindness to the fact that I was, in fact, keeping him, rose to the surface and caused lots of tension between us. There was this one occasion when it really hit home how he was treating this arrangement. Tom was staying with me and on this particular day had asked me for some soup. I immediately said yes and went to the kitchen to sort this for his lunch. As much as Tom was fairly aware that Dad was skint, I always prided myself with the fact that he didn't know the extent of my skintness! When he was with me, though a stretch, I always made sure I had food to give him and life around me was as "normal" as possible. It was obvious to him that I was struggling and, obviously, I couldn't give him the life he'd had with me when he was growing up. BUT I always have done the best I can for him, always will do. Now I was sure there was ONE tin of Chicken soup left in that cupboard and I was so delighted that I could fulfil my boy's wish to have Chicken soup for his lunch! I COULD DO THAT, I could give him chicken soup! THANK Christ he'd asked for soup and nothing else! Then I opened the food cupboard (my old Mum used to call it a larder!) and to my dismay ... NO CHICKEN SOUP! I knew straight away that David had had it, it must've been him ... "Sorry Tom, don't have any chicken soup, thought I did, sorry mate, toast ok?" ... he moaned and reluctantly said "ok Dad" as I looked at David in utter disgust, sat there on my settee in my house, watching footy on my telly ... with Tom's Chicken soup tucked away in his belly, bastard. I did Tom his toast, got through the rest of the day, bided my time, dropped Tom home then got back to mine ... David, still sat on my settee, in my house, watching my TV. "David, a word mate" . . . "Anything to tell me, anything to say?" . . . "What Malc, what are you talking about?" There you go, complete and utter disdain, total ignorance to what had happened that day and the bigger picture of it all. "David, it's not just about a fucking tin of soup mate, it's about the fact you have been living in my house, eating my food, driving my knackered out old car for two months now and then you take . . . without asking or mentioning it, my boy's tin of soup, the ONLY tin of fucking soup in the whole damn house. The bottom line is mate, when I CAN'T feed my boy because YOU have TAKEN his food, that's it, this HAS TO END" . . . "You are now taking the piss out of me and my family and the kindness I extended to you." I had to rip into him some more to make him realise he was a very selfish man who, in my opinion, had grown up in a middle class, probably veering towards upper class family and then gone on into adult life to have, at one time, a wealthy lifestyle. This meant that when "thrown" into the lions' den of real life where you have to dig in, fend for yourself and come down off that pedestal where he perhaps thought he still was, he had to buy himself some humility and grow some balls. At least, think of others and what they had tried to do for him to stop him going under. It was at that moment, when he just seemed to meekly take everything I threw at him, that I realised I was maybe dealing with a spoilt brat here, a man that was so used to TAKING, he didn't even know How to give back? It didn't seem to come on his radar . . . he'd been so used to getting what he wanted and having people run around for him, when friends like me and those before me gave him stuff to get him through this lean period, he was conditioned to just TAKE! It really didn't matter that I had bloody nothing, he was going to bleed me dry if I let him! Well he nearly already had as we WERE out of soup now! The guy didn't even pick up a hoover or clean the shower out . . . I am not accusing him of being a slob as this was a guy that had once had good, high class living standards and to an extent he still looked after himself but around the house he did nothing apart from washing up after meals. I feel a pattern forming here! . . . lived with 3 guys now and became a skivvy to them all! But I just like to be clean and tidy. Meticulous and organised and, despite everything, I have standards that I set myself to live by.

So we had the two boxes going on here, the living together box and the work one. I had to get firm with David after his first couple of months of Taking, taking. The reality was I had NOTHING left to take anyway. Sure, I wasn't by now paying the mortgage as those bastards weren't getting any more money out of me now I could see the "finishing line" of losing the house. So what I "saved" on that sort of funded the £700 you have to find to go bankrupt (in cash, without fail... what a system that you have to find £700 you haven't really got to officially declare you haven't got no money!). Any other money I could scrape up, I just put into the pot of life... food, bills, Tom etc. The kick up David's backside had worked (shame he had to be told at all, grown man and all that); he'd gone and signed on now and was starting to get Jobseeker's allowance, albeit a pittance but beggars and all that... This meant he could give me a little bit towards stuff... and I only took a meagre sum as I was very aware he had a Son too and needed a bit for him. Anyone else would've just said Sod you, I want the lot but this is Me, soft old Me! Also, miraculously, he started to get some help from his family... So where were they over 2 months back, these rich relatives, when he needed them? Instead of leeching from me and dragging me further down, why didn't he go to them then? I never quite knew where I was with him and, though he came across as genuine and sincere, I always had an aura of mistrust around him. He somehow negotiated to move out to a flat in a month's time... hooray, I was getting my house and my life back!... Hold on, what house, What life? But it would hopefully mean a return of my sanity away from this strange situation.

This meant that we could just concentrate on being business "partners", in the loosest sense of the word! But him moving out was a good, positive thing and gave us the space away from each other to just focus back on the business. As it happened, the little business was starting to show some promise and make us a few pennies. We attracted interest from an investor in London, a brother of a friend of David's . . . I was instantly dubious about This contact but as it turned out the 2 guys who showed the interest were good people, sound businessmen and as soon as we had pitched properly to them, they were on board! Maybe life was now turning for the better; perhaps I was now going to get a bit of luck come my way after all the turmoil of the recent years. I had said when I made the decision to "throw in the towel" that I needed to reinvent myself, go along a different path . . . well it seemed that this was exactly what was happening with the new business. Now I just had to wait to be evicted from the house and then the little matter of finding somewhere else to live! . . .

David gone to his flat the other side of town, Bankruptcy now a couple of months behind me, it was time to start to deal properly with the matter of the impending repossession of the house. With all the paperwork and main aftermath of the bankruptcy behind me now and the fact that the guys in London had agreed to set us up with a proper office from which to run their business, this meant that I could close up my garage office and, generally, start to pack things up or have a good clear out (again) in readiness for my vacating the property. At first, I was a little oblivious to the fact that I was actually losing the house and concentrated solely on just tidying it, throwing out stuff, just the "flushing out" exercise I was now becoming accustomed to with all my moving around! I had become a serial mover in the last few years and very skilled and adept at doing it efficiently . . . and on the cheap. Besides, I don't do clutter at the best of times and, as I have probably mentioned a few times before, came out of my marriage with very little so moving out was going to be a minimalistic exercise. I think my agenda of remaining, in the main, very practical and matter of a fact at this juncture, deflected me from the reality of the situation . . . very soon I was going to be losing my house. At this stage it was easy to live there as the eviction notice had not been issued so I guess I was kidding myself it wasn't really happening or, at least, wasn't going to happen for a long time yet. This gave my mind a little peace and allowed me also to put a lot of effort into working hard at building the little business. It was a good thing to get up in the morning and go to an office away from the house and do a day's work ... I almost started to feel normal, like a Real person for a change! Got into a nice little routine, even started to build a good relationship with David as we no longer had that pressure and contention of living together AS WELL as working. I remember we even went out a couple of nights for a few beers ... something we'd never done in those 3 odd, gloomy months he'd been in the house. Away from all the pressures and our personal problems, we managed to "escape" and respected each other's needs to switch off and have a good time. Aside from all we'd been through, we both had a common goal to be happy, fulfilled ... and successful again. We'd both been "somebody" in our day and earnt a few bob, raised our children, looked after our Wives ... now, at our time of lives and after having sunk so low, it wasn't about materialism, being rich, just about achieving something, proving at least that we could do it still, run a business, do something worthwhile.

Life then had reached a plateau. A seemingly slightly better place to where I'd been for a while. Though the year had started with the devastation of the Bankruptcy, the impending repossession and the David debacle, somehow a little bit of normality had crept back in! We were running a business, even getting paid to do it, the guys in London believed in the product ... There was HOPE, a sense of optimism for the future amidst the adversity.

However, as often seemed to be the case in my life, when I achieved a modicum of happiness and positivity, another arrow of doom came hurtling in to inflict a wound into my equilibrium. My leap to a scant of normality was to be short lived. Two major things happened in the next couple of months ... David left the business for personal reasons. But, more importantly, the eviction date was set for May 24th that year ... I was going to be HOMELESS! Boy, do I get some challenges thrown at me but, what do they say ... "It's all character building!." ... I don't think I've heard THAT one before! ONLY a million times!

So, I had a date, a couple of months to get a roof above my head! Of course, I had done a little bit of searching by now ... and come up with nothing. I did look at a couple of places but they were worse than the Bedsit! I had spoken with friends and family and none of them would see me homeless but, let's be honest, people say these things at times like this but they don't REALLY want you to turn up at their house and invade their privacy for an indefinite time, this time with a big black Labrador in tow! If I was going anywhere, Frank was coming with me; I wasn't giving up my best mate again ... we were in This together ... And I had promised him! I continued with my "flushing" out exercise at the house, involving several trips to the dump in the Bean Tin, cleaning, sorting. Anybody else planning to leave a house that was being repossessed would probably just give up on it, trash it, not bother to leave it in a nice, tidy position. Not me. I even continued to mow the grass and keep the garden as best as I could, dog poo Free of course! Must admit, perhaps in the last month or so in there, I think I stopped deep cleaning the bathroom and kitchen and let go a few of my normal weekly chores in an effort to distance myself from it all ... and **fall OUT of love** with this house that held so many memories.

Then, I had a stroke of luck in my pursuit of a new abode. I bumped into a lady on a dog walk who, the year or so before, I had had a very brief liaison with. She was a scatty American lady, Linda, who lived in the adjoining cul de sac to me ... the posh, red brick houses we had always called them! She was a lovely, bouncy, attractive lady, just turned 40 who I had spent some time with the previous Summer. I loved her personality and she made me laugh. Like lots of Americans ... she was A BOX OF FROGS! Nuts! We'd shared a few dog walks, even a couple of Wine nights, once in my house and once, no twice in hers. We did get a bit close ... for 5 minutes I think! But, this lady could never keep her mind in one place for a second and one minute we were arranging to meet up for a walk or drink or something, then I wouldn't hear from her for days or weeks sometimes! In the couple of months or so that I knew her, she flitted back to the States at least twice!

There was never ever a chance of a relationship with this lovely, but bombed out lady! So when I saw her on the dog walk after not seeing her for at least 6 months, we just swapped stories and updated each other on our lives. She was in the midst of planning to go back to America full time, was sorting out all the legalities, mainly the welfare and custody of her 2 kids (she too was divorced but had till then had both her children living with her). One, her daughter, was going with her, her Son was looking to stay in this country with his Dad. She had a place to go to in the States lined up and, obviously, had all her family out there. She was deciding on what possessions to take or sell before she went and, like me, having a Flush out. I shared with her my new challenge and my pursuit of happiness in a different direction. I didn't **really** Know this lady, so was not too forthcoming with all the details! She knew from our brief liaison that it was a struggle for me alone in that house so I just said I was looking to sell up and go into Rented. With that, a penny dropped and I remembered She was actually Renting her house here, she didn't own it. I asked her what the situation was with it as it would be ideal for me to rent when she left (if I could afford it), being that it was only around the road from where I was, would make an easy move . . . and I wouldn't have to change Frank's daily routine of getting up to the field twice a day! She told me that she thought her landlady was intending to sell the property when she returned to America but she would find out. I thanked her and left her to it. I did offer to help her in any way I could to move out, though regretted that statement of intent, albeit just a friendly gesture as I knew her life was full of madness at the best of times and I didn't need to go to her Circus! As it turned out, she had plenty of help with her move so I wasn't really needed. She had all areas covered including selling off most of her stuff on E-Bay or something. She had a chat with Mrs Pellow, her landlady and I think put a good word in for me, saying how clean and tidy I was even with a dog and that I'd make a good replacement tenant. Mrs Pellow was at this time unsure of what she intended to do when Linda left, sell it or rent out again or even just leave it vacant whilst she did some major maintenance and decorating. However, with an open mind, she agreed to meet with me to see what I was all about and discuss the situation. She was also seeing a couple of other potential tenants with the same view. She came to my office first and, secondly, met me at the house . . . I think this gave her a firm understanding of where I was in my life. She could see that I ran a little business (not Virgin!) from a small, attic office, sub- let from an Insurance company, and how I was living in my damp, under maintained house. Though she took on board the down side of these 2 mediocre places I worked and lived in, she could also tell that I kept them both clean and tidy and made the best of both of them. She could tell I had standards and was a proud, upright, hard working person. I was abundantly honest with her about why I was living like this and the background to my life thus far. I didn't see any point in holding anything back . . . I needed this lady to trust me from the off and so I needed her to know I had gone bankrupt, was divorced and was being repossessed . . . SOON! This obviously meant my Credit file was shot so if this was going to happen, she would have to agree a private arrangement between us. She had to process all this and go away for 48 hours before coming back to me with her decision. To her word, she did this and I was amazed to hear that she had decided to take a punt on me! We had hit it off from the word go in our couple of meets and, from that moment, we struck up an immediate friendship, a rapport, a bond that still exists today and will always last. We have the perfect set up in that we both agree to compartmentalise our business relationship with the house away from our very special friendship. Paula, as she now lets me call her, is an amazing lady who has been through so much in her life that has made her the person she is today. We discuss life and though she would never tell me all her stuff and vice versa, we know we are there for each other and always will be. I call her my Guardian Angel! She seemed to fly into my life just when I needed her . . . she took a chance on me renting her lovely house because she likes me, respects what I am all about, loves my dog (thank God, as most rented properties don't allow them) and she opted for me as opposed to the other people she interviewed.

So, I had a smashing, airy, clean and tidy (and NOT DAMP!) property lined up to move into, a fantastic landlady, the business was doing ok, no great shakes but we were getting there slow but sure . . . Just one major thing to contend with now: the ACTUAL move from the house to Paula's and all that entailed. Loopy Linda was busy flushing out her stuff at her end, I was doing the same . . . we were both working towards her leaving to go to the States a few days before the bloody Bailiff's were due to take mine on the 24th May. As it happened, this all went to plan and Linda did in fact get on her 'plane 4 days prior to this, though it was uncertain right till the last, as these kind of plans normally are. With her issues surrounding her move, I had in fact made contingency plans to stay with Big Mike, my friend from football . . . I'd softened up his Wife down the pub after footy one night and, after she'd had a couple of wines, got her to say "she'd never see me and Frank homeless and I could stay with them if we had to in the interim!" Preyed on her love of dogs to get me in there! It never came to it but it was comforting to know the dog and I had a place to go to if needed . . . and that would've been like going on holiday as they have a plush bungalow in the posh part of town!

In that last month or so of being in the house, it was a mixture of emotions going around. I made a huge effort to "fall out of love" with it. After all, I kept telling myself, it was only Bricks and MORTAR . . . Just a house, everybody moves house. But the reality was now setting in. I had lived in this house for 21 years, less the nearly 2 years I had been away after leaving the family. I was bound to have some affection for it and, most certainly, huge amounts of memories there. I don't mind admitting that in that last month, I nearly changed my mind, nearly undid all the stuff I'd set in place to move out. I was on the verge of 'phoning the mortgage company to ask for another chance, nearly told Paula I'd decided to stay, started to think of unpacking boxes I'd packed! But I knew in my head . . . And my heart I had to go. It was time, I'd done my time . . . this was the Right thing to do no matter how upsetting it was going to be. It was time to start afresh. Every day in the lead up, every bit more of stuff I packed made it Real that this was

IT . . . I was NEVER going to live in that house again, my whole life was going to change completely. That bit should've been ok with me as I had now moved more times in the last few years than gypsies do! But it was turning into a huge wrench . . . I was really struggling with it; this was once MY HOME where I had lived with my family, brought up my boys, had a normal, MOSTLY happy time. Now, it was going, I was losing it all . . . THIS WAS THE FINAL NAIL IN THE COFFIN. Al the Pal from next door popped round a lot in those last few weeks and shared my anguish . . . he too, was sad to think I was going (again) and knew that this time, I would NOT be back . . . EVER. We pledged to keep our strong friendship intact . . . after all, I was only moving bloody 300 odd yards up the road . . . though out of eyesight, we said we'd probably see as much if not more of each other as we'd now make a bigger effort to keep in touch and have to drink more beer down the little local!

Eviction Day was creeping up very soon. By now, a lot of my gear was tucked away in Paula's garage where she'd allowed me to store it to break down the labour on actual Move day. As I said, my old house was only a few hundred yards down the road from the new house! So in these preceding weeks, I found myself on my early morning dog walks carting boxes of junk up through the lane and depositing them in the garage. Sometimes I used my little red trolley I'd had for years for bigger items like the telly and stuff so I must've looked like a burglar with his haul on those dark mornings! This meant that the house was getting emptier and hollower and SAD. All I had in the house on the last day to move was my bed and the white goods which I had a mate helping me with. Paula let me move these final items in as soon as Linda had left so this meant I had 4 days in the new house before the Bailiff's were due to take mine. That should've been That, I know, but Paula was using those few days to get her plumber guy in to finish off some jobs, including the bathroom so I had no water! This meant, reluctantly, I went back to the Old house to shower for those last couple of days, thus giving me a further chance to mull over the massive move I was now making. It just added to the heartbreak, seeing my now shell of a house, clean but perilously EMPTY . . . just waiting for the vultures to take it. I think, if I am honest, whether I had the water problem or not, I would've not been able to resist going back for one last look before handing the keys over. What happens is, on eviction day, the Bailiff turns up at his appointed time (think he was due at 11 a.m.) with a locksmith and, If they have to, they break in and seize the property then go onto change all the locks. There are horror stories of having to drag people out of their repossessed properties, violence, properties left trashed in more ways than one, all of that stuff, but this was going to be an easy one for Mr Bailiff. I was going without a struggle and the house, aside from the basic maintenance needed and normal wear and tear, was in a good order and VERY CLEAN! ON THE DAY, I was going to meet the Bailiff and pass him the keys, though you don't have to as, like I said, they have the right and power to break in. Right up until the day before, I had planned to do this. However, I just couldn't go through with it, just could not face the horrible man who was going to take my old home away. I knew that if I had to face him and talk to him, I WOULD just break down and maybe not say the politest of things, given the circumstances. The couple of weeks lead up to this day, despite keeping exceedingly busy with all that was going on, were terribly emotional. The sheer reality of what was happening here was truly sinking in. On The day, I had told David I wouldn't be in to the office till the keys were handed over (he was still working in the business at this point; we were still another month or so away from his leaving). I'd slept at my new abode the night before and returned to the old house for my shower as planned, intending to stay there for the handover. After my shower, I just looked around, as I had done a hundred times over the last couple of weeks, at the empty shell of a house. This is probably where I was stupid to myself, but I just had to do this (more self –hurting, more torture) . . . I told myself at that point, at that very moment, I was going to spend the last hour or so I had in that house, going from room to room, "taking" a Memory, Just ONE memory from each room! I don't mean physically ripping out something to take (by this time there was nothing left anyway, and I wouldn't of been so sad as to take strips of wallpaper!). No, I was going to "put" into my head, my Memory bank, the thought that jumped into my head as I entered each room. Mad I know, but I was just overwhelmed by a sea of emotion and some strong, overpowering, perhaps spiritual soul telling me I had to do this. I started upstairs as I figured the bedrooms would hold the most powerful memories for whatever reason. Started in Daniel's old room and the memory that jumped in was of the night we had found a little field mouse in there! He was about 13 or 14 at the time . . . Daniel, that is, haven't got a clue how old the mouse was! Just got a glimpse of the little pest scurrying under Daniel's bed whilst he slept like a baby . . . Daniel would've slept through a volcano erupting! We couldn't go to our bed aware there was a mouse in the house. We didn't know what to do though to capture it? I panicked and grabbed the first thing I Could see to hit it with . . . a big chunk of wood with 3 nails sticking out of it! This was a remnant from some work we'd been doing upstairs . . . I was like a man possessed running around the room trying to beat this poor, maybe only an inch-long creature with my foot-long weapon with Nails! Needless to say, I couldn't catch the bloody thing. There was only one thing to do now . . . Molly the Mouse Catcher had to come to the rescue! The wife left me to watch guard over our vermin intruder whilst she popped around to Al and Claire's to ask for the loan of Molly, their cat. We knew Molly was adept at these kind of things, seen many a "present" she had brought home for them! Al duly came around, Molly in his clutches, a lovely looking cat, predominantly white but with slivers of brown and black to give her a classy look! We decided at this juncture to remove Daniel from his bed, though he was Still not awake! We shuffled him to our bed where he immediately fell back into a deep sleep . . . not sure if he even woke at all in the very brief "journey" between rooms! Then we let Molly loose, closing the door behind her. Her pursuit and capture of said mouse was all over in a minute whereas I'd been on the case for well over half an hour! Just a funny old night and, though not a cat lover, I looked at that cat with utter respect every time I saw her thereafter.

Onto Tom's old room . . . the smallest room in the house. What entered my mind here was the times I had read him a story to get him to sleep when he was little. Then, as he got older, jumping onto his top bunk with him to watch telly or watch Him play a Playstation or X-Box game; I was never any good at these bloody things so it was just a case of me watching him go through the motions. All the games seemed the same to me, especially the football ones and many a time I found myself nodding off, bored with the repetition, then shaking myself to stay compos mentis enough to share his excitement! Happy days.

Funnily enough when I went into THE main bedroom, my takeaway memory here was lying in bed with the wife, eating our breakfast and watching GMTV, **every** morning! This was our daily routine and, I guess, was a bit of Us time before we turned into Parents to get the kids up and ready for school (that was mainly her job) and then I was off to work. That was it, my nicest of memories I could take from that bedroom? Weird, no thoughts of love making, laughing or, now stretching it, even decorating together! Just eating cereals and having a cup of tea . . . Simple but nice!

Moving downstairs, my thoughts were generally family filled times, everyday stuff. Watching the telly together, helping with the kids' homework, the boys rushing in singing, laughing, Tom "a bull in a China Shop!" There were many Christmases, Birthdays and celebrations whirling through my head and, though I have already said I hated my boys spoiledness, I also, perhaps hypocritically, loved to see the massive smiles on their faces, their eyes wide with excitement and happiness when they opened their mountains of pressies! Happy times . . . look at the Credit card bill later to see what we'd spent!

The kitchen filled me with the fuzzy thought of Saturday Pasta Nights! . . . Pasta, Wine and the X-FACTOR, sad man, creature of habit! Back then, I never did any of the cooking, such was our ritual, team understanding, just the way it was. Never seemed a sexist thing, it worked . . . and she was a good cook! Of course, we also entertained a lot in the old days and I allowed myself this memory when I went into the conservatory which backed off from the kitchen ... all our friends sat around the big table, loads of laughing, talking and drinking going on ... great nights full of fun.

Finished my Tour in the garden and finally the garage. The garden was an easy one ... Football. Not the dog, not the parties we'd had out there but Playing footy with my boys in that garden. I got both of them into the hallowed game from an early age ... Daniel was a natural. He moved in with me at 3 and hadn't really been into it before, with his real Dad not being an avid fan of the game ... I soon had Daniel kicking a ball around. He took to it like a Duck to water and was really good even from that young age. We had photos of him kicking this big orange ball around that seemed bigger than Him! It was in that garden he did his record breaking, earth shattering, mesmerizing, **1200** "Kicky- uppies" while I watched every one of them, willing him to do more! Took him about an hour and he got cramp in his calf doing it ... a Momentous Day! Tom, on the other hand, though eventually he went on to find his Natural talent for the game, it was never seen in That garden! Much to the neighbour's furore, he was the typical pain in the ass kid that would consistently kick the ball over into their garden! Their patience wore thin after the 6th or 7th trip to their door asking for permission to retrieve it. Greenhouses, plants and PEOPLE were not safe when Tom was playing! But, my mind recollected MANY happy, fun-filled, hours and hours of play time with my boys in THAT garden. And then, also, I could not forget the endless hours I spent with Frank that 1st. pivotal Christmas training him, playing with him ... the tears were coming now; this was all getting to be a painful journey into the past.

The garage didn't prompt any immediate thoughts of my time spent working in my office up there as I thought it would. Given that I'd just spent the last 2 odd years working from home in there, built two businesses and been probably 1000's of hours in those four walls, it would've been the obvious thought now. No, what jumped into my head was hearing Al the Pal singing away whilst playing his organ in his garage next door! He was (is) a good musician and did many local gigs. I never let him know he was good; our banter is based around me being his No. 1 heckler! He thrives on it and we still laugh about it. "You only get gigs in Nursing homes or the Conservative Club cos they're all too old to hear you!" . . . "I'll come to your next one Al, I will swell the numbers by 100%!" . . . Stuff like that. Many a times in the good old days, I'd heard Al in his garage rehearsing and banged on the door to "keep the noise down"(!) and then he'd open up and I'd join him for an impromptu karaoke session and a few beers that would fill a few happy hours! . . . We'd only done that once since I'd been back in that house for whatever reason and it was at that point that I REALISED . . . **ALL** the memories I had stored, those that I'd allowed to jump in at the pivotal point of entering each space of the house I'd set myself to go to were **ALL** things that had occurred in the 16 years I had lived in that house with my Family. Not from the 2 or 3 years before she moved in with me and, most definitely not from these last 2 years! This was bizarre to me as, come on, 2 years living in that house, surely there was one good memory? But, no, these last couple of years had just been an endless struggle to exist, to survive and that house was just that, **A house, not a happy Home**. What a bloody waste of 2 years of my life, why the hell had I even gone back I asked myself . . . at the end of the day I was losing it ANYWAY . . . **TODAY!**

Now the tears flowed, the flood gates opened. This was like a bereavement of a sort. I was never ever going to step foot into that house again, never create another memory there. I was shaking, weeping, just totally overcome with the whole build up and place my mind was in. I had worked so hard over the years to make this my home, keep it and protect it and now it was slipping away from me. It felt like someone was turning off my Life Support machine. I should've called someone to be with me, someone close to share this with. I decided just to call David and let him know where I was at with it all. Now, he had been through this, losing a home to repossession (as I have said, one with a few more digits on than mine!) and **he**, probably more than anyone else in my life at that time, understood how I was feeling at that precise moment. He could hear my heartbreak, sense my anguish over the phone. He was there, with me at the house in ten minutes. He too could not do the next bit when he had lost his house and physically hand the keys over himself so he offered to do this bit for me. Despite all we had been through up till then, which we had actually sorted and worked through as Men and adults, putting aside my reservations of him as a person, at that moment he came up trumps and I could not have thanked him anymore profusely than I DID for taking that burden away from me. I gave him the keys. Left him to it and went back to work. He duly carried out the simple, but for me, massive, task of presenting the keys to the bailiff in a quiet, controlled manner so as not to stir too much gossip from the neighbours and that was it, Job done.

21 years of my life, line under, in the past well and truly . . . it was now time to start to go down another road, literally! I was working on the reliance of something I had read recently . . .

"Your future is always more valuable than today; the sooner you realise that the better."

Now for another challenge! Living in someone else's house, adapting to another routine and life but virtually passing my old house every day on the way to work! It took a few weeks to ween myself off the habit of driving to the old house instead of veering off right to get to 99, my new abode. And I can't deny, those first few weeks were emotional, the reality setting in, waiting for the "cut to heal" and just leave a scar. Time, the old cliché', heals all and it's just so true . . . Time does its job, heals the wounds and just gets you to get on with it. There were still lots of jobs going on in the new house so a hive of activity for the first few weeks anyway to take my mind of things. Paula, my lovely landlady, had a little team of tradesmen she whipped into shape to get things done . . . I had plumbers, sparkies, decorators and a carpenter popping in and out all the time. But this was a Circus I COULD deal with! This was just practical stuff that was happening and, by the time they had carried out her orders, I had a plush new bathroom, nicely decorated house and all of the niggly jobs that get left behind normally, done and dusted! Paula had let me have a say in colours and an input to the jobs going on and I had chipped in to helping with some of the labour and cleaning up so it almost felt like it WAS my home! Paula understood completely what I had lost and what I was feeling at that time and her empathy and sensitivity will never be forgotten. This theme continued and I know it was a rented house but, on a day to day, because of that relationship with her, it felt like mine. It also goes without saying that wherever I had lived, Dan's, the bedsit, the igloo, the old house and now 99, I always had my standards and my pride would not let me live in a dirty house! Even in the bedsit, which definitely WAS NOT a "home", I had my weekly ritual of household chores to keep it spick and span! But, this place, 99 felt different . . . perhaps because of the journey I Had been on to get me here, I was now ready to settle somewhere, put the past behind me, just make the best of what I had and put my energies into what lay ahead, not look back. This was the 5th place I had lived in as many years and I hoped and prayed this would be the end of my gypsy like existence!

The Business was ticking along, slow but sure. I was making a few pennies out of it, enough to pay my way and, again, after all I'd been through, that was certainly enough for me. Never wanted to be a millionaire anyway! . . . Well, perhaps once, many moons ago but that was in another life, pre all the crap in my life and, maybe, when I looked at life another way. Back then, when I EARNT good money and my Business was doing well, it just seemed the natural thing to do to "chase the dollar" as they say. My whole lifestyle was built on that philosophy it seemed, working damn hard just to earn as much as possible so we could do and have as much as we could. Though never a wealthy, rich man, it did seem the most important thing in the world to have enough money to have expensive holidays, nice cars, a lovely house, smart clothes and plenty of treats, eating out in nice restaurants and so on . . . We used to live by the motto, "work hard, spend hard" . . . It just seemed that no matter how much I earnt, we always seemed to live up to it . . . not putting Any away for the rainy days and certainly didn't live to a budget! Looking back, I should've been harder and though I moaned and groaned when she spent far too much or extravagantly spoiled the kids, nothing I said or did changed the situation. Instead of moaning, being the clever businessman (?) in the house, I should've frugally put aside at this time amounts of money so that when the hard times hit, we had enough to cope. But, as I said, this was another life and I've come to terms with all that now. I will look back briefly here but I have now learnt Not to dwell upon the past. It happened, it was the way I lived back then and this was an area of my life I was NEVER comfortable with. Though I have to admit I enjoyed all the things we did and bought, inside I cringed at the amount of money we'd spent. It was totally against the grain of the way I had been brought up in a Council House with not much in the pot to go around and definitely no lavishness. Every penny Mum and Dad had they BOTH worked damn hard for, my Mum holding down a full time job even when she had 4 kids to bring up! We never went without, always had presents, albeit inexpensive ones and had our week away Every year in a Caravan in Swanage, Dorset to look forward to! My kids don't understand it when I tell them stories of playing with the tins from shopping night as make-shift cars, pretending twigs down the park were my trains and painting faces on hard boiled eggs to create a game we all played at Easter! There was, though, lots of happiness in my childhood, plenty of love and a sense of values and morals when it came to money. I revisited those values in the years after the split up. Don't get me wrong, money is important and we all need it, but scraping by as I had to do on my own has replenished my awareness of money and what it does. Having and spending money back then **Never** made me happy. Having the nicest car in the street and the sharpest suits, Designer clothes, holidays to fantastic places . . . these are all short term things and bring you short term happiness. I lived in a world of materialism where these things were at the Top of the Agenda of the people I lived with . . . I went along with it but it did not make me happy. I love them but I don't live with them anymore and the way I live my life now . . . SIMPLY, makes me happier than craving and living up to all that falseness. Whatever happens, even if I came into money or suddenly starting earning the big bucks again,

I will Never go back to living as I did back then. There is as much, if not more enjoyment in going out for a long walk, coastal path or moors or wherever, than throwing money at a shopping trip or lavish restaurant meal! HAPPINESS, true happiness cannot be bought . . . my years of struggle have made me see that again and appreciate it. People, places and doing simple, natural things are what count.

Have the years after the split up affected my Sons and my Relationship with them? This is a question I constantly ask myself, almost on a Daily basis! They are the most important people in my life without a doubt, the single, most important thing I worry about. I still suffer guilt twangs about leaving back then and have worked so hard since to rebuild and maintain a healthy relationship with them both. I have not over compensated, not forced myself on them, just tried to achieve a Normal Father / Son relationship with them. In the early, raw days of the split up they were both understandably very angry and couldn't understand what was happening after their happy, idyllic childhood had been, in their eyes, destroyed by my leaving. They also lived with their Mum, so only really saw directly **her** suffering, her take on all this. In their innocent, yes naïve perception of it all, I was the perpetrator, the ONLY one to blame for all the sadness. I guess from their side of the fence they saw that Dad was the bastard that had broken up a family. Black and White . . . no Grey, kids don't get grey anyway, not until they've had a few life experiences of their own and, I have to say it, grown up. So, yes, at first it had a huge effect on their lives and probably WILL help to formulate some of their opinions on relationships going forward. But I HOPE what they can take from all this into their adult lives, whether that involves marriage or not, is a sense of reality . . . an awareness that life is hard and relationships have to be compatible and worked very hard at to work. After that initial surge of lust, desire and, if you're lucky, love, when the relationship settles down into the everyday stuff, there are pressures and challenges to cope with to keep it going. They've seen this first hand now and, if they'll let me, I can pass on my life experiences, my lessons learnt to them to help them go forward. I have a great relationship NOW with them both. It is very natural. I never for one minute get complacent about that and take it for granted and, never, ever forget what they had to go through when I left home. Now, though as young men, entering the jungle of life, I hope they can still respect me as a Dad first and foremost, a good one who never let them down in that department and has and always will put them first, whatever or whoever comes into My life. Secondly, I hope as they get into Manhood themselves, they will also see that we all make mistakes, have imperfections, insecurities and, as a Man, I sought something in life that, unfortunately, I felt was missing in my Marriage. I hope, in the proper fullness of time, they will understand I never meant to hurt their Mum or them because of it all. I Hope also that they will in time get a real sense of value for money and how hard it is to earn it and get enough to do all the things they want to do! . . . One of the major reasons I was unhappy in my relationship with their Mum, was the constant need I felt I had to satisfy her and the kids with material things, which, as I have already talked about, I went along with to some degree to keep the peace. Money, or huge amounts of it can fuel greed, spoildness, arrogance and selfishness. On the one hand, I want my boys to have everything they want (and I used to give it to them) but I also need them to have a grounding and understanding of money's worth and how you have to work bloody hard to attain it. That has been a tough one to preach to them or even lead by example over the last few years. When I try to say to them "work as hard as you can to build careers and earn good money", it has no credibility when they see a Dad who has done just that ALL HIS LIFE, never claimed dole money (I think they still call it that?), worked his absolute guts out and ended up with very little to show for it. I hope, though, they will remember their childhood and how my working so hard gave them everything they wanted . . . and more, too much more! How I built a Business and just always tried my hardest to be a Dad they could look up to. Followed them and supported them in everything they did. I know I hurt them deeply when I left but I am Still **that Dad,** still that Man that loves them and will Always give them what I can when I can. The Greatest Gift I can give them and have even more so in these last few years is my TIME. Not money, not gifts or lavishness, but TIME and support. Whenever they need me, I am there, whatever problems or things they come across in their lives, I am there. "No problem at all" is always my motto with my boys . . . whether I am feeling happy, sad, stressed, skint . . . "**No problem at all"** . . . Unconditional. I am just so happy we have come to a place, after All that's happened, where they still want me in their lives and are comfortable spending quality time with me.

A Huge learning curve, a Master lesson in Character Building . . . those first few years after leaving home were a turbulent, colossal time in my life. At the beginning, some wise soul told me it would take at least 2 years to "work it out" and move on from my massive decision to leave. The average is 2 – 3 after a split up involving children, I was informed. Well, I'd say the first 4 were a minefield for me, the fifth spent amalgamating the events of the first 4 and coming to terms with it all! Have I ticked ALL those boxes? . . . **Not a chance, don't think you Ever do!** But There's the thing . . . I probably spent those first 4 beating myself up so much for what I'd done and therefore trying like a crazy man to tick all the boxes, dodge all the arrows and attempt to redeem myself with Everyone involved or who became involved, keep everyone happy I guess. But, when I finally "came up for air", saw the light, I fully realised and made sense of why I had left, what I had been through and understand you'll never keep everyone happy, you can't get everyone to understand your decisions or like you. There will ALWAYS be people (including some friends) who will judge you based on their perception of how it was and guided by their own life experiences. Nothing you can do about that, no point wasting time and energy on it. I tried that! Most definitely, there will ALWAYS be boxes to tick. There will always be life experiences and lessons to learn from. That's the key

. . . **understanding just that and embracing the fact you have to learn from everything that happens, good or bad.**

Chapter Eight

We'll be alright Frank!

So me and Frank got to grips with living in our new abode!... Another house, another routine to get into. Though, to be honest, we were now even closer to the field I used to take Frank up to twice a day. In fact, the field, with its adjoining woods was so close to this new house, I would tell people I owned it as an add on to the house! Frank, being the brilliant dog he was, soon adapted to our new way of life. Paula had been around to the old house and seen my routine with him. As before, this new house allowed him to have his own space in the utility room, just off the main kitchen area. Nice and warm... and dry! Also, he had his own "living quarters" and garden outside for during the day!... i.e. a very well maintained and spacious wooden shed where he could have his other bed, food and water bowls. The garden was just a square bit of grass with small, tidy, ample borders and just the odd sprinkling of hardy plants or bushes. Compared to the old house where we'd had an 80-foot garden, this was fine for me as I am no gardener and never will be! Of course, I had painstakingly taught Frank that the garden was not the place to empty his bowels! Well a pee was acceptable but not the dreaded poos!... I had worked hard over the years to get him out of that habit of just doing it in the garden. I was proud of the fact I now had a dog who appreciated his routine and was clean enough to wait till I took him up the field or out for a walk somewhere else. As much as I loved him and he was Frank, he was still a dog and they do still have to be disciplined sometimes in certain aspects. In fact, he already knew from our short walk to the field from before that he was not allowed to wee or poo until we actually got up there. He would walk right by my side to the command of "Come by" (picked that one up from "One Man and his Dog", a programme that had been on telly donkey's years ago about Sheep Dog trials . . . Showing my age now!). Turns out, this command to a dog really means run off to the left, not keep by my legs! But Frank was a blimmin' lab anyway not a sheep herder and he knew my lingo! No need for a lead, he knew his place, walking alongside me, looking up sheepishly, excuse the pun, to see if it was time for him to be "let free!" . . . Never peeing in people's houses, not a cock of a leg though he must've been bursting! . . . Then, as soon as we saw the field in view, I would make him sit, I'd lean down to wipe the sleep from his eyes (quite why, I don't know!), then I would command him to "GO!" . . . then, in a sprint he was gone, up that field and peeing for England! The field was a big one, a mix of rough, unkempt grass, bushes and tall trees at the back which signalled the start of an expansive woods behind. There were defined paths but not as tidy or clear as the local National Trust Estate which was the field's "neighbour." . . . it was **Frank's Field!** HIS back garden! Unfortunately, we had to sometimes share it with other dog walkers which was a pain as we just liked doing our own thing but there were many many times when the field just "belonged to us!" As we sauntered through it some days, it was just easy to imagine it was ours, we owned it, not a soul in sight . . . it changed with the different seasons, frosty and hard ground in the depths of Winter, soggy and slidey after downpours of rain, fresh and full of bluebells and snowdrops in Spring and just a delight to be up there in the hot Summer days! Frank and I respected and appreciated this field . . . yes, he would wee wherever, but he would take himself off into the woods, bushes or long grass to do his no. 2's! He just knew it was not nice to do on the paths or the main field . . . although this field's predominant use was for dog walkers and in the main other owners didn't care where their dogs deposited their stuff, Frank did! . . . and he liked his privacy of going off to do it alone! Of course it also meant that the majority of the time, I didn't have the hassle of picking it up in those horrible poo bags! BRILLIANT.

The little Business I had been running for the guys in London was now starting to struggle. In essence, as I had encountered in my life a lot over the years, people in the West country do not have the money, the ambition or the foresight to see or invest in something that is a great idea and my experience of their apathy in supporting this venture was another blot in my life. The money guys in London backed it for as long as they could and gave me personally what I needed to just keep it going, income and car but, creeping towards Christmas, they started to intimate that in the New Year we'd have to have crisis meets to discuss its viability. So, less than a year after moving into Paula's lovely house, and beginning to feel settled for the 1st. time in years, the business was closed down, leaving me with no income and back to driving around in the Bean Tin . . . thank God I had kept it! Paula was brilliant . . . we talked in depth and she totally understood my situation and, far from just throwing me out, she empathised and wanted to help me through this . . . yet Another step back when I had thought my life was getting back on track. She was grateful that, in me, she had found a good guy who looked after her house pristinely, as his own and, in fact, we had become Very good friends and allies in Life, despite an 18-year age difference. I respected the tribulations and sadness she had encountered in her life and in confidence I had shared my life experience with her as well. As I have said, before, in her I had found my Fairy Godmother . . . but she knew that I NEVER took her kindness and patience for granted and, although when the business closed, this meant I now effectively had no regular income stream, I reverted to getting in some print work and doing whatever I could to get by and be able to give her what I could and put food on the table. My mate, Dan, was the manager of a furniture shop so he would give me the odd Delivery job to help out and to earn a few bob . . . this was my food money! But, yes, it was back to square one mode, scratching by to earn a living . . . again though, I am a survivor and this was not going to beat me. I had been in far worse places and I WOULD get through this set back . . . and, thanks to Paula, at least I was now living in a great house, the first abode I had called "home" in 5 years! All the other places were like "stop gaps" on my journey to this place. I was happy under this roof, content and at peace in my life . . . **I had to keep it. I must.**

On the woman front, well I had been on Tinternet periodically, more OFF than ON! . . . though pretty disillusioned at this time as to would I Ever meet anyone ever again that I would be happy with? Quite honestly, with the move and the business going down, women and relationships were way down the list at this time and not a priority. I had a busy life just surviving again, still seeing my boys, keeping on top of my house and looking after Frank! Not much time to fit a relationship in there! But I did meet the odd lady and went out on dates and walks but it just seemed I couldn't or wouldn't let anyone in completely to my life . . . it was perhaps a "protection barrier" . . . I had been through so much in the previous few years and come through it and here I was, aside from the job situation, of sound mind and ALIVE! . . . I was, I guess, very wary of sharing that with anyone, letting a woman come in to mess it up, hurt me, destroy my equilibrium . . . warp my mind, take me back to the black places I had fought so hard to come away from. I don't know, I certainly didn't dwell on it or try to analyse too much . . . overthinking had been part of my downfall in the past and a contributory, negative influence. These days, I lived for the now and the future. Just One Day At a Time! But, yes, I wanted female company at times and sought it occasionally . . . being very selective this time around, I met a couple of ladies from the dating site which both developed into very nice friendships, both maintained to this day.

Then, on one of my Tinternet sessions, I was messaged by a lady whom I had known 30 plus years back! But this was a bit different because me and Steph had actually "got it together" all those years ago! . . . Though we'd never actually been an item, a mutual flirting in our youth when she was a Greeting Card Sales rep. and I a young Manager in a Newsagents, led to us popping in and out of each other's lives over the next few years ... between our respective Divorces (our first ones ... we called these early marriages our "practice runs!"). With Steph, because of the history between us, we just had a very natural, easy connection from that "first date." It didn't seem like a date, just two old friends catching up ... and lots of catching up to do, 30 plus years of stuff! We met in a local pub for a couple of drinks and, because we knew each other, decided to just cut to the chase and blurt out our highlights AND lowlights since we'd last seen each other, probably 20 odd years back! ... "2 Divorces, 2 great kids, 2 Businesses, 2 Bankruptcies" ... it seemed **2 was my theme!** ... Steph had been through the ringer too and had reached a time in her life, like me, where she was just looking for some peace and happiness, not much to ask we thought. So because of our past connection and the ease of that first night, we just from then on seemed to slip into a very comfortable, what we consistently termed "simple, uncomplicated friendship." Steph understood I was struggling again for money, scratching around to survive and now actually claiming Working Tax Credit to put food on the table! This was a Special, genuine lady who, again like me, appreciated that money doesn't make you happy anyway. Although she had a good job, she was not materialistic, had been brought up with good values and lived a simple life. We hardly ever went out but when we did I tried to pay my way but Steph and I were more content with getting out in the air to walk the dog. Oh my, did we have some tumultuous walks with that dog! That became one of our favourite words ... **Tumultuous!** Frank definitely became a major benefactor of this period in our lives as Steph and I discovered some amazing new places to walk. We got into a Very nice habit of making Sunday OUR DAY to set off early and walk most of the day. Steph and I would pre-plan our Sunday during the week, picking out a desired walk. She would print off a walking route and encapsulate it so it was weatherproof. On the Sunday she would pack up a little picnic (I'd provide the water and choccie bars!). Walking gear on, away we'd go! We would mix it up a bit, perhaps one week a coastal walk, the next maybe on the moors. But wherever we went, it was a New adventure, an exploration of the simple pleasures that the countryside holds. We covered a lot of the South West Coastal Path, a fair chunk of Dartmoor and on a couple of occasions went away for the weekend, camping once at Talland Bay, near Looe and another time Steph found this idyllic little holiday chalet in Marazion, not far from St. Michael's Mount in Cornwall . . . we called it our little Love Shack! We had a few amazing walks around the Tamar Valley, one in particular where Frank went on a train for the first time! Excellent stuff. Wherever we went Steph was happy to take Frank . . . in fact she insisted as he was a massive part of what we did together. She had owned dogs before and missed having one now so Frank sort of filled that gap for her perhaps. She thought the world of him and I am sure the feeling was mutual . . . after all, he was getting some fantastic exercise and fun from all this! When we camped at Talland, Steph borrowed a tent that had a "Special bedroom compartment just for Frank!" That was a great weekend . . . the walk around that beautiful bay and encompassing Looe seemed to go on forever and we were shattered at the end of the day. So, despite the fact we had brought plenty of wine to drink in the tent, we broke one of our spending rules and decided we deserved a few drinks up at the noisy club house on the holiday camp . . . not really our style but we joined all the crazy campers and mingled in, getting quietly drunk and singing along to the, let's say, adequate camp entertainment! . . . Of course, as parents, we had both been there and done all this stuff with our kids as they were growing up so knew what to expect. It's funny that the more we drank, the funnier the comedian's jokes were and the better the singing was! Could have been Michael McIntyre and Frank Sinatra on that stage for all we knew! . . . At the end of the night, in our happy, drunken state, we meandered our way, arm in arm back through the camp to somehow find our palatial . . . Tent! Frank had been brilliant as we knew he would be and had stayed quietly in his "bedroom" . . . well he'd had a ten odd mile walk so think he was shattered too . . . Though Not drunk, like us!

So me and Steph shared some great, great times. But more than that, we just revisited and took up to another level the bond we had all those years back. This time, we were grown adults who both had been through so much to bring us together at this stage of our lives. Steph understood me, supported me, shared all that I was going through at this time . . . and, simply **JUST GOT ME!** She, above anyone in my whole life, just accepted Me for who I am, faults, weaknesses, my past, all of it; she just wanted ME in her life unconditionally . . . what a Lovely Lady. I in turn, supported her as best I could. In the time we were together, she was going through the sale of her family home . . . a place she had lived in practically all her adult life, brought up her kids in and a place that held many memories for her. After a lot of soul searching, Steph had decided she had to sell now that her kids had grown up and it made so much sense for her now to change her life, sell while she could make a little bit of money (after paying off her ex) and now rent a much smaller place where she could be in control of her future. Having lost My house, albeit in different circumstances, I could help Steph through this emotional occurrence in her life. It was a massive decision for her and, like in my situation, contained the dividing "boxes" of Practical and Emotional. I helped her with this . . . we both cleared the garden and did a couple of dump trips and, of course, I was a shoulder for her when she hit those inevitable black moments in this life changing event. These reciprocate supportive feelings just came naturally for us both and were unconditional in our relationship.

Yes, it also became a physical relationship too. Especially Sundays after our tumultuous walks! We just relaxed into the evening, praising ourselves for our achievement that day and "celebrating" with a few wines to boot!

In all, it was in lots of ways a perfect relationship really . . . Two people that had developed a friendship into a seemingly beautiful relationship that encompassed contentment and satisfaction on many levels . . . intellectually, humorously, physically. What more could I want? But, then, despite this being something in my life that was really good, special, I go and just destroy it. It was never as simple as that and in my defence, I just had to be totally honest with Steph, as I always had been . . . there was Just Something missing for me, I wasn't feeling the fireworks and, after 11 odd months together I thought I should be blindingly in love with her. Whatever Love meant at our age? I certainly loved what we had, craved it even, the affection, the caring, the quality time we spent together, talking, sharing, walking (100's of miles of walking!), . . . Malc, "what the fuck more do you want from life after all you've been through?" . . . We used to say WDFK . . . Who Da Fuck Knows! . . . So apt. But based on my insecurities, indecision, doubts, whatever, I called it off . . . let her go, told her I had to for both our sakes. **FUCKWIT!** IT has been a decision I have lived to regret as I have profoundly missed Steph and all that we shared. I have discovered feelings for her that I just could not or wouldn't embrace in our time together . . . bloody idiot, bloody LIFE.

Meanwhile, things had picked up on the income front. I actually got one of those job things! I had obviously been applying for lots of things whilst scratching around on Working Tax credits etc., had a couple of unsuccessful interviews and then, finally, got myself in front of a Printers who saw the benefit in taking someone on with my experience and credentials. They gave me a chance to get "back out there!" Good, established, family run business, MD looking to retire soon so my role was to work in liaison with the Son to take the Business forward. Excellent, all positive . . . could not have come at a better time for me as my Self- esteem and confidence had started to dive towards the bottom again and I was abundantly aware of the Black places those emotions can take you. I NEVER want to sink that low again. I was still with Steph when I got the job (this was a few months before our split). She, again, was so super supportive. She just boosted my moral and gave me the belief that I could do this, I could get this . . . or any job . . . she erased my doubts. For the record again, THANKYOU so much Steph for that. I would not have pulled it off without her. On my first day, this company presented me with a brand new car, new laptop and all the other bits n' bobs I needed to hit the ground running . . . a sign they believed in Me and trusted and respected me. I remember driving home at the end of that day; I called Steph and she just knew, telepathically, how I was feeling and that she needed to drop everything and come round to mine. I got home, within minutes she was there. And I just cried like a baby in her arms, just completely overwhelmed by this tumultuous day's events. SHE more than anyone in my life at that time, knew where I had "been" in the last few years and what a massive turnaround to my life this signalled now. Though not a big wage, (in fact, I had been on the SAME wage the last time I had been employed over a decade ago!) perhaps now with regular monthly income coming in I could start to pay my way properly again, pay back some of the people I had borrowed from to survive, eat better, get me teeth done(!),buy better wine(!), clothes . . . who knows, maybe have one of those holiday things again . . . but, most importantly, get my Pride and esteem back to where it should be. Yes, a gigantic day for me and the emotions just took me over. But she was there to share it. Thank you again Steph, a wonderful lady.

Having made that monumental decision to let Steph go, I simultaneously decided that if I didn't want her, let's JUMP straight out of that frying pan into the Fire! . . . Went back on Tinternet. Idiot! Predominantly out of curiosity initially, to see who was still on there, who wasn't . . . who was in the pond! I came across Louise, a lady whom I had "spoken" to on there around 3 years previously . . . in fact, She had rejected me back then because her observation, and rightly so, was that I "was not in the right place" for a relationship. She had just picked up on that reading between the lines of my messages I guess. But, now things were different, weren't they? My mind was sorted, I wasn't depressed, I had no hang ups about my Ex anymore and, yes, I had a job now with money coming in . . . Surely I was right to cast my net again? And if I didn't want Steph, surely I wanted someone else? Yeh, I must do . . . come on Louise, give me a chance to show you I am not the nutter you spoke to 3 years ago! After a bit of persuading, Louise agreed to meet me! We got on great and we jumped like a bull in a China Shop head first into a whirlwind, action-packed relationship . . . perhaps TOO quick! We hadn't even come up for air really after the 1st. month of going out, throw in a Christening, an Engagement Party and endless wine drinking! . . . Then it was Christmas to boot and, well, let's just say 2 months in the cracks were showing . . . or the drink was wearing off! We parted over Christmas and that was that . . . my first taste of the "outside world" so to speak since my year or so with Steph.

After this, I guess I just gave up on having a proper relationship again. Happy to have female friends, old and new ones, whom I talked and walked with, shared quality time. Maybe I was scared to commit. Was I really "CURED" from my past, or had the mistakes, hurt, setbacks, mistiming etc. etc. tainted me for life, perhaps making me immune to EVER committing again? . . . Who knows?

ALL I really knew at that time was that I had to JUST focus on keeping positive, keep my confidence levels up, beat the insecure demons that sporadically jumped into my head and draw on all my strength to keep this job, keep the house and somehow forge a future for me . . . AND FRANK! After all, I had discovered by now that, quite frankly, the thing that I enjoyed the most, the simplest pleasure in my life was spending time with That DOG! . . . Pressure at work, stress, financial worries, loneliness, they just all paled into insignificance when we just got "out there" . . . my life was full of hang ups, complexities, worries and concerns and the weeks just went by at 100 miles an hour, but when I took that dog out, it just all didn't matter. A dog just wants to be walked, just needs to get out in that fresh air and embrace the simple, easy pleasures of just living! Why the hell can't we all be dogs? . . .

We lived for 3 years at 99 but then Life was changing and evolving. Mine, My Sons, Paula's, even Frank's! He was 8 now (8 x 7 = 56, apparently that's the way they work it out for dogs?). He'd actually caught me up and surpassed me in years! Still a Puppy at heart and bounding around as if he was one! However, the reality was Frank, with now a little tint of grey on his chin, was in the Prime of his life. I WAS abundantly aware that he was heading towards the "run in" . . . by my research on this, perhaps had another 3 or 4 years tops left in him. I had read that labs live on average to 11 / 12. Ok, he was in great health and all the walking, exercise, routine and love had paid off. He was a magnificent animal, so strong and vibrant. He could live even longer than that average, maybe 15 or 16 I was told. Whatever, at this stage of his life, I had decided I just wanted to make the most of the quality time I had left with him... **ANOTHER MOVE, ANOTHER CHANGE OF LIFE WAS IMMINENT!**...

Chapter Nine

The Journey Ends

Eight years old, 56 in real Money! . . . But Dogs have no perception of age, no thoughts about getting older, have absolutely no awareness of the concept. Their mind set NEVER changes from the day they come into this world. They eat, they sleep, they wee and poo . . . They play, swim and have as much fun as they are allowed. And they just Run, Run and Run! They simply just **Live for the moment**. They grasp every bit of excitement they can and don't let anything beat them. Well, that was my experience with Frank anyway . . . this dog had been a character from the day we first picked him out of that litter as the dog for us! The one that stood out in a crowd, the most boisterous, mischievous and with a zest for life that we could all learn from! Nothing had changed throughout his whole life really . . . if you took him out for ten minutes he'd love it, ran and ran . . . if you took him for 10 hours, he still didn't stop! And at 8 years old, he was still showing off, capturing everyone's hearts with his Party trick of diving down in the deep water to retrieve a stone! Loved it, couldn't keep him out of the water. I got huge pleasure in seeing people watch in awe at this dog, swimming like a seal and surfacing around 10/11 seconds later! To be honest, I would more and more find myself purposely taking him to the places I knew he loved doing this. There was one place on the moors where he dived off the wall and belly flopped into the water! It was great to excel in the expressions on people's faces at this unique sight. When he did it in the sea at the beach it was also comical to see the waves wash him in as if he was bodyboarding! He loved it. "Mister, your dog's drowning!" or "I cannot believe what that dog just did" . . . "Never ever seen a dog do that before!" . . . these were a few of the observations from the many people I saw on my walks. He became a little celebrity locally and I am sure he too lapped up the attention.

As I said before, life for us all was moving on though and, as settled as I was now, in the house, job and, most importantly, in my mind(!), circumstances were about to dictate Yet another move for me and Frank . . .

The thing is TIME takes care of so many things and everybody's lives evolve with age and maturity . . . we all hope anyway! Both my boys had now turned into strapping young men, both of whom were enjoying life to the full, discovering what it's all about and carving out futures. Careers, partners . . . it was all taking shape for them. They still popped in and out of my life when they could and we had (always will have) a close relationship. The Chels and football generally brought us together and will always provide quality, bonding time for us . . . whatever happens in all our lives or wherever we live! We have had some pivotal Pizza nights watching the Chels and visited the home of football, Stamford Bridge on many an occasion! My communication with my Ex Wife had now reached that very comfortable, perfect place that a broken marriage has to reach eventually . . . a place where you can be friendly, without necessarily being best friends . . . a place where the only contact you need to have is purely about vital things concerning the boys and nothing else. This too had become extremely minimal now the boys were men, both driving, working and pretty independent really. So all in all, **time had done its job** and, hopefully, all the bad times way and far behind in the past. So it was a time for me to reflect, consider and try to perhaps plan **MY** future, look at what I really wanted from this perennial prime time in my life. I had to be very pragmatic and an absolute realist at this time . . . financially I was still not as stable as perhaps I should be at this time of my life. My ups and downs, decisions, misjudgements, whatever, had left me with no savings, pensions, assets . . . nothing really! Had it, lost it, was never going to get it all again . . . didn't really want it really! It don't make you any happier and you can't take it with you . . . But, you do need a certain amount of money to get by and, in my 50's, if I was lucky I had another 15 / 20 years to provide for myself and carve out a life, yeh? . . .

In my marriage, we had always said we'd retire to Cornwall, a little place by the Sea. Well, this notion had stayed with me. I had Always loved the sea, the coastline and my explorations with Frank had just further fuelled this dream. Now, it was to become a stark possibility that I could "finish our journey" in this way. As I said, reality had to kick in and what I was now considering was a caravan, a static somewhere. . . . I knew I wouldn't be able to afford anything fantastic . . . some of these dwellings could cost as much as a Real house . . . £150k upwards but these were not in my league! I'm a man that had learnt to live frugally, basically and just needed a roof above my head to operate from. So I needed something nice but within, let's say . . . a very modest budget!

. . . And WE found it! . . . and it turned out to be in Devon and not Cornwall after all! But still by the sea. About a year before we moved, I came back into contact with another lady I had met about 3 years previously. . . . and, yes, I DID meet her on the Tinternet Site! Tracey had "popped" up again on there and we rekindled a friendship with a few drinks, some lovely dog walks and a bit of gardening, would you believe? Me . . . gardening! Well, on one of our days out, she took me out to Bigbury on the South Devon coast where her Brother owned a caravan and, in fact, she'd been to the site many times with a view to buying one herself. Well I was smitten with the area, the site, the beach and the many walks around the coast from there . . . a lot of them managed by the South West Coast Path in liaison with the National Trust and other organisations (both of which I had joined!) . . . it had become a "Bucket List" entry to walk the whole 630 miles of the South West Coast Path . . . before Frank, or me, or both of us died!

Well, let's cut a long story short here . . . we (me and Frank) found our perfect caravan, just big enough for the two of us and it had a small spare room for my boys to come and stay whenever they wanted and, in fact, that's just what happened! This site was only about 45 minutes from Plymouth, but just far enough for it to become an "escape" for them! . . . almost a "Safe House" away from their girlfriends, family, their problems and stresses. Even to get away from their mates, work and, just to give them an alternative lifestyle for a few days, sometimes just a few hours! I'd had a huge worry that This move might damage our closeness but, in reality, the distance thing actually brought us closer together because when they visited now, they had to make a concerted effort to get there or just a spontaneous urge to escape and be with their Dad! Of course, there were visits with their girlfriends too, the "normal" family stuff but, in the main, it was Tom or Daniel on their own, sometimes together, just popping out to see their old man and lap up some of the idyllic Country lifestyle and embrace the pure simplicity of it all!

It was a completely **New** life out there in the country, by the sea. My love affair with this lifestyle had been pushed along by my relationship with my dog. Since leaving home several years prior, Frank and what we did together had become the pivotal aspect in my life. As I have said before, re –evaluating my values and learning that the simple, natural, pure things in life are the happiest ones. This made this move (the Final move) that much easier.

Conscious that Frank was now in the prime of his life, I wanted to share as much time as possible with him and, let's not deny it, I had probably reached my Prime time too! Of course, as always, he knew his boundaries, we had our routines, strong and good habits I had got him trained into from an early age that had made him such a well behaved, respectful dog. But now living in a caravan, albeit a lovely caravan, gave us the chance to live on the one level . . . space was a bit more limited and as a result, I allowed Frank to have the run of the place, do his own thing, be in the lounge with me evenings, though he still had his bed area and I didn't allow him on the sofa ALL the time . . . and the bedroom was, as ever, totally out of bounds to him! I guess I just mellowed a lot more and decided that now he was getting older, he deserved a bit more of my time and affection. He always knew he was loved but in the old house he had his living area and I had mine and that worked with my busy lifestyle and my paranoia about keeping that house tidy and clean. I was still busy of course and worked long hours but now, on the days (generally a couple a week) that I worked from home, he could be near me and have my company, as well as in the evenings. It just brought us even closer together and the bond grew stronger.

Over the years, Frank and I had shared many momentous walks. Yes, there were a lot of the "routine" ones, the morning / evening ones, before and after work but we had discovered some amazing places to walk, coast and country. Of course, my enthusiasm to explore more and find new walks had really been inspired by my time with Steph and the quality of our days out in that period. Now, at the caravan, we were surrounded by beautiful coast and countryside and, even the routine walks were a joy . . . and I have to say, became longer and longer! Weekends and Spring / Summer evenings were ALL about my time with Frank and we just covered so much ground over the years. Sometimes I would just plot a walk, chuck Frank in the back of the Bean Tin and go for it! Occasionally we'd go further afield and jump on a train and camp away for the weekend . . . Just me and my dog. We visited Snowdon, and walked it, up and down (I'd done that years before with friends but never with Frank!), the Lake District, a week in Scotland and, of course, the many and varied walks in Devon and Cornwall . . . covered even more of the beautiful South West Coast Path.

But of course, inevitably Frank was getting older and, as much as he was a "Puppy" in his head and heart, his body was showing the signs of old age. People said to me I perhaps should've cut back on the walking, the excessive exercising . . . I disagreed profusely as I had a dog here that just Did Not want that, he didn't want to stop or curtail his activity. **Every** walk for him was like his first one and you could see the excitement in him, that "helicopter" big black tail swirling around at ten to the dozen! As I have said before, if you gave him 10 minutes he ran and ran . . . if you were out for 10 hours, he'd never stop, always on the go, thrived on it, craved it. LIVED LIFE TO THE FULL! . . . And this amazing dog "dragged" **me** along to keep up with **him,** much to my absolute Pleasure! . . . No, Frank and I shared the same positive view on life, that it is too short to be boring . . . get out there and Smell it!

In fact, this dog had been extremely healthy ALL his life and, thank God, had cost me little or nothing in Vet's fees because of that! It was only when he reached 11, about 3 years after the move to the sea, that I noticed any sign of infirmity in him . . . as is quite normal with the breed, he just started to become a little slower in his movement (on occasion, not all the time). He was going a bit deaf . . . or was he just pushing his luck Even more when he didn't answer my calls to "Come here Frank" when right over the other side of the field and I was in a hurry to get back! . . . He never strayed too far from my view but had always tried to extend his walk as much as possible! As he was getting older, his "selective hearing" became more apparent! His legs were showing signs of arthritis and there were days I could see he was suffering a little. But we both soldiered on . . . I was in my late fifties and I too was full of aches and pains, sciatica always a niggle and, yes, not as sprightly as I had been. The pair of us were determined old sods though and we carried on regardless, 2 decent walks a day, topped up by the **tumultuous "Memory Makers"** at the weekends!

However, there was this ONE pivotal day when I woke up in the morning to take him out as normal but he simply did not want to get up. I didn't think too much about it at first as Frank never got up straightaway, never really stirred at all as he waited for me to "be ready" for him. This, he knew, involved me going through my own morning routine before I got to him! We had gone through the SAME routine for so many years that we were BOTH conditioned to it by now! Switching on my computer, checking e-mails, going through my OCD controlled checks around the caravan, tidying this, tidying that, all this whilst the kettle was on to make that vital FIRST cup of tea of the morning which I always took out with me on our walk! SO, cup in hand, this was normally the cue for Frank to bound out of his bed and head for the door but today, nothing, not a movement, not a whimper. He just lied there lifeless with no intention to move. He was awake, those big, deep brown eyes glaring at me. They still had the life in them of a puppy but the body was not having any of it. I reached down to pat him on the head gently, trying to coax him softly from his bed. "Come on Frank, it's morning mate, it's YOUR favourite time of the day, come on, let's be having you!" . . . But still nothing, a hint of a yawn but his body was just like a stone, as if he was attached to that bed. I stroked his fur, got down on my knees to be at his level and just carried on talking to him. It was at this point, I realised a few spots of blood on his blue bedding, nothing major, just a couple of stains really next to him. I didn't panic at first but then, after stroking him some more, his body moved a little off the cushion and this revealed a bigger stain of blood near the end of his bed . . . this was fresh and was A LOT of it. Now I was worried. Somehow though, he got himself to his feet and dawdled towards the door . . . HE was not letting this, whatever it was, beat him. He WAS having his morning walk! Okay, it took longer to get him out and he wasn't himself but, once we got up to the grass, he was gone, as usual! Over into the long, rough grass and did his stuff. As usual, sniffing around for England and, generally, running as best he could. I kept looking at him to see if he was okay . . . but he was adamant, seeing out his walk in his normal vibrant way. But on our return walk, he slowed up again. This wasn't hugely unusual as he had Never wanted to come home from a walk! This was different though . . . On THAT walk he looked like an old dog to me, for the first time ever really. I had never looked at him in this light before. As he walked sluggishly, I noticed very small specs of blood dripping from his stomach area, almost like he'd just grazed himself on a bush or something. But, of course, I sensed it was more than that. I got him back to the caravan and went through the normal routine of rubbing him down with his favourite towel and then putting his food down. I wouldn't say he waffed it back as normal but he certainly cleared his bowl . . . eventually!

However, I knew he wasn't right and I decided I had to get him to the Vet... Made the call and got him booked in for later that morning. I Decided to take him in the Bean tin rather than my Company car. He'd been in that many times by now but, it just seemed right that THIS JOURNEY was done in "his" car. I let him sit in the front with me this time, which was normally only a treat saved for our trips to the Dump or when I was really feeling in a good mood! As always, he revelled in this, sitting up proudly and sniffing out of the open window, taking in the fresh Spring air. He just sat there proudly staring ahead, looking magnificent and quite regal, watching the road ahead as if he was my navigator!

We got to the Vets in about 40 minutes... though I had not had to use a Vet much over the years, I decided to use the one where we'd had him vaccinated as a pup and I had been to a few times, perhaps 3 or 4 in Frank's life. I had no real loyalty to them, though I did know a lady that had worked there for years on Reception and she had been the reason for us using that particular Vet in the first instance. On this day, as fate would have it, Tracie was working... she booked us in and said hello to Frank. I had over the years gone out with Tracie for the occasional walk with her and her faithful Border Collier, Maddie, to whom she was doted to until Mads had died a couple of years prior. Trace knelt down to pat Frank and give him a cuddle; she saw the faint stains of blood on his otherwise still Jet black body. Outwardly, the only signs this magnificent dog was ageing were the giveaway grey streaks under his chin and around his mouth. Apart from that, you would Never know he was a nearly 12-year-old dog. "You're looking good Frank, are you still swimming and diving for stones?" Trace remembered Frank's party trick from our walks and how mesmerized she had been at seeing this. As she got up from the floor after giving him lots of attention, she just glanced at me, knowingly, as if to say "You ok too, Malc?" ...

We went into see the Vet, a small, softly spoken lady in her early 60's I would say. She introduced herself and I did remember seeing her once or twice before on a visit there but, unsurprisingly, she didn't remember us... at first. Fiona beckoned Frank to a canvas mat near her surgery table . . . she could already see he was Not happy to be in her environment! Like me, he just didn't do sickness; I don't do hospitals, he hated Vets! But she was great with him and settled him relatively quickly, starting to examine his tired body. She saw the specs of blood and felt his under carriage gently, looked into his eyes and mouth, all the normal stuff. Then, whilst she was doing this, she suddenly exclaimed loudly and excitedly . . . "I KNOW who you are Frank! You're that dog that swims like a Seal aren't you? . . . I've seen you on Facebook and I have had lots of people in this Surgery telling me about the famous Diving Dog!" . . . She was talking to him, NOT ME, as if he was human. Well of course **I Knew** he was but I didn't know anyone else did! Frank seemed to know what she was saying and instinctively starting to wag his tail and lick her profusely! That Happy tail, the helicopter blade . . . yep, that had been in only second gear recently, but this brought a smile to the old boy's face! Fiona had to compose herself and get her professionalism back in check now! . . . She turned to me and said, "can we have a word." I knew it wasn't going to be good news. The fact she then asked me to come away from Frank and out of his view while she talked to me meant a lot to me as she was respecting Frank in a human way after the "chat" she'd just had with him and didn't want him to hear this conversation. "It's not good Mr. Collier . . . I can feel an obvious growth; I am certain it is the latter stages of a large tumour in Frank's stomach . . . He is an incredible dog in that he seems to have 'HIDDEN' the symptoms of this disease until he was ready to share it with you . . . and he was ready to accept it for himself." I had told her before the examination began that Frank had not been particularly unwell, I had often felt for lumps and found nothing. My friend from Gables (Cats & Dogs Home) had also checked him out regularly on our visits there and no signs of this illness whatsoever. She had told me that dogs can deteriorate quite quickly with tumours and not necessarily show any symptoms to the last minute but they'd normally have some indication of sickness in the final run in. He'd obviously got tireder as he got older but had still carried out his normal walks, lost no weight and only really been sick or had diarrhoea on the very odd occasion. Nope, until perhaps this last few days and, specifically, TODAY, Frank was in fine form. It was as if Today, for whatever reason, he decided it was time to "come clean" . . . none of this labouring the point, playing the victim malarkey, just got on with it! Fiona explained that, despite his braveness, this dog must be in dire pain inside as the tumour was well advanced. She confirmed this with an X-Ray and then gave me the obvious options. It was a "Marley and Me" moment . . . that point in the film where John Grogan is told it's a choice of (in Marley's case) another op (think he'd had a couple before that point) or to gently put the dog out of its misery. In John's case, Marley had shown signs of old age and illness, preparing him and his family for the inevitable . . . but in this situation, although I knew this day had to come ONE day, FRANK had not let on, just given me no indication, till TODAY! But hadn't we lived our lives like this eh? Me and that dog had given life Everything we could together these last few years and EVERY DAY had been special and vibrant. We'd made the most of it . . . TOGETHER! He didn't want that, those memories to be blemished, spoilt by a long illness, a dragging out of the misery.

"Ok Fiona, I understand what you're saying, I really do . . . but could, if possible, could you just give me TODAY, one LAST day with him? Some stuff we need to do, is that ok?" . . . Fiona understood but reluctantly agreed and the compromise was I would get him back there for evening Surgery, no later than 8p.m. when she finished her shift. ALL THIS time I had been talking to her, Frank had layed quietly on the mat. He KNEW, he just KNEW we had been discussing him. And I think he knew what was coming . . .

"Come on boy", I softly whispered to him . . . "let's get out of here, stuff to do." I didn't put his lead on to walk him out . . . didn't need to; he just walked close to my side, only looking up to acknowledge Tracie as she stroked him. She didn't say good bye, didn't say anything. She gave me a hug and could see the tears welling up in my eyes. She just nodded her head and we went out the door to the car. Do you know what, that bloody dog still jumped into that seat and resumed his proud, pole position in the assistant Driver's seat! I was crying but I had to contain myself to drive and, after all, I was in the company of the bravest animal in the whole world at this moment so how COULD I crumble!

I knew what I had to do . . . where we had to go for one last time, well 2 places actually. Before we got going, I called 6 People . . . My boys and their Mum, Steph, Ruth from Gables and Paula. I explained what had happened and what I was doing now. They ALL agreed to drop everything, work, whatever and meet me at what had been Frank's favourite diving place! . . . a local walking track, down by the river. We all met, as agreed at the Car Park by the bridge. I wanted them all to see Frank for the last time and, more importantly, if I COULD get him in, witness his Last swim! I know I was pushing it but I just sensed this is what **HE** wanted. He loved it so much, his favourite thing! Tears flowing all around, everyone was assembled at the bridge and Frank just lapped up the attention, AS ALWAYS! He knew where he was going and he wasn't going to let no fatal tumour stop him from having a dip! It was an eclectic mix of people, but to be fair, ALL the people in his life that at one stage or another had been REALLY close to him and cared about him. Especially Steph, whom I had that Special relationship with and shared some wonderful, quality time with this dog. It was great to see her again, albeit in sad circumstances. As I had always done, I let him off his lead once we'd got into the woods . . . it was remarkable, like this dog was oblivious to pain, as if he was half his age! He careered off into the wild bushes to do his stuff, as was his habit and the discipline I had taught him. With the exception of Steph, none of the others knew his routine on our walks and, for them the best was to come! Whilst we walked, we all talked exclusively about Frank, the Wonder dog! EVERYONE shared their memories of him and their love of the happiness he had brought into all our lives . . . BUT THEY ALL KNEW, he was MY dog ultimately, my best friend, the one thing that had been CONSTANT in MY life all these years.

Well, again by habit, Frank found his favourite "watering hole", the part of the river he loved the most. There was a little "beach" clearing next to a quite deep part of the river that was flanked by some trees. The Spring Sun was shining through the branches and onto the water and created what was like a natural "spotlight" for Frank to swim into! . . . And he didn't let us down. Quite by instinct, he sprinted into the water, swam out to the deep bit and did his dive! Sure enough, surfaced with a large stone in his mouth and swam back out to present it to us! They were ALL amazed and could not believe what he'd just done . . . Steph just smiled with pleasant satisfaction. Tears overtaken her by now, she just looked at him admiringly. I let him do it a couple more times, then it was time to get back. It took a little while to make that sombre walk back to the Car park but I was determined to let Frank enjoy every minute of it and lap up the air. Back at the car, again, he didn't let me down but jumped into his seat after a brief rub down. I opened the window so his head could peak out to lap up the goodbye pats from everyone. Not much was said between us all but they knew what was happening next. I drove off with Frank, leaving behind me a barrage of tears and 6 distraught people.

BUT this last part was just between me and Frank. "Well mate, here we go . . . there is ONE place I know you want to see for one last time isn't there?" . . . he just looked at me but if he COULD talk . . . I drove Back to Where it All began . . . THE FIELD, up that hill just up from the old house we'd lived in, where he'd had his VERY FIRST proper walk and many others after that! We parked up and he now stepped out of the car, carefully, rather than jumping. He looked around, looked at me and then we walked together, side by side towards the entrance to the field. Somehow, he managed to climb up that steep hill where we stopped to rest near the top. We sat, together, overlooking the view . . . silently, in awe of . . . EVERYTHING . . . after what seemed like an eternity, IT WAS TIME . . .

"Frank, I love you and I always will. THANKYOU for what you've brought to my life; you saved me Mate, I COULDN'T have done it without you . . . We've been through so much together; you've seen it all! People have come and gone but you, YOU have been with me throughout. You've taught me so much Frank, I'll be eternally grateful for that and I'll never forget you mate . . . but we have to go now" . . .

He really DID NOT want to leave that place . . . he just wanted to hold onto his last time there. By now, he was weak from his day's exploits and had pushed himself to his limit. I just couldn't hold back the tears now. They were streaming down my face as I virtually carried him down that hill to the Bean Tin . . . now having to lift him into his seat for the journey back to the Vets . . .

***OUR LAST PART OF OUR JOURNEY TOGETHER* . . .**

I found this story by a Vet on a link to a website . . . it is quite apt to the end of my story . . .

*　*　*

Being a veterinarian, I had been called to examine a ten-year-old Irish wolfhound named Belker. The dog's owners, Ron, his wife, Lisa, and their little boy, Shane, were all very attached to Belker, and they were hoping for a miracle.

I examined Belker and found he was dying of cancer. I told the family we couldn't do anything for Belker, and offered to perform the euthanasia procedure for the old dog in their home.

As we made arrangements, Ron and Lisa told me they thought it would be good for six-year-old Shane to observe the procedure. They felt as though Shane might learn something from the experience. The next day, I felt the familiar catch in my throat as Belker's family surrounded him. Shane seemed so calm, petting the old dog for the last time, that I wondered if he understood what was going on. Within a few minutes, Belker slipped peacefully away.

The little boy seemed to accept Belker's transition without any difficulty or confusion. We sat together for a while after Belker's Death, wondering aloud about the sad fact that animal lives are shorter than human lives.

Shane, who had been listening quietly, piped up, "I know why."

Startled, we all turned to him. What came out of his mouth next stunned me. I'd never heard a more comforting explanation. It has changed the way I try and live.

He said, "People are born so that they can learn how to live a good life—like loving everybody all the time and being nice, right?" The Six-year-old continued,

"Well, dogs already know how to do that, so they don't have to stay as long."

AUTHOR UNKNOWN.

__Remember, if a dog was the teacher you would learn things like:__

When loved ones come home, always run to greet them.

Never pass up the opportunity to go for a joyride.

Allow the experience of fresh air and the wind in your face to be pure Ecstasy.

Take naps.

Stretch before rising.

Run, romp, and play daily.

Thrive on attention and let people touch you.

Avoid biting when a simple growl will do.

On warm days, stop to lie on your back on the grass.

On hot days, drink lots of water and lie under a shady tree.

When you're happy, dance around and wag your entire body.

Delight in the simple joy of a long walk.

Be loyal.

Never pretend to be something you're not.

If what you want lies buried, dig until you find it.

When someone is having a bad day, be silent, sit close by, and nuzzle them gently."

AUTHOR UNKNOWN.

"I AM HEALED, I FORGIVE MYSELF, I FORGIVE OTHERS THAT HAVE BETRAYED OR JUDGED ME. I HAVE FOUND A WAY TO DEAL WITH MY PAST. I LIKE **ME** NOW; I NEVER USED TO. I AM A SIMPLE MAN LOOKING FOR SIMPLE HAPPINESS. IT COSTS NOTHING AT ALL, IT NEVER DID. I KNOW THAT NOW! I AM AT PEACE".

Malcolm Collier

money can't buy healing, health and wellness

money can't buy happiness, love, joy

money can't buy clarity, grounding, faith

money can't buy friendship, truth, respect

although; money can buy fancy shoes, new clothes and a trip to the moon

but how long will that fleeting moment last?

find something deeper, something of substance, something real

eternal happiness, that's the kind that comes from within

it's worth your time investing in:

in side you

inside you

AUTHOR UNKNOWN.

Afterword

If mine IS a unique tale and no one out there can relate to what I have gone through and experienced, I apologise for my ramblings! But, this is **my** story, the truth of what I have experienced since leaving my family and my home. I do so much hope that, perhaps, maybe it will help others in this situation. . . . to show that there is Always light at the end of the tunnel. Even when you are at your lowest low, in the darkest, gloomiest, saddest place in your life, there is hope and something, some other life out there. I have learnt so much about myself, life, human nature and know that no matter what, adversity can be turned into positivity even though sometimes it can seem impossible! My life is far from settled even now and perhaps never will be. There are still so many things I would like to do, to learn, to experience but maybe will run out of time trying to achieve them all! For now, though, I remain content that I have come through the worst possible stage of my life . . . AND SURVIVED to tell the tale! I now, on a daily basis, play the GLAD GAME . . . Glad to still be here, glad to have my two special sons in my life, glad to have my health, my own teeth and hair still(!), glad to appreciate life and have the opportunity to make the best of it I can . . . NO LONGER THE **SAD** GAME! . . .

And GLAD for Red Wine!

PEOPLE . . . people are important . . . I have mentioned a few of the people in my circles but there are many more that have dipped in and out of my life. People can shape your life and, as everything happens for a reason, every person (and dog) that comes into your life, whether for 5 minutes, 5 months or many years, I believe also makes an appearance to bring something in for you to learn from. I today have a very open mind about anyone I meet or who wants to "come in." I have to admit, my experiences have made me super wary of everybody and their agendas but I also know that they could, potentially, "bring something to the table" and could enhance my life. Equally, they could encourage damage or negativity but, to be honest, think I have learnt to spot ***those*** ones pretty quickly! I have made myself strong again and I don't let others take ME over anymore; I have spent far too many years in my life doing just that, trying to play the role that was expected of me. I'm not arrogant or selfish . . . God, haven't got a selfish bone in my body. I just don't do anything anymore I don't want to do just because I think I have to, to make people around me happy. Though curtailed by money, I still can be my own man and as independent as possible.

EVERYTHING happens for a reason, even the shit stuff! . . . Having learnt so much about me, people and life, I feel now, finally, I have found a kind of peace, an acceptance of everything that has happened and, indeed, of what the future holds. That is of course still uncertain, my path is not entirely clear but now that I know you don't Have to "take on the world", I can go about dealing with my future with a sense of nonchalance if you like. Not an I DON'T CARE attitude, just one of not worrying too much or planning out the future because I don't think that helps. I am very task orientated, organised and, yes, plan my daily time out to get things done but I don't look months or years ahead anymore or stress over the future. It will be what it'll be. It's all mapped out for you anyway! One Day at a Time . . .

I spent far too long "serving a sentence" for the life crimes I felt I'd committed. It almost seems like I went to "Prison" for years and, now, having done my time, I am now in rehab! A lot of that time, especially in the first two or three years after the split, I just thought the whole world hated me and I had to somehow make it up to them. I felt alienated, depressed, so out of everything, a hermit. I would peak at Facebook, don't use it avidly and just scroll down the Wall to see all of the people I know just LIVING their lives ... Without Me in it, doing normal things that I was not part of like I had always been in the past; socialising, parties, gatherings, eating out, weekends away, holidays. It was like the world had forgotten me, parked me, left me behind. A leper, an alien with rabies ... don't invite him to the party, you'll catch depression or something ... Paranoia, I know, but I just didn't think I fitted in anymore, lost all confidence to mix with people in social situations.

There is a lot of content in this book I have managed to keep intensely private until now. It has been a massive, soul searching decision to put all this down on paper and share it with the world. But for me, this has been a therapy, a guiding light, my reminder to myself that we Are all on a journey that has its trials and tribulations but, with perseverance and lessons learnt along the way, can lead to a better place. Revisiting all the things I have been through has allowed me to properly destroy my demons, by exposing them again then eradicating them forever. Writing intensely about my past now allows me to bury that past and not live in it as, again, I think I probably did for far too long. I have found peace in my mind, heart and soul now and, in achieving that, know that everything else will eventually fall into place. I have a faith now in my future that was not at all prevalent in my troubled times. There were times I didn't think I had a future.

I have learnt to LIKE myself, respect myself for my past and how I have lived my life. I don't like or condone some of the things I have done in my life, but I have learnt from them and the effect they have had on other people. I have done some bad things but I am NOT a BAD person. It took me a long time to realise that. I am a Good person who cares for and loves those that are special to me and always tries to do the best for them. That word **learn** is pivotal. The secret to life is learning and continuing to learn by our mistakes, misdemeanours, misjudgements and bad decisions. I never have and never will forgive myself for any hurt I have caused to anyone, my Ex Wife and children especially but I have learnt to live with my failings and understand why they occurred and know I would not let them happen again. I've hurt and been hurt in return. **ENOUGH.**

CALM (Charity)

The Campaign Against Living Miserably, CALM, is an award winning charity dedicated to preventing male suicide in the UK. Founded in 2006 the charity seeks to prevent suicide by providing a service for men who are down or in crisis, and by fomenting cultural change so that any man considering suicide feels able to seek help. There were 6,109 probable suicides in the UK in 2014 of which 76%, or 4,623, were male. Suicide is the biggest single killer of men aged under 45 in the UK (NISRA, GRO, ONS 2014).

CALM receives around 5,000 webchats and calls each month to its helpline and webchat service. Calls and chats are free, confidential and anonymous. CALM's helpline is accredited by the Helplines Partnership, and its webchat and helpline service is available every day of the week from 5pm to midnight, staffed by professionals, on 0800 585858 (national) 0808 802 5858(London) and www.thecalmzone.net.

CALM supporters and advocates include Professor Green, Dizzee Rascal and Frank Turner, and its offbeat brand and challenging advertising have proven effective in reaching men across the UK.

Being Silent Isn't Being Strong

CALM are pleased to have been involved in a BBC Panorama documentary about male suicide, by journalist Simon Jack, broadcast on April 13th, 2015 on BBC 1.

Having lost his father to suicide, Simon Jack wanted to look further into the rising issue of male suicide in this country and the problems arising from a culture where men are expected to be strong at all times, where asking for help is seen as a sign of weakness.

The delicate issue of male suicide was brought to UK homes as the BBC's Panorama showed Simon Jack's film, "A Suicide in the Family." The film is of personal interest as Simon's father took his own life when Simon was only 19. Twenty-five years on, the same age his father was when he committed suicide, Simon wanted to use the film to explore the reasons why this tragic event happened that shook his whole family. As he put it, "One January morning my father left the family home and took his own life."

It was not an easy project for Simon and involved asking searching questions amongst his family. Initially, his brothers were not keen to discuss the issue as it was too raw. Eventually, his mother agreed to be interviewed on film and Simon described how he found out more about the challenges his father was facing a quarter of a century back. Rather than being angry, Jack admits to being sorry for his Dad that he had arrived at such a place - the point of no return.

Whilst investigating his own family history, he was able to discover that male suicide is the biggest killer amongst men under 50 and that his Dad was in the most vulnerable age group. Indeed men are four times more likely to kill themselves than women. Even amongst younger men, it is responsible for 25% deaths amongst men between the ages of 20-34. The figures show that it causes on average 100 deaths a week amongst men. In the filming, Simon Jack tried to explore why it is particularly men who suffer. Whilst there are no hard and fast causes, it is generally perceived to stem from men's inability to express themselves or to speak openly about their feelings. Too often, men feel under pressure to be seen to be coping and to appear to be outwardly strong. Admitting that there is a problem is seen to be demonstrating a weakness.

This was borne out during his interview with former hardman, Rugby League star Ian Knott, who used to play for Warrington Wolves. Following a career-ending injury, Knott found readjusting to life impossible to cope with, despite having a wife and children and led to his attempting to end his life. He now is a spokesman for State of Mind where he encourages former sports stars to open up and share their experiences.

Former PFA chairman Clarke Carlisle also brought the issue of depression into the spotlight when he helped Nick Clegg launch The Mental Health Charter for Sport and Recreation. He admitted in an interview to the Sun that he had attempted suicide by stepping out in front of a moving lorry, stating that "I had to die." Following six weeks recuperation in a hospital, Carlisle is now able to speak out openly about the subject and encourage others to come forward.

The Author (Malc Collier) is donating a % of his Royalties from this book directly to the CALM Campaign.

www.ingramcontent.com/pod-product-compliance
Lightning Source LLC
Chambersburg PA
CBHW070054110526
44587CB00013BB/1571